SACRED WONDERLAND

SACRED

THE HISTORY OF

WONDERLAND

RELIGION IN YELLOWSTONE

THOMAS S. BREMER

University of Nebraska Press
Lincoln

For customers in the EU with safety/GPSR
concerns, contact:
gpsr@mare-nostrum.co.uk
Mare Nostrum Group BV
Mauritskade 21D
1091 GC Amsterdam
The Netherlands

Library of Congress Control Number: 2024060717

Designed and set in Adobe Caslon Pro by Lacey Losh.

To the memory of my father, David A. Bremer,
who first took me to Yellowstone,
and for Melanie, who found me there.

CONTENTS

ILLUSTRATIONS

ACKNOWLEDGMENTS

I returned to Yellowstone National Park in the summer of 2004 on a final road trip with my father. Neither of us knew when we set out from his home in Oregon that it would be his last visit to the park he so much loved. But by the time we arrived at Yellowstone's south entrance, it had become abundantly clear to me that future road trips would be out of the question for him. My father's dementia had progressed to the point that made travel an insufferable challenge.

As we drove across the arid landscapes of eastern Oregon and Idaho on our way to Yellowstone that summer, I was wondering what writing project I should be turning to next. My first book was nearing publication, and I had no idea what my next undertaking would be. In one of his more lucid moments, my father suggested I write about Yellowstone. The idea at once seemed obvious to me.

When we arrived in the park, I arranged to meet with Lee H. Whittlesey, who was Yellowstone's official historian at the time. As we sat in his office at the Heritage and Research Center in Gardiner, Montana, I shared with him my original inspiration for a book about religion in the history of Yellowstone. Lee encouraged me, saying that the topic of religion was absent from the considerable historical literature about the park. By the time I delivered my father back to his home in Oregon a week later, my new book project was underway.

Now, two decades later, I am humbled by the many people it has taken to bring this book to fruition, from the first suggestion from my father and that initial meeting with Lee Whittlesey to the wonderful team at the University of Nebraska Press who transformed my work into an actual book. The common truism about the lonely nature of writing is misleading at best. Yes, putting words onto the page is a solitary occupation, but the research, getting feedback from trusted readers, and the eventual transformation of the writer's words into book form involves multitudes.

Among the many people who helped me with research for this book were several National Park Service employees. Besides Yellowstone National Park historian Lee Whittlesey, I also received help from archives specialist Harold Housley and his able staff at the Yellowstone Heritage and Resource Center during my stay in Gardiner, Montana, in the summer of 2006. Additionally, assistant archivist Shawn Bawden helped me during my 2015 visit to the center. Tom Olliff and Bill Berg, both with whom I worked at Yellowstone Park Service Stations in 1978, made my time in Gardiner more enjoyable.

Staff at other research collections were invaluable in finding additional primary sources. These include archivists, librarians, and others at the Huntington Library Rare Books Collection, San Marino, California; the Department of Special Collections in the Charles E. Young Research Library, University of California, Los Angeles; the Historical Society of Pennsylvania in Philadelphia; at the Theodore Sedgwick Wright Library Special Collections and Archives of the Princeton Theological Seminary in New Jersey; at the University of Delaware Library Special Collections in Newark; and in the Montana State University Library Archives and Special Collections in Bozeman. In Ohio I benefited from the help of the staff at the Rutherford B. Hayes Presidential Center in Fremont; at The Ohio State University Special Collections in Columbus; and at the Ohio Historical Society (subsequently renamed Ohio History Center), also in Columbus. Additionally, I found valuable sources at the St. Anthony of Padua Catholic Church in Cody, Wyoming.

I am especially grateful for help from John Kleberg of The Ohio State University. He oversaw the "castle" that the nineteenth-century financier Jay Cooke built on the island of Gibraltar in Lake Erie, an island now owned by the university. John's considerable knowledge about Cooke not only assisted in finding sources at Ohio State, but he also steered me to other collections, where I found little-known details of Cooke's life and his role in creating Yellowstone National Park.

My investigations of A Christian Ministry in the National Parks (ACMNP) benefited from a phone conversation with the late Gordon D. Compton, who was the assistant director of the ministry when we spoke.

He provided valuable historical context for the organization. In addition, my interview in 2006 with Rev. Dr. William R. Young offered valuable insights about the practical aspects of the ministry from his more than twenty years as the ACMNP resident minister of Yellowstone.

Originally, I had decided to not include Church Universal and Triumphant (CUT) in this book since the group does not operate inside Yellowstone National Park. A chance meeting, however, with Leighton Quarles at a Western History Association meeting convinced me otherwise, for which I am grateful—CUT turned out to be one of the most intriguing aspects of Yellowstone's religious history. Leighton put me in touch with church members and officials, which made my visit to their Montana property in 2016 both possible and valuable. Much of that trip's success was due to the hospitality and insights of Destyne Sweeney, who served as my host and arranged tours of the Royal Teton Ranch and other CUT locations. She also facilitated numerous interviews with CUT officials and members, and I thank everyone who took time to meet with me during my visit. I am also grateful to Richard Parks of Gardiner, Montana, for sharing his views of CUT and the group's relationship with the local Montana community. I also enjoyed the kind hospitality of Richard and his wife, Nancy, at the Gardiner Guest House, a delightful home base just a short walk from Yellowstone's north entrance. In addition, Venetia Charles was helpful in supplying a former member's perspective on CUT, and I also learned much about the church from a conversation and correspondence with Erin Prophet, daughter of the church's founders.

Travel for research requires money, and I have been fortunate to have funds available from several sources at my home institution, Rhodes College in Memphis, Tennessee. Additionally, a research award from the Huntington Library Rare Books Collection, San Marino, California, enabled a sabbatical stay for study in its collections.

All writings benefit from the comments, questions, and suggestions of readers, and this book is no exception. Leighton Quarles read the chapter on CUT and offered useful comments, including some corrections of minor inaccuracies. I also am thankful for feedback from the participants in the Religion in the American West Symposium of 2022–23, led by Brandi Denison and Brett Hendrickson and cosponsored by the Clements Center for Southwest Studies at Southern Methodist University and the Eiteljorg

Museum of American Indians and Western Art in Indianapolis, Indiana. Especially helpful were comments from my reading group cohort of Carleigh Beriont, Lynn Gerber, and Joshua Paddison in the summer of 2022. Additionally, Jim Bennett offered useful perspective on the Church Universal and Triumphant.

One suggestion that came as I was finishing the manuscript changed the tone of the book. Laila Rall and Lee Davis, my writing group partners, pushed me to include a more personal perspective on both Yellowstone and religion. Because of their comments, I added the prelude and postlude as frames for the historical narrative.

Transforming my writings from plain documents to beautiful book relied on the expertise, experience, and professionalism of the staff at the University of Nebraska Press. I am especially grateful for the patience of editor-in-chief Bridget Barry, who allowed me as much time as needed to finish. Also, copyeditor Elizabeth Gratch's expertise and careful reading significantly improved the text.

Sometimes it felt that this project would never be finished, but the support of so many kind people sustained my determination to get it done. Twenty years is an exceptionally long time to write a book, and I did not work on it all those years. Long periods of dormancy intervened as I turned my attention to other writing projects. However, the encouragement and enthusiasm of those who continually asked me about the Yellowstone book kept me coming back to it. And though I may not recall everyone who has taken an interest in this work, I am forever grateful for their confidence that I would complete it. I can only hope that when they finally open its pages, the book will not disappoint but instead will justify their trust.

Two people in particular have nurtured and sustained me, not only in writing this book but throughout my life. Both are profoundly connected to my relationship with Yellowstone, and to them I have dedicated this book. Besides providing the spark that ignited this project, my father, David A. Bremer, first introduced me to the park and all of its wondrous possibilities. Our long summer camping trips throughout the western United States and Canada were truly magical times for a young child, and Yellowstone was one of our favorite destinations. When I was a young adult casting about for a path to follow in life, my father suggested I go work a season in Yellowstone. That long summer in 1978 changed my life. Many years later, as I took up his idea for a book on Yellowstone, his love of the park, an affection that he had imparted to me, provided constant encouragement. With great sadness, I regret that he never was able to read any part of the book before he left this world.

In addition to my father, I dedicate this book to Melanie, whom I first met in Yellowstone. She has been the love of my life from the moment she greeted me with "You must be Tom" as I walked into her room in the dormitory behind Yellowstone's Old Faithful Snow Lodge. Our first encounter came near the end of my long summer of employment in 1978, and it turned into a magical day of getting to know each other among the geysers and scenic vistas of the park. In the subsequent decades of our life together, we have returned to Yellowstone numerous times, including several research trips. Without her presence, this book would not have been possible.

My final acknowledgment must go to Yellowstone itself. Of course, the sacred wonderland on the high plateau at the headwaters of the Yellowstone River is the central character and exclusive focus of this book. On a more personal note, I would not be the person I have become without having known the park over the many years that it has been in my life. Yet I know that Yellowstone is far more than what I have experienced of it, far more than what any visitor, resident, researcher, guide, ranger, or other person can know of it. Yellowstone, as other commentators have emphasized, is an idea, one that resides differently in the minds, hearts, and experiences of anyone who has ever been there. But more than that, Yellowstone is a place unto itself, a dynamic land that will never be fully contained in whatever we might say, think, or feel about it. Both sacred and profane, inspiring and terrifying, familiar and strange, Yellowstone endures as a place of wonder, danger, and mystery that forever escapes whatever we might make of it.

SACRED WONDERLAND

PRELUDE

Rites of Passage

I stood alone in the snow-covered meadow in the heart of Yellowstone National Park, my eyes closed, perfectly motionless, with my boots firmly rooted in the crusty ice on the snow's surface, absorbing the immensity of the land, settling into a tranquility I had never before known. Though springtime bloomed at lower elevations, Yellowstone had not yet shaken its long winter. The park had opened just a week earlier and was still nearly empty of visitors. Not a single car ventured down the highway; no other person intruded on my moment of solitude. A slight westerly wind brushed coldly across my cheeks, and I stood motionless, silent, unhurried and patient. The universe paused.

After several minutes that seemed much longer, I finally opened my eyes. The meadow appeared oddly different, transformed into a sparkling field of welcome, inviting me into a new life. A fallen tree branch lay at my feet, half-buried in the snow. I knelt to pick up the bent stick and proceeded to etch in large letters in the snow, "I am born here." I paused again to absorb the perfect stillness and harmony of that Yellowstone morning.

I had wandered out to this large field on the other side of the park's main loop road from my room in the dormitory behind the Canyon Village service station, where I was employed for the summer tourist season in 1978. The sun shone brightly, hinting at warmer days to come that eventually would melt the thick white blanket still lingering in the higher elevations of the Yellowstone Plateau.

When I crossed the road that cold morning, the meadow welcomed me with a calm quiet, anticipating the solemnity of this auspicious moment in my young life. No longer confined by the anxieties and expectations of the busy suburban life that had nearly crushed my soul, I paused in the delight of having arrived in the immense tranquility of Yellowstone.

Having sold my few possessions, I had boarded a Greyhound bus just days earlier in my escape from the demoralizing atmosphere of my childhood environs of Santa Ana, California. The long journey over deserts and mountainous terrains had landed me in an entirely different universe in the wilds of the Rocky Mountains. As I wandered out to the snowy meadow that first morning in my new home, I found myself alone in the world, a solitary figure in a sprawling landscape beneath a wide, clear spring sky that stretched my horizons to eternity.

A potent magic engulfed me on that long-ago spring morning as I was reborn to a new life in the Yellowstone wonderland. The extraordinary sensation of that propitious moment as I bent down to write my ephemeral proclamation of rebirth in the snow has stayed with me through the intervening decades. Indeed, my liminal encounter with a more profound experience of the park fundamentally changed me. I returned that morning to the barren walls of my dormitory room as a changed person.

Only later, in reflecting on my solitary rite of passage, did the opening line from John Denver's most famous song occur to me. "He was born in the summer of his twenty-seventh year, coming home to a place he'd never been before." Not quite yet summer, and I was only in my twenty-second year, but that May morning, I found myself coming home in a park I had long known and loved but now experienced differently, connecting to a larger universe of wonder that my young life had never known before.

In the waning days of the Yellowstone summer season some forty-three years later, I returned to the park for another rite of passage as I carried the gray powdery remains of my father into the wilderness he so loved. My father's affection for wild places had found its utmost fulfillment in this earliest of the world's national parks. Throughout our childhood he had brought me and my siblings on regular summer camping trips to Yellowstone, where we, too, began a long romance with wild, untrammeled places far from the anxious busyness of our suburban upbringing. More than summer recreations in faraway places, these mountain sojourns of my early years introduced me to the imaginative potentials of a life that contrasted to the numbing despair of American suburbia. I owed my father a debt of gratitude for this gift of possibility.

I had grieved for my father long before I carried his remains to Yellowstone. He had been gradually losing his grasp on the world for a number of years, and I felt a gnawing despair as I witnessed the slow loss of my father, my friend, a lifeline of support throughout my life, to the ravages of dementia. When his wife of twenty-five years finally gave up on him, it was up to me to get him into a secure facility where he would be safe and cared for. Once I delivered him to the Alzheimer's unit that would become his new home, I could no longer contain the emotional strain. My grief poured out.

With two thousand miles between us and the restrictions of COVID lockdowns, I did not see my father the last eighteen months of his life, another deep pain that fate had delivered us. When the call came notifying me of his death, my sadness was marked less by grief and more by gratitude for having had him in my life as well as by the relief that his final years of confusion and suffering were at a merciful end. The father I had known and loved had finally left this world for good.

The following year I honored his wishes to return him one last time to Yellowstone. With all the solemnity of a religious ceremony, I tossed the last remnant of my father's long life into the soft breeze wafting across the heart of the land he so loved. The river sang a final hymn as the pines stood in respectful tribute to a life that had introduced so many others—his children, his students, his many friends—to the treasures of nature's sacred lands. As his ashes settled into their final resting place, I contemplated the memory of my father's life—the times we had shared in this park and elsewhere in the American West, his exuberance hiking across wild lands, in deep forests and over high mountain ridges, paddling on rivers and lakes far from highways and towns, telling stories around campfires on dark moonless nights in the great outdoors. He took every opportunity to heed his hero John Muir's wisdom "that going to the mountains is going home; that wildness is a necessity; and that mountain parks and reservations are . . . fountains of life."[1]

Yet alongside these happy remembrances were recollections of sadnesses and disappointments that had punctuated his life—the tragic loss of his father at a young age, the failed marriages, and especially the dreadful final decade as he descended into the dark pit of dementia, losing all recognition of who he had been and the many adventures that had defined his life.

In these meditations on his life, I let go of my father on a sunny autumn day in a place we both loved and had often shared.

These two occasions frame my attachments to the Yellowstone wonderland. They remain among the most profound religious moments of my life. My career as a scholar of religions has involved many years of thinking about the numerous traditions that make up the diverse religious landscapes of the Americas. As such, I have long adopted an agnostic disposition, often claiming to be a "religious tourist" of sorts, not bound by any particular faith but endlessly curious about and fascinated by how religion structures virtually all human experience. Yet despite a wariness about identifying myself religiously, I cannot deny the profound impact of transformative experiences that continue to influence who I am. No one, I have come to realize, not even the most committed atheist, can avoid habits of belief and practice that generate ultimate meaning and purpose in life and provide a moral lens for ethical living. We all find a faith, conventional or otherwise, deliberate or accidental, to guide us through our days.

My faith found its center in Yellowstone.

INTRODUCTION

A Sacred Wonderland

The thin air clawed at my lungs, my aging legs ached at the steep incline, but I made my way steadily toward the summit. We were ascending a holy peak, Maitreya Mountain, a prodigious nexus connecting faithful pilgrims to the Ascended Masters, the spiritual guides of the Church Universal and Triumphant (CUT).[1] The two CUT officials who were my hosts guided me up the back side of this sacred mountain looming above the church's Inner Retreat. One step at a time, I made my way toward the summit of spiritual energy.

Atop the holy mountain a pair of shrines bore witness to the devotions of previous pilgrims. A bare wooden frame held seven Buddhist prayer wheels that appeared to be products of a children's craft class. The brightly colored buckets spun steadily in the constant wind blowing across the mountain's top. Nearby a circular stack of rocks balanced a makeshift Christian cross fashioned from two weathered gray sticks possibly gathered on the trek up the mountain. The shrine evidenced a ritual celebration, likely performed in gratitude for Maitreya's benevolence.

The vista from Maitreya Mountain offers a clear view of the heart of CUT's sacred geography in Montana. The mountainous terrain stretches in every direction. To the south looms Electric Peak in the northwest corner of Yellowstone National Park. Mol Heron Creek cascades down the winding valley below as it tumbles toward the Yellowstone River. Along the banks of the creek at the foot of Maitreya Mountain, the grounds of the Inner Retreat rest empty and calm, a contrast to the crowded and lively camps convened each summer beginning in the 1980s. The quiet of this spring day mutes an ominous past; across the gravel road from the Inner Retreat, traces of an elaborate complex of underground bunkers punctuate the deceptive calm of a grassy meadow. An army of CUT members had carved the massive subterranean shelters in 1989–90 in anticipation of a predicted nuclear holocaust. The global war never materialized, but the shelters remain, fully stocked and ready to save the holy community from catastrophic calamity.

The Church Universal and Triumphant came to Montana in the 1980s, although CUT had had its sights set on relocating there a decade earlier.[2] The Ascended Masters, the spiritual guides who CUT followers consult in regular communications, had destined their arrival in this piece of wildland adjacent to Yellowstone National Park. Besides its sheer beauty and its relative isolation from the controversy the church had stirred up in previous locations, the Royal Teton Ranch, the sprawling Montana property that it purchased in 1981, had auspicious meanings for this community devoted to a religion that combined Buddhist, Hindu, and Christian traditions in its own uniquely eclectic religious practices. CUT's new Montana home fulfilled the promises of the Ascended Masters.

Besides the religious significance of the Royal Teton Ranch itself, another even more auspicious site lies not far to the south of CUT's Montana church headquarters. The Teton Mountains, centerpiece of Grand Teton National Park directly south of Yellowstone in Wyoming, has been the gathering place of spiritual beings for tens of thousands of years, according to the I AM tradition that spawned CUT. The Grand Teton Mountain, in particular, ranks as the most sacred location in the Western Hemisphere for the church community. And between these two most holy locations of its sacred geography, the ranch and the Grand Teton, lies Yellowstone, which holds its own sacred meanings for the Church Universal and Triumphant.

My CUT guides were feeling the energy of this place as we made our way up Maitreya Mountain. On the summit, Destyne Sweeney, a CUT official, walked to the north-facing edge and raised her arms skyward. I watched her lean into the steady wind on that cool spring day as she absorbed the spiritual powers of this land.

The Many Places of Yellowstone

The followers of the Church Universal and Triumphant have incorporated Yellowstone National Park into their sacred geography according to communications received from their Ascended Masters. Their religious

FIG. 1. Destyne Sweeney of the Church Universal and Triumphant on Maitreya Mountain, June 2, 2016. Photo by T. S. Bremer.

reinterpretation of Yellowstone, though, is not as unusual as many people might assume. Yellowstone National Park carries a variety of meanings and uses for different groups, and religion has been a prominent element in creating the significant places that make up Yellowstone. Tourists in nineteenth-century America traveling to the park entered a "wonderland" that promised sublime experiences bordering on religious. Some of these adventurous travelers brought overtly sectarian frames of religious reference for interpreting their experiences in the wilds of Yellowstone. Others adopted less obviously religious aesthetic lenses for seeing the national park, but even the dominant aesthetic views that gave the park meaning for so many nineteenth-century travelers derived in large part from American Protestant traditions of the day. For nearly all early visitors to Yellowstone National Park, religion figured prominently in their experiences, interpretations, and memories of this western wonderland.

The role of religion has not diminished for contemporary visitors to Yellowstone National Park, although its presence has become less pronounced. The interpretive frames by which many twenty-first-century visitors find value and meaning in Yellowstone have deep religious roots. Although some visitors turn to their traditional confessional orientations to interpret their experiences of the park, many others refrain from imposing sectarian significance on Yellowstone. Yet the vast majority of visitors engage in practices and traditions that derive from distinct religious orientations, some more directly than others. At the most generic level, conventional travel practices involved in experiencing the park stem from a long history of ritualized devotional travel stretching back to ancient times, a history that transforms traditions of religious pilgrimage into modern practices of leisure travel. As part of this history, Yellowstone has been a destination of profound sublimity and for many travelers a sacred wonderland.

Like virtually all places of any recognizable significance, Yellowstone National Park is a "simultaneity of places." It is, in other words, made up of multiple distinct places of different meanings, different uses, different experiences, for the variety of people who visit and inhabit the park.[3] In this regard Yellowstone's significance reflects the variety of ways that people find meaning and value in their own lives. There are as many Yellowstones as there are people who enter the park, and even people who have never been there imagine the park to some extent in relation to how they imagine themselves.

How people imagine themselves eventually turns to religion, at least according to how some scholars have described it.[4] Religion, whether regarded as formal sectarian traditions and institutions or merely as one's personal guiding philosophy of life, underlies how people find significance in their lives. Consequently, it guides how they live, what they value, and their relations with others and the broader worlds they inhabit. At the same time, their religious orientations, attitudes, and commitments also confer significance on the places they inhabit, visit, and find meaningful.[5]

All religions everywhere have material contexts. The sacred, regardless how abstract it may be in any particular tradition, always has a material side. Gods, spirits, ghosts, animating energies, and other conceptions of transcendent powers all figure decisively in the economic and material aspects of believers' lives. This relationship between materiality and perceptions of the sacred explains in part the appeal of places like Yellowstone. By declaring the region at the headwaters of the Yellowstone River as a "park," the U.S. government transformed its wildlands into a domesticated extension of the nation's civilized, Christian society. The subsequent development of roads, accommodations, and other infrastructure made possible experiences of aesthetic awe for visitors to the park. Both the wonders of nature and the built environment joined together in creating the possibility for encounters with the sacred in Yellowstone.[6]

When visitors find the sacred in places like Yellowstone, they value their experiences according to the religious undertones of meaning that they perceive in their encounters. Consequently, the attraction of the Yellowstone region for religious people like the CUT community parallels its appeal for leisure travelers. Both religious devotees and tourists alike experience transcendent meanings in the Yellowstone landscape. Indeed, this place has been a sacred wonderland from its earliest days as a federal reserve set apart "for the benefit and enjoyment of the people."

A Reverence for Nature

The transcendent meanings people find in Yellowstone National Park typify the many ways the people of the United States have turned to nature for religious and spiritual needs. The Church Universal and Triumphant has been a latecomer to the parade of spiritually oriented seekers who have found uplifting treasures in the natural wonders of the world's first national park.[7] CUT's insistence that divine beings reside inside, above, and beneath Yellowstone is just one of a multitude of religious beliefs, orientations, and attitudes that people have brought to this wonderland of natural features high in the Rocky Mountains. Its religious element coincides with effusive descriptions of the park as a beautiful, strange, and wondrous landscape of divine creation, but its holiness also reflects other realities. Like all things religious in the United States, the spiritual legacy of Yellowstone National Park bears witness as well to modern socioeconomic realities tied to legacies of conquest, dispossession, and colonization. This iconic national park rests on the bones of displaced peoples, and its value relies as much on the consumer ethos of our modern world as it does on any divine presence that people may perceive in its sublime natural attractions.

The attractions of Yellowstone and the regrettable realities of its past mirror a larger story of the American nation. Religion has been the prism through which many in the United States have found national purpose and meaning in the face of the ironic, contradictory, hopeful, and malignant realities of modern democracy. In this regard popular attachments to the treasured lands and astounding features of the world's first national park are a complex product of spiritual practices and orientations, nationalist sentiment, gendered attitudes, racist assumptions, and economic ambitions. And lying at the core of these cultural forces is nature, the gravitational center of the Yellowstone idea.

Throughout their history the people of the United States have had an ambivalent and conflicted relationship to the natural world. On the one hand, nature's bounty has been a source of national wealth. The rich resources of the American land—its minerals, petroleum, wildlife, timber, water, and nearly a billion acres of fertile soils—have fueled the growth of the U.S. economy into the largest in the world. On the other hand, the dominant Protestant religious culture of the United States has repeatedly turned to nature for comprehending the Christian God and as evidence of divine national purpose. More than material resources for economic gain, the riches of nature have contributed to a public confidence in righteous intent.

The ambivalence toward nature in the history of the United States arrived with the earliest Puritan settlers. The English dissenting Protestants who established colonies in New England in the seventeenth century introduced a rigorous Calvinism that pervaded every wrinkle of their social life. Their attitudes toward nature included a typically English perspective that regarded the uncultivated "wilderness" as savage, uncivilized, and dangerous. William Bradford, who arrived on the *Mayflower* and later served as governor of Plymouth colony, described their newfound homeland as "a hideous & desolate wilderness, full of wild beasts & willd men."[8] This new land, where the Puritans intended to build their gleaming "City on a Hill," posed for them a frightening challenge as a source of demonic chaos.

At the same time, the Puritans remained devoted to a Calvinist reverence for nature. The sixteenth-century Protestant reformer John Calvin had turned toward the natural world as the most important source outside of the Bible for Christians to know God. He declared "that it can be said reverently, provided it proceeds from a reverent mind, that nature is God."[9] Calvin's reverence for nature became a central component in subsequent Reformed Protestant doctrine. The 1646 Westminster Confession of Faith, which has been an influential statement of doctrine for Reformed Protestants in the English-speaking world, begins by affirming "the Light of Nature, and the works of Creation and Providence do so far manifest the Goodness, Wisdom, and Power of God."[10] Their Calvinist emphasis on God's providence inspired Reformed Protestants to find God everywhere in nature; to them, as environmental historian Mark Stoll observes: "Nature was egalitarian. At every moment God sustained, ordered, cared for, and guided the tiniest creature individually as well as the vast universe as a whole."[11]

For English Puritans who traveled to North America to build a new Christian society, the Calvinist interpretation of providence instilled an ambiguous attitude toward the natural world. Initially, they framed the American wilderness as a dangerous land where Satan and his minions resided. But its demonic character had a providential purpose. Here the Puritans' spiritual worthiness would be tested in the tradition of early Christians who fled into the desert to be tempted by the devil and ministered by God's angels. "The wilderness," religious historian Catherine L. Albanese notes about Puritan settlers in seventeenth-century America, "was still a place of testing, the backdrop for a spiritual purification in which the corruption of old England might be permanently purged." This purging in the untamed lands of their new settlement, Albanese concludes, "might also protect them from worldly evil and even invigorate them."[12]

As their new homeland became more settled and tamed, the descendants of these first American Puritans tended to regard nature less as demonic and more in Calvin's reverent terms. By the 1720s Puritan minister, writer, and scientist Cotton Mather could invite readers to join him in the "Publick Library" of nature: "Walk with me into it, and see what we shall find so legible there, *that he that runs may read it*." For Mather the natural world stood as a divine edifice, a "*Temple* of GOD, *built* and *fitted* by that Almighty *Architect*."[13]

American Parklands

The Puritans as a distinct religious group gradually faded into the growing complexity of U.S. religious history, but their values and ideas have had remarkable enduring influence, not only among their Congregationalist successors but as part of the fabric of American cultural life. By the nineteenth century a conservationist ethos had emerged from the Reformed Protestant values rooted in the Puritan past of the Connecticut Valley. In particular, a doctrine of Christian stewardship developed into three areas of practical concern among nineteenth-century New England Protestants: agricultural improvement, the conservation of forests and natural resources, and the development of public parks.[14] Although all three of these themes had interconnected moral overtones, the first two derived from more practical apprehensions about agricultural prosperity and conserving the woodlands that supplied timber and firewood for nineteenth-century New England rural society. Parks, though, responded more directly to moral and aesthetic concerns in the Reformed Protestant tradition. This Puritan ethos underlying the U.S. parks movement is plainly evident in the work of Frederick Law Olmsted, widely hailed as the originator of American landscape architecture, most famously as the designer of New York City's Central Park.[15]

Olmsted's childhood education in Connecticut had instilled Reformed Protestant values that became foundational in his subsequent career as the nation's preeminent landscape architect.[16] His vision for New York's grand park articulated these Christian moral values in deliberate design principles. He wrote, "It is one great purpose of the Park to supply to the hundreds of thousands of tired workers, who have no opportunity to spend their summers in the country, a specimen of God's handiwork that shall be to them, inexpensively, what a month or two in the White Mountains or the Adirondacks is, at great cost, to those in easier circumstances."[17] Olmsted sought to provide the laboring masses an Edenic refuge from the urban "Hell," as Mark Stoll puts it, that characterized their working-class circumstances.[18] He regarded his parks as sacred places, even resorting to the Christian imagery of humankind's original paradisiacal garden; in 1881, for instance, Olmsted cautioned against overdeveloping the park he designed for Mount Royal in Montreal: "If you can but persuade yourselves to regard them as sacred places and save them from sacrilegious hands and feet, the original Gardener of Eden will delight your eyes with little pictures within greater pictures of indescribable loveliness."[19]

Olmsted exerted enormous influence on subsequent generations of landscape architects, including those involved with developing national parks. As a member of the commission overseeing California's newly established Yosemite park, he proposed a plan in 1865 for development based on his principles of landscape design. Although park officials never implemented Olmsted's specific plan for Yosemite, its underlying principles became canonical in later national park development. His proposal first emphasized a holistic experience for visitors that required careful preservation of the whole area rather than highlighting isolated encounters of disconnected features. Olmsted argued, "The union of the deepest sublimity with the deepest beauty of nature, not in one feature or another, not in one part or one scene or another, not any landscape that can be framed by itself, but all around and wherever the visitor goes, constitutes the Yo Semite the greatest glory of nature." The second principle in Olmsted's proposal recognized the importance of public access. The park and its attractions, he insisted, "should be laid open to the use of the body of the people." Third, parks offered therapeutic benefits as places of recreation: "The enjoyment of scenery employs the mind without fatigue and yet exercises it, tranquilizes it and yet enlivens it; and thus, through the influence of the mind over the body, gives the effect of refreshing rest and reinvigoration of the whole system." Finally, Olmsted realized Yosemite's value as a civilizing force for U.S. society at large. Although Congress had delegated care of the park to the State of California, Olmsted regarded it as the nation's park, what he described as "a trust from the whole nation." This exquisite scenic paradise, in Olmsted's view, would have a transformative, beneficial effect on visitors, much like his intentions for New York's Central Park, where landscape serves social reform. Unlike the urban park, though, Yosemite's landscape was a product of divine arrangement, the "greatest glory of nature" created by the Christian God.[20]

Olmsted's Reformed Protestant background colored his design principles for parks, both urban and the more spectacular natural places like Yosemite; a Calvinist propensity for reading nature as God's book encouraged Olmsted to utilize landscapes for moral purposes aimed at improving society. These underlying moral intentions became canonical among subsequent generations of designers. Consequently, U.S. landscape architecture, beginning with its most influential progenitor, relied significantly on park design principles derived in part from a Reformed Protestant religio-aesthetic vision of nature in its Edenic purity.

This reverence for nature rooted in the Calvinist tradition of Reformed Protestant Christianity helps explain the early appeal of places like Yellowstone, where the grandeur of God's creation beckoned those seeking sublime experience.[21] It also bolstered nineteenth-century nationalist sentiment in the United States, particularly in the years following the Civil War. The providential magnificence of the natural world on display in Yellowstone legitimized the self-understandings of the American people as the chosen nation destined to fulfill God's preordained intentions for humanity. For many elite citizens of the United States in the postbellum period, the sublime experience of nature justified their devotion to Manifest Destiny. The splendor of natural wonders gave witness to God's hand in this new Promised Land of the American nation.

But like most cultural attitudes, regard for the natural world in the United States harbored significant tides of ambivalent crosscurrents. Indeed, both reverence and conquest defined the relationship to nature.[22] Gilded Age concerns about gender roles made the great outdoors a key proving ground of maleness, which in turn encouraged the manly national effort to subdue nature. This also included subduing what many in the United States regarded as the "savages" who inhabited nature's wild places. Conquering and civilizing wild places and the people who had been there for centuries would be rewarded, many influential Americans believed, with endless prosperity from the natural bounty that God had provided for his chosen nation. Divine favor as evidenced in the land and what seemed the inevitable prospect of the United States "to overspread and possess the whole continent" pillared the nineteenth-century ideology of Manifest Destiny, an ideology that tested the strength of the nation's manliness.[23]

By the 1870s, with Civil War behind and with optimism about expansion and boundless prosperity on the horizon, Yellowstone National Park emerged in the tension between the two orientations to nature, as God's gift to enrich the chosen nation and as aesthetic experience evidencing God's promise. This tension eventually would plague the entire national park system as it became, in later decades, an open conflict between recreation and preservation—between, on the one hand, use of the resources for human pleasure and benefit and, on the other hand, protecting and preserving lands in their natural "unimpaired" state for aesthetic appreciation in perpetuity. To a large extent, national park management policies have attempted to steer a delicate balance between the hazards of these two views of parklands. Underlying the struggle to compromise between recreation and preservation in Yellowstone has been fervent devotional attachments to the park as a sacred wonderland.

"Only God Can Create a National Park"

This book traces the religious dimensions of this epic struggle over the meanings, purposes, and best uses of Yellowstone as the nation's premier national park. It treats the various religious permutations of Yellowstone with chapters arranged in chronological order, each focused on a particular element of the park's religious history. The story begins in the nineteenth century as the young nation discovered "the nakedness of our sleeping Yellowstone Beauty" in the wilds of the Rocky Mountains.[24] It follows the story of religion through the controversies surrounding the Church Universal and Triumphant in the latter decades of the twentieth century.

Though Native Americans have had religious associations with Yellowstone for generations, this book does not delve into their traditions. Numerous Indigenous peoples have long known of Yellowstone and its unusual landscape features, and several tribal groups engaged in devotional practices there long before it was a park. A community of mountain Shoshone people commonly known as "Sheep Eaters" lived year-round inside the boundaries of what would become the national park. Others regularly entered the Yellowstone Plateau on hunting or raiding expeditions. In their impressive study of American Indians in and near Yellowstone, Peter Nabokov and Lawrence Loendorf note that "the park clearly marked the meeting place for all three cultural regions, with Plateau, Plains, and Great Basin peoples using this upper corner of present-day Wyoming at different times and bequeathing different legacies upon it."[25] They document Bannock, Blackfeet, Crow, Flathead, Kiowa, Kootenai, Nez Perce, and Shoshone as all having associations with Yellowstone. Many of these people, if not all, had religious connections with the land. The ethnographer Åke Hultkrantz found, for instance, that the "scene of interaction" between the Sheep Eater people and the spirit entities of their religion included the "wooded areas of the Yellowstone Park."[26]

An entire book could be written exploring Native American religions in relation to Yellowstone. Others more suited to the task have taken up that topic in their own books.[27] The story in these pages does not delve into Native American religious understandings of Yellowstone. It is more concerned with the Euro-American displacement of native peoples by an invading Christianity confident in its divine mission of Manifest Destiny. This is not to say that Native Americans have not been part of the story of religion in Yellowstone or to claim that they are no longer relevant. They show up often in the chapters of this book. Their presence in the story, however, is in relation to the Euro-American religions that came to dispossess the Yellowstone region from its aboriginal peoples.

Since its beginning, in 1872, Yellowstone National Park has been a repository of meanings and aspirations for the people of the United States, an alluring destination with significance beyond its stunning mountain scenery, abundant wildlife, and the world's largest collection of geysers, hot springs, and other thermal features. Deemed "America's Wonderland" by nineteenth-century railroad promoters, Yellowstone's significance has made it a place of religion that mirrors the religious nature of the United States. Its religious history spans nineteenth-century U.S. Christian ideas of Manifest Destiny in addition to the religiously informed preservation movement that is often associated with national parks. Yellowstone's religious history also touches on white supremacist interpretations of the park in the early twentieth century as well as the eclectic religious sentiments of the Church Universal and Triumphant community, whose members arrived on the scene in the 1980s. Certainly, the story of religion in Yellowstone has as much variety and intrigue as the natural attractions of the park.

Horace Albright affirmed a religious foundation for parklands when he proclaimed in 1930 that "only God can create a national park."[28] As director of the National Park Service, Albright lent an air of officiality to this view of national parks as preserves of divine handiwork. Like so many Americans of his era, Albright regarded the protection of these stupendous landscapes, unique natural features, and other special attractions of national parks as a civic obligation, our collective duty to the god that had manifested the American destiny.

Yet national parks have always been very human creations, despite confessional claims of a creator god establishing natural preserves for the benefit and enjoyment of recreational travelers.[29] They are the products of an aesthetic appreciation of natural beauty (and more recently, of historical importance and national heritage), political will, economic development, and the assertion of social privilege. Moreover, they are sites of contestation in which conflicting political views, economic interests, and moral priorities do battle.[30] As such, national parks have been occasions for struggles over essential meanings of the American nation itself.

Consequently, the story of Yellowstone National Park is a story of the United States. And like the story of the country itself, religion has been an inextricable foundation of the Yellowstone tale. Pulsing through the heart of the Yellowstone story are the many ways that the people of the United States have been religious, especially in regard to how religion structures their self-understandings of nationhood. Whether glorifying nature in the remarkable features of the park or envisioning an alternative spiritual world of underground chambers inhabited by Ascended Masters, Yellowstone has been a sacred wonderland reflecting the very foundations of the United States as a nation and a people. Indeed, the cultural mirror of Yellowstone reflects an image of nationhood that includes the bewildering array of religious forces that course through the arterial fabric of U.S. society. Through the magic looking glass of the Yellowstone wonderland, we can view some of the religious foundations of America itself.

1

WHERE HELL BUBBLED UP

Fr. Francis Kuppens barely mentions how, in 1866, he first heard from his Pikuni hosts about the mysterious, enchanting land at the headwaters of the Yellowstone River. We can only guess what he initially imagined. In his recollections some three decades afterward, he recalls only that "many an evening in the tent of Baptiste Champagne or Chief Big Lake the conversation, what little there was of it, turned on the beauties of that wonderful spot."[1]

Perhaps on first hearing of that "wonderful" place, the tall, muscular Jesuit missionary lay back and let the images sit awhile in his mind as he watched the smoke from the lodge fire curl through the opening where the poles protruded into the night sky. Taking rest in Chief Big Lake's lodge as they camped in the darkening woods along the banks of Montana's Judith River, Father Kuppens likely listened with curious fascination as his companions spoke of steep canyons shimmering in an array of brilliant colors, crowned by roaring waterfalls, and of restless waters brimming with fish in a vast sparkling lake rimmed with snowcapped mountains. We can imagine their excitement as they described a land of boiling springs that would sometimes erupt in tall fountains spewing steam and water hundreds of feet into the mountain air. Pulling up a thick bison skin blanket against the chill evening, the young Flemish missionary probably was not certain of the details that his Pikuni companions related, still lacking confidence in his grasp of their native language. The images they evoked, though, were clear enough to rouse his imagination. Perhaps on one of these winter nights, as he lay in the smoky tent of Chief Big Lake in the dark wilds of Montana Territory, the young Jesuit resolved to see this enchanted place for himself.[2]

While traveling with a hunting party in the spring of 1866, Father Kuppens probably had no difficulty urging his American Indian escorts to show him the place that they had spoken of all winter long. An excursion up to Yellowstone may have sidetracked the small party of Pikuni huntsmen from their pursuit of the vast herds of bison on the plains farther east, but they likely were eager to show him the wondrous sights at the headwaters of the Yellowstone River. Unfortunately, the details of their trip are left largely to our imaginations. Kuppens's recollections some thirty years later merely hint at the elation he felt touring that magical land. His account offers very little regarding the specifics of his adventure, revealing only that he and his Native American companions saw "the chief attraction, the Grand Cañon," as well as "hot and cold geysers, variegated layers of rock, the Fire Hole, etc." In an understatement tinged with the modesty of an aging missionary recalling a youthful adventure, Kuppens concludes, "I was very much impressed with the wild grandeur of the scenery."[3]

His experience as the first non-native person of a religious vocation known to have visited Yellowstone's wildlands came scarcely a decade after the youthful Kuppens had first imagined his life in these mountains. He was little more than an adolescent schoolboy at the Jesuit school in Turnhout, in his native Flanders, when he heard the inspiring message of the charismatic Jesuit missionary Pierre-Jean De Smet.[4] The renowned missionary had returned to his European homeland to recruit new evangelists to serve American Indians in Montana; De Smet spoke passionately and insistently about adventures awaiting dedicated young missionaries willing to work among the native peoples of America. As the youthful Francis Kuppens sat enthralled in the crowded lecture hall listening to the venerable missionary's tales, the thrilling possibilities of adventure and piety in America excited the boy's passions; he determined to enter the Jesuit order and follow Father De Smet into the wild regions of Montana in the far western territories of the United States. His path was laid before him as a warrior for Jesus in strange lands far away.

Kuppens was barely nineteen years of age when he made his way across the Atlantic Ocean to the Jesuit novitiate in the village of Florissant, near St. Louis, along the western boundary of the United States. There, in 1857, he began his training for the priesthood, still determined to serve Indians in the Rocky Mountains. After six years in the novitiate, Kuppens was ready to enter the missionary field.

Before he could go west, though, Kuppens first needed to travel east to receive formal ordination into the Catholic priesthood. He arrived in Boston at a moment when the United States reeled under the heavy toll of civil war. All of America, it seemed, was abuzz with news of dramatic fighting in Gettysburg, Pennsylvania, combat that exacted more loss of life than any battle on U.S. soil before or since. But as he underwent the sacrament of ordination in July 1863, Francis Kuppens had little interest in ministering to the casualties of war. He was a warrior for Jesus who harbored no concern for the political and moral contentions that had ruptured the American nation. Instead, the twenty-five-year-old Belgian had his sights set on the wilds of the American West, and he would not linger in the war-torn eastern states. His ministry was to be among the native peoples of the Rocky Mountains.

By November 1864 Father Kuppens had arrived at his mission assignment, St. Peter's, a remote religious outpost on the Missouri River in Montana Territory. There the strong, youthful Catholic turned his pious enthusiasm to evangelizing among the Pikuni people, a nation notoriously inhospitable to the intrusions of Euro-American explorers, trappers, and settlers.

The newly arrived "Black Robe," as Jesuits were often referred to, quickly earned the respect of both his Native American hosts and white settlers alike. Father Kuppens distinguished himself as an esteemed religious figure among the ambitious, the unsavory, and the hard living settlers of mid-nineteenth-century Montana. Just over a year following his arrival in the territory, he officiated at the first Catholic mass in Helena, a growing mining town that would eventually become the capital of Montana. But although he represented the church in the Euro-American settlements of the territory, Kuppens had come to Montana less to officiate the rites of Catholicism among white settlers and more to bring his holy faith to the native peoples of the region.

The Jesuit missionary Francis Kuppens took to his vocation with zeal, following literally in the footsteps of his mentor, the elderly Pierre-Jean De Smet, a fellow Belgian Jesuit of some fame who had established the first Catholic missions among the tribes of the Northern Rocky Mountain region. Like De Smet, Kuppens did not settle into a sedentary mission life but instead followed the example of "flying missions" used by the earlier Black Robes who had Christianized the eastern tribes of New France (now eastern Canada) in the seventeenth century. Rather than imposing the lifestyles and values of European Christians on the Indigenous cultures of the Americas, this strategy involved Jesuit missionaries entering native worlds to live among the people they sought to teach, learning their languages and adapting the Christian message to native perspectives.[5] Embracing a similar strategy of evangelization, Kuppens was soon living and traveling with Pikuni people. It was while living this "nomad life," as he called it, that he first heard from his native hosts about Yellowstone.[6]

We cannot know for certain what motivated the young Flemish missionary to depart from his usual missionary efforts among the Pikuni people in order to undertake an excursion up to the Yellowstone Plateau. Perhaps it was from his evangelist need to better understand the people he served and what they held sacred; maybe it was a pious inner impulse to witness the magnificence of God's creation; or maybe it was just a tourist's curiosity to undertake a rare and special sightseeing excursion. Most likely, it was some combination of these and other motives that inspired his resolve to experience this special place for himself. Whatever his reasons, the young missionary persuaded members of a Pikuni hunting party "to show me the wonderland, of which they had talked so much. Thus I got my first sight of Yellowstone."[7] Their sightseeing tour, it is clear, made a profound impression on the young Father Kuppens. Upon his return to the St. Peter's mission, he could hardly contain his enthusiasm as he excitedly related his experience to his Jesuit colleagues. He even claims to have convinced Thomas Francis Meagher, the acting territorial governor of Montana, that he should go see the Yellowstone attractions for himself.[8] It seems that this enchanting land had cast its spell on the young missionary.

Father Kuppens, though, was silent about the Pikuni companions who accompanied him on his first visit to Yellowstone. His report offers no clues about how they felt entering the enchanted land. His silence suggests that he thought of them merely as his guides on this fabulous tour. According to his recollections, they showed no reluctance to take him there, belying claims that Indians feared Yellowstone, a widely held notion among misinformed Americans and Europeans that persisted from the nineteenth century through the latter decades of the twentieth century.[9] At the same time, we can only speculate on whether the young hunters who guided Kuppens up the Yellowstone River engaged in any sort of devotional practices or performed any obligatory rituals in this land they regarded special enough to share with their missionary friend. Whatever reverence they may have felt toward Yellowstone remains absent from the record that Kuppens left.[10]

Kuppens's account, however, makes clear that his Pikuni guides were willing to treat the Jesuit missionary to a tour of the chief attractions of Yellowstone, making him in all likelihood the first non-Indigenous person of a religious profession to visit this wonderland. But in the annals of visitation there, he certainly was not the first Euro-American to enter this enchanting place. In fact, numerous Euro-Americans had been there long before his 1866 visit, although reports of the spectacular attractions of the region were just beginning to circulate much beyond the settlements of the Montana Territory. Indeed, awareness of the Yellowstone wonders came slowly to the people of the United States.

The story of how Yellowstone first entered the U.S. public imagination takes us to the early and middle decades of the nineteenth century. The experience of the Jesuit missionary Francis Kuppens is especially instructive for understanding the role of religion in how Euro-Americans interpreted Yellowstone as a sacred wonderland. Much like its effect on millions of visitors since, Yellowstone cast an enchanting spell on the young Jesuit missionary who had gone into the wilds of western North America to bring God and civilized ways to what he regarded as the pagan people who inhabited the mountainous regions.

Tall Tales

The earliest hints about a place of strange and marvelous attractions in the western mountains came initially from the tales of trappers and other mountain men in the early decades of the nineteenth century. In the wake of the Louisiana Purchase, which more than doubled the territorial extent of the United States, a handful of ambitious Euro-Americans began seeking their fortunes in the regions between the Mississippi River and the western shores of the continent. The most lucrative pursuit at the time was trapping beavers, whose pelts were in high demand in European and American markets. Western waterways were teeming with the large aquatic rodents, and fortunes awaited those who could endure the hardships of outdoor life in harsh mountain environments. In fact, the earliest explorations by non-native people of much of western North America, including the Yellowstone Plateau, were done in pursuit of beavers.

The first of the trappers to enter Yellowstone initially came west with the famed Lewis and Clark expedition. John Colter had been an early recruit into their Corps of Discovery in the summer of 1803, joining the enterprise as Meriwether Lewis made his way from Pittsburgh to the initial staging area for the expedition just upriver from St. Louis.[11] Over the course of their westward explorations, Colter gained the trust of his commanding officers and fellow explorers on the Corps of Discovery, serving the expedition well as a reliable and resourceful comrade. His enchantment with the people and lands of the West, though, exceeded his loyalty to his fellow expeditioners, and as the famous explorers neared the end of their epic journey, Colter itched to return to the wildlands of the American West. On the final segment of their trip in August 1806, they met a pair of adventurers, Joseph Dickson and Forrest Hancock, intent on finding their fortune trapping furs in the western mountains. The two men enticed Colter to join them on their venture, and after securing his early release from the Corps of Discovery, Colter returned westward.[12]

In the ensuing years of wandering the Northern Rocky Mountains, John Colter earned a reputation as a towering figure among the mountain man trappers of the early nineteenth century. He became intimately aware of the land, its moods and textures, the flora and fauna, and its people. Colter also was known to share some incredible tales of his ramblings in the American wilderness. Among the many fanciful stories he told over the years was a description of a perplexing landscape reminiscent of the underworld. Colter told of coming across a "volcanic tract" of "gloomy terrors, [with] its hidden fires, smoking pits, noxious steams and the all-pervading 'smell of brimstone.'"[13] This hellish precinct, according to the stories traded among the trappers of the era, could be found on the Stinking Water River (today known as the Shoshone River) above the Big Horn River. The place became known as Colter's Hell, a threshold to what one later visitor described as "the back door to that country which divines preach about."[14] Colter also found even more widespread and varied "gloomy terrors" of volcanic tracts when he became the first non-native person to cross the Yellowstone Plateau farther west. The fabulous stories that he told of these places added to his notoriety among fellow trappers and traders in the Rockies.

Some of these early explorers and trappers who worked the Rocky Mountain region came to realize that Colter's stories were, if anything, understatements of the curious oddities to be found in the mountainous western territories. There were many entrances to hell in this forbidding land. At the same time, though, the scenic vistas and stark beauty of the diverse Rocky Mountain landscapes offered doors to heaven as well. Terror and fascination melded into a majestic sublimity for sensitive observers of the American West.

The Yellowstone Plateau, in particular, inspired a sublime awe for at least some of the few non-native travelers who ventured there in the first half of the nineteenth century. As their stories began to circulate, a vague awareness of the bizarre landscapes in this peculiar corner of the American West started to seep into public consciousness. Pangs of curiosity began to gnaw at the collective imagination in a few corners of U.S. society.

The first stories of Yellowstone's wonders began making their way to U.S. readers in the East as early as the 1820s. First mention came in an intriguing little news item that went largely unnoticed. It appeared as a letter from trapper Daniel T. Potts to his brother Robert back in the eastern states, and it told of the young adventurer's exploits in the Rocky Mountains, hunting furs and fending off hostile Indians. The epistle's appearance in the *Philadelphia Gazette & Daily Advertiser* in 1827 also included the earliest known published description of Yellowstone.[15]

Daniel Potts had been taken by the allure of adventure and fortune in 1822, when he answered a bold call from Gen. William H. Ashley for "one-hundred young men to ascend the Missouri River to its source" to establish a fur trapping operation in the Rocky Mountains. A letter to his brother after several years out West presented a lively account of his adventures as a trapper. It told of being rescued from starvation by friendly Indians, killing a bull bison with just a spear, and entering a valley of the Big Horn River that presented "the most beautiful scene of nature I have ever seen."[16] His next correspondence a year later continued his lively narrative with a harrowing tale of "passing through a narrow confine in the Mountain [where] we were met plumb in face by a large party of Black-feet Indians," from whom he and his companions narrowly escaped. Potts also mentioned "a large fresh water Lake" at the headwaters of the Yellowstone River that lies, he explained, "on the verry top of the Mountain which is about one hundred by forty miles in diameter." On the south edge of this lake, Potts wrote, "is a number of hot and boiling springs, some of water and others of most beautiful fine clay and resembles that of a mush pot and throws its particles to the immense height of from twenty to thirty feet. The clay is white and of a pink and . . . appears to be entirely hollow under neath." He goes on to tell of "a number of places where the pure suphor [sulfur] is sent forth in abundance." Potts told of a companion who was investigating one of the hot springs when "the earth began a tremendous trembling and he with dificulty [sic] made his escape when an explosion took place resembling that of thunder."[17] Without relating it specifically to the underworld, Potts's letter gave readers their first inkling of a land brimming with frightening wonders.

Subsequent decades brought additional stories about Yellowstone to public attention. Among those that enjoyed more widespread circulation were the amusing tales of Jim Bridger. Like Potts, Bridger had counted himself among the "hundred young men" who went west as part of General Ashley's Rocky Mountain Fur Company in the 1820s.[18] He distinguished himself as one of the most colorful and widely known of the mountain men, and he became a key figure in introducing the Yellowstone region to the U.S. public. Foremost was Bridger's fame as a storyteller, and he featured Yellowstone in some of his most widely known "tall tales." Stories credited to this legendary and colorful character include anecdotes of fish caught in Yellowstone Lake and immediately cooked by plunging them into a boiling spring while still on the line. Bridger also told of a mountain stream that flows in two directions, toward both the Pacific and Atlantic Oceans, so that a trout could swim up a stream in one drainage and cross over to the other. Among the more witty and often repeated of Bridger yarns is the description of petrified trees in the Specimen Ridge area of Yellowstone, where "petrified birds sing petrified songs." Bridger sometimes appealed to religious sensibilities in his tales, as when he characterized the numerous thermal features of the Yellowstone Plateau as "the place where Hell bubbled up," echoing Colter's earlier descriptions while invoking Protestant evangelical religious imagery popular in U.S. culture.

A taste of Bridger's fantastical tales of Yellowstone appeared in an 1852 book by Lt. J. W. Gunnison, an army topographer. Bridger, according to Gunnison, "gives a picture, most romantic and enticing, of the head-waters of the Yellow Stone." Gunnison goes on to relate Bridger's descriptions of the thermal areas and rivers: "The ground resounds to the tread of horses. Geysers spout up seventy feet high, with a terrific hissing noise, at regular intervals. . . . In this section are the Great Springs, so hot that meat is readily cooked in them, and as they descend on the successive terraces, afford at length delightful baths. On the other side is an acid spring, which gushes out in a river torrent."[19] The publication of Gunnison's book lent authority to Bridger's tales of Yellowstone for a mostly skeptical reading audience.

Yellowstone's First Tourist

Although a largely incredulous public easily dismissed such tales as the wild imaginations and entertaining exaggerations of illiterate mountain men, a few bold souls determined to find out for themselves if the stories held any truth. Probably the first person to visit Yellowstone out of a purely touristic curiosity was a clerk with the American Fur Company by the name of Warren Angus Ferris.[20] At a summer rendezvous of trappers and traders in 1833, Ferris heard the excited tale of mountain men who had discovered what they described as "remarkable boiling springs" at the source of the Madison River. Ferris resolved to see these boiling waters for himself.[21]

The following spring, Ferris found himself on a trading expedition along the Snake River in the vicinity of the Teton Mountains. He realized that they were not far from the headwaters of the Madison, the place of boiling springs that he had heard of, and that he may not again have such a convenient opportunity for seeing the remarkable sights that had captured his imagination at the previous summer's rendezvous. Ferris left the trading party in May 1834 and, with two Pend d'Oreille guides to accompany him, set out for Yellowstone. Upon arriving, the young trader was astounded by the area's collection of geysers, hot springs, and other thermal features. He reports what he saw in a book that gave the world its first tourist account of the attractions of Yellowstone:

> From the surface of a rocky plain or table, burst forth columns of water, of various dimensions, projected high in the air, accompanied by loud explosions, and sulphurous vapors, which were highly disagreeable to the smell. The rock from which these springs burst forth, was calcareous, and probably extends some distance from them, beneath the soil. The largest of these wonderful fountains, projects a column of boiling water several feet in diameter, to the height of more than one hundred and fifty feet . . . accompanied with a tremendous noise. These explosions and discharges occur at intervals of about two hours.[22]

At one point Ferris approached one of the fountains as it rested between eruptions and attempted to put his hand in the water, but quickly realizing the danger, he "retreated back precipitately to a respectful distance." Ferris's boldness in approaching the boiling waters so closely made his Pend d'Oreille companions anxious, which he interpreted as religious dread. Despite his encouragements to join him beside the boiling waters, they were, in his words, "quite appalled, and could not by any means be induced to approach them." His account speculates that they clung to superstitious attitudes toward the hot springs and fountains, that "they believed them to be supernatural and supposed them to be the production of the Evil Spirit. One of them remarked," Ferris reports, "that hell, of which he had heard from the Whites, must be in that vicinity."[23] In Ferris's imaginative estimation, Yellowstone was a place of unusual attractions that could frighten those of a superstitious mind.

Ferris's interpretation of the Pend d'Oreille' reluctance to approach the geysers also stayed in the U.S. imagination of Yellowstone. For more than a century, most people assumed that Indians harbored a superstitious fear of the Yellowstone Plateau as a place of evil powers. This presumption would later serve efforts to rid the park of Native American threats and to quell tourist fears of being attacked by hostile natives.[24]

Curiosity about Indian superstitions and native regard for Yellowstone did not concern most of the trappers, miners, and other explorers who entered the Yellowstone Plateau in the early part of the nineteenth century. Intent on finding profitable beaver colonies or mining prospects, they also showed little appreciation for Yellowstone's beauty. But a few early visitors were able to see beyond the strangeness of the bizarre and frightening landscape to consider the area's features in aesthetic terms reminiscent of romantic poets. Trapper Osborne Russell, originally from Maine, went to Yellowstone on five different occasions, and his 1835 description of the Lamar River Valley borders on the poetic in its sublime imagery. It anticipates what visitors have said about the place ever since. He wrote, "There is something in the wild romantic scenery of this valley which I cannot nor will I attempt to describe; but the impressions made upon my mind while gazing from a high eminence on the surrounding landscape one evening as the sun was gently gliding behind the western mountain and casting its gigantic shadows across the vale were such as time can never efface from my memory."[25] Among his peers, however, Russell's affection for Yellowstone's wild scenery was not widely shared. There was little regard for such laudatory sentiments among the nineteenth-century mountain men pursuing a fur-lined wealth in an unforgiving land. Few of them shared Russell's fondness for "wild romantic splendor." In fact, Russell himself chastised his fellow trappers for their "humbug" attitudes about his idealized notions, which they regarded as "vain and frivolous."[26]

Osborne Russell's aesthetic appreciation of Yellowstone scenery marked a prescient turn toward the romantic in the public imagination of the American West. Romantic notions of sublime experience began to show up in numerous accounts of western landscapes during the middle decades of the nineteenth century, and this included reports of fantastical wonders at the headwaters of the Yellowstone River. By 1866, the year that the Jesuit missionary Francis Kuppens accompanied his Pikuni companions to see the enchanted wonderland for himself, a local newspaper in Montana was able to publish an enticing description of the Yellowstone region, remarking that it displays "some of the most stupendous scenery amid the Rocky Mountains. . . . [It is a place] of wonderful grandeur and sublimity."[27]

At the same time, recreational pursuits heightened the potential appeal of Yellowstone. The same article hints at opportunities for fishing and hunting, noting that the Yellowstone River "is full of fine trout and bass, and the numerous sedgy islands are inhabited by a great variety of water fowl." Thus, even the earliest renderings of the mysterious Yellowstone Plateau depict it as both a place of sublime spiritual experience as well as a playground for recreational activities.

Black Robes and the Book of Heaven

Before romanticized images of Yellowstone and the recreational possibilities of the region began to circulate, Christianity had established itself in the Rocky Mountains. Father Kuppens's arrival came in the wake of the initial wave of Christian missionaries. But their presence had been predicted in a Salish prophecy. Long before stories of Yellowstone pricked the consciousness of the American public, decades before Lewis and Clark would set out on their western explorations, a religious prophecy foretold a new religion that would come to the Rocky Mountain region, according to oral traditions of the Salish people. Xalíqs (Shining Shirt), an eighteenth-century Salish holy man, predicted that "fair-skinned men wearing long black robes would come to the [Bitterroot] valley" in what is now Montana. He said they "would teach a new way of praying and a new moral law." These men would wear a cross and never marry, and although they would bring peace, "their arrival would signal the beginning of the end of all the people who then inhabited the land."[28]

Fulfillment of Xalíqs's prophecy would deliver unprecedented upheaval to the Salish homeland. Catholic Black Robes, as Jesuits were sometimes called, would come to build Christian settlements among them. These evangelists would be in bitter competition with Protestant missionaries, who would bring their "Book of Heaven" to the Northern Rocky Mountains and the Pacific Northwest of the United States. The Salish and other native peoples would be caught up in rivalries between these Christian foes.

Xalíqs rightly predicted the coming of Christian missionaries, but the story of how Christianity first arrived in the Rocky Mountains is not what many people assume. It is not a tale of zealous Christians going west to impose their own religion on unsuspecting natives. On the contrary, the wave of Christian missionaries who went west beginning in the 1830s came at the invitation of Indians: native peoples who had come east asking for religious instruction first enticed Christian evangelists to the mountains. At least that is the story that has come down to us from Christian historians. The native version remains untold. We likely will never know for certain what complex circumstances and conditions motivated Native American tribes to send emissaries east seeking help from the Euro-Americans. What we do know is that four American Indian delegates arrived in St. Louis in the fall of 1831.[29]

Protestants tell a different story of these four Indians than what Catholic historians say about them. Their respective historical accounts, though, reveal little about the actual circumstances of Native Americans in the western mountains, nor do they offer much insight into why native peoples would find it advantageous to send a delegation to a U.S. frontier town asking for help. But the differences between the Protestant and Catholic versions say quite a bit about the contrasts between these rival groups of U.S. Christians in the nineteenth century.

Catholic and Protestant sources agree that a delegation of Native Americans arrived in St. Louis in the fall of 1831 (originally thought to be 1832 in early Protestant versions) pleading for missionaries to serve their people. The two religious groups differ, however, on motives for the Indians' request and what they actually were asking for. According to the Protestant version, these Indians desired the Book of Heaven that they had heard about either in Protestant schools or from fur trappers. In contrast, Catholics tell of Iroquois trappers from Canada who migrated to the Upper Columbia River basin and introduced the religion of the Black Robes (Jesuit missionaries) to native peoples there. In the Catholic telling of the story, the Christian tale captivated these tribes in the U.S. territories of the intermountain West, and they subsequently sought Black Robes to come teach Christianity to them in their native lands.

Probably neither of these two versions of Indians pleading for Christian missionaries is wholly accurate. Their respective stories emphasize details that have more to do with intra-religious rivalries between Catholics and Protestants, and they reveal very little about Indigenous motives for dispatching a series of diplomatic missions to the American outpost of St. Louis in the 1830s.

Protestant historians emphasize that Indians came to St. Louis seeking the Christian Book of Heaven. In typical anti-Catholic fashion, they stress the preeminence of the Bible while condemning the material and ritual trappings of the Catholic Church. A common Protestant rendering of the narrative appears in an 1883 history of Oregon. In his telling of "Four Flat-Head Indians in St. Louis," author William Barrows portrays the "always religiously inclined" Flathead Indians of the Washington Territory as obsessively consumed with the Christian teachings they had heard from "mountain trappers." The Indians deliberated intently on Christian notions of God, Heaven, and especially the Bible in what Barrows describes as "their rude processes of investigation." He imagines the scene in somewhat poetic but deeply patronizing terms: "In those ancient groves which no axe had mutilated, God's first temples, or where solemn and sublime mountains shut them in like grand old cathedrals, we see them sitting about their dusky camp-fires. They think much and say but little of the white man's God and Book—stealthy worshippers—feeling after the true God, if haply they may find him."[30]

Barrows speculates on the Indians' decision to send a delegation to St. Louis: "It was gravely and anxiously settled that some of their number should go on the long trail to the rising of the sun to find the Book and bring back the light."[31] For a Protestant like Barrows, the source of truth and light is "the Book."

Barrows's distinctly Protestant orientation remains evident in his recounting of the delegates' experience once they arrived in St. Louis. Impressed as they were with "this world of new sights" in the U.S. city, "their sacred errand was uppermost, and they must deliver to one man." They sought out Gen. William Clark, the former leader of the Corps of Discovery, who now served as the superintendent of Indian Affairs headquartered in St. Louis. Lewis and Clark had enjoyed affable relations with the people of the Upper Columbia River basin on their epic expedition a quarter-century earlier. When they called on him in St. Louis, the aging general gladly received the weary delegation of Indians who now solicited his help.[32]

In their initial meeting, the envoys "made known distinctly the fact that they had come their long journey to get the white man's Book, which would tell them of the white man's God and heaven." Shortly after arriving, two of the delegates became ill and died, while the remaining pair pressed on in their search. But, Barrows continues, finding the Book of Heaven in St. Louis was a futile task: "In what was then a Roman Catholic city it was not easy to do this. . . . It has not been the policy or practice of that church to give the Bible to the people, whether Christian or pagan." Barrows reveals a Protestant anti-Catholic sentiment when he explains that the Christianity the Catholics gave to native peoples "was oral, ceremonial, and pictorial. In the best of their judgment, and in the depths of their convictions, they did not think it best to reduce native tongues to written languages, and the Scriptures to the vernacular of any tribe."[33] Consequently, Barrows laments, "the poor Flat-Heads could not find 'the Book.'" Although their hosts lavished them with gifts and hospitality, the Indians faced the prospect of returning west to their mountain homeland empty-handed. In a farewell address to General Clark, Barrows tells us, one of the two surviving delegates expressed disappointment in their mission:

> I came to you over a trail of many moons from the setting sun. You were the friend of our fathers who have all gone the long way. I came with one eye partly opened, for more light for my people, who sit in darkness. I go back with both eyes closed. How can I go back blind, to my blind people? . . . My people sent me to get the white man's Book of Heaven. You took me where you allow your women to dance, as we do not ours, and the Book was not there. You took me where they worship the Great Spirit with candles, and the Book was not there. You showed me the images of good spirits and pictures of the good land beyond, but the Book was not among them to tell us the way. I am going back the long, sad trail to my people of the dark land. You make my feet heavy with burdens of gifts, and my moccasins will grow old in carrying them, but the Book is not among them. When I tell my poor, blind people, after one more snow, in the big council, that I did not

bring the Book, no word will be spoken by our old men or by our young braves. One by one they will rise up and go out in silence. My people will die in darkness, and they will go on the long path to the other hunting-grounds. No white man will go with them and no white man's Book, to make the way plain. I have no more words.[34]

The two surviving Indians, according to Barrows's account, then boarded a steamboat of the American Fur Company as it embarked on the first ever steamer voyage up the Missouri River to the mouth of the Yellowstone River. From there they would return overland to their homes.[35]

Barrows composed his account of this initial delegation of "Flat-Head" Indians roughly a half-century after the events. His tale is a mixture of historical fact, apocryphal Protestant imaginings, and concerns of his day.[36] Clearly, in the fall of 1831, four Native Americans from the Upper Columbia River area arrived in St. Louis, where they sought the counsel of Gen. William Clark (Barrows and most nineteenth-century Protestant accounts mistakenly list the year as 1832). Only two of the Indians survived the winter, and they left in the spring to return to their people with only vague promises of missionary help to follow. The historical record indicates, however, that the unnamed Indian orator described in Barrows book most likely never addressed General Clark at a farewell gathering, if such an event even took place at all. Perhaps someone in St. Louis sympathetic to Indians penned the eloquent oration as a tactic to arouse Protestant benevolence and to motivate the establishment of a missionary effort in the American West. More likely, the Indian's purported speech was a later invention; in fact, the speech did not appear at all before the 1880s, when it began showing up in various Protestant histories such as Barrows's book. It eventually became a staple of the Protestant missionary narrative through the early decades of the twentieth century, providing justification for missionary activity among native peoples of the Pacific Northwest. It also served Protestant self-congratulatory affirmations in their long-standing rivalry with American Catholics.

The Catholic sources for their part reveal a somewhat different account of Indians arriving in St. Louis in 1831. In contrast to Protestant versions that emphasize the Book of Heaven, Catholic accounts insist that the native delegates specifically sought Black Robe missionaries. The Jesuits heard this cry for help emanating from the American wilderness, but their precarious circumstances in St. Louis postponed any Christian help coming from them. The pleas of the Jesuit superior for additional resources to serve missionary needs beyond the Rocky Mountains fell on deaf ears. It would be a decade, well after Protestant missionaries had gone west, before Fr. Pierre-Jean De Smet would establish his wilderness kingdom among the Indians of the Rocky Mountains.

The Catholic tale of Indian missions in the American West, as told by Jesuit historian Gilbert J. Garraghan, maintains that the first delegation of four "Flathead or Nez-Percé" Indians who arrived in St. Louis in October 1831 had "travelled all the way from their home in the upper Columbia Valley to ask for Catholic missionaries."[37] These Indians, in the Jesuit version, came looking for Black Robes to bring them the spiritual powers of the Christian religion.

In Garraghan's telling of the story, the native peoples of the Upper Columbia Valley in Oregon Country first learned of Christianity when two dozen Canadian Iroquois left their home in Caughnawaga, near Montreal, in 1816 to go west. They settled and intermarried with the Salish people, who eventually adopted these Canadian newcomers into their tribe.[38] Among this group of Christian Iroquois was a particularly fervent Catholic devotee by the name of Ignace La Mouse, and he introduced Catholic Christianity to the Salish, teaching them the Lord's Prayer, how to make the sign of the cross, to baptize their children, and to "sanctify the Sunday." Garraghan emphasizes that Ignace impressed upon his adopted tribe the need to have Black Robes come "to teach them the white man's prayer." The Salish people consequently took up the quest for Catholic priests to "bring among them the blessings of the religion."[39]

Garraghan's Catholic version of events insists that the Indians arrived in St. Louis specifically looking for Jesuit priests. After visiting General Clark, according to a contemporaneous letter from Bishop Rosati, the prelate overseeing the Catholic Church in St. Louis in the 1830s, the Indian delegates went to see the church "and appeared to be exceedingly well pleased with it." The bishop goes on to report that two of the Indians became ill, and they sought and received baptism before passing away. Both were buried "with all the Catholic ceremonies."[40] The remaining two departed from St. Louis the following spring, but Garraghan insists that the tale of a farewell banquet featuring an impassioned plea by one of the Indian delegates was a Protestant invention.[41]

The Jesuit bishop in St. Louis regarded the tribes of the Far West ripe for missionary activity. He wrote at the end of 1831: "These nations have not yet been corrupted by intercourse with others. Their manners and customs are simple and they are very numerous."[42] The Catholics in St. Louis, however, were shorthanded and could ill afford sending missionaries west.[43] Their failure to send Black Robes prompted a second Indian delegation to St. Louis in 1835. According to Garraghan's Catholic version of events, the Salish people prevailed on Old Ignace himself to travel to St. Louis to plead for Catholic missionaries. Ignace went in the fall of 1835 with his two sons, ages fourteen and ten, who were baptized by the Jesuits in St. Louis. Ignace wanted to leave his sons at the college in St. Louis, but the priests declined to accept them, nor were they able to send a missionary back with the delegates to minister to the Indians in the Rocky Mountains. So, Garraghan reports, Ignace and his sons returned west without success in securing a priest for their people.[44]

Ignace later met martyrdom in yet another failed attempt to get a priest to work among the native peoples of the Upper Columbia basin. In 1837 he led a third delegation to St. Louis, but hostile combatants attacked them on their way east and killed Ignace and his companions. Undeterred, the native peoples dispatched a fourth delegation in the summer of 1839 to obtain a Catholic priest to bring them Christianity. Two of the Iroquoians still living among the Salish, known as Pierre Gaucher and Young Ignace, volunteered to make the journey in the company of trappers heading east. As they descended the Missouri River, the Native American delegates rested at a Jesuit mission among the Potawatomi people, in a place known as Council Bluffs. Their brief stop at this Iowa mission before proceeding on to St. Louis would have momentous consequences for bringing the Catholic religion to the Rocky Mountains.

The Jesuit mission at Council Bluffs had begun just over a year before the Indian delegates from the West stopped there on their way to St. Louis. In the spring of 1838 the Jesuits had initiated plans for new missions along the Missouri River, and with the support of the super-intendent of Indian Affairs, Gen. William Clark, they sent three missionaries into the Indian territories.[45] Among them was Fr. Pierre-Jean De Smet, who, after seventeen years in America, was "burning with a desire to go among the Indians," according to his superior.[46] His fellow missionaries left him at Council Bluffs to singlehandedly evangelize the Potawatomi people.

Initially, Father De Smet tackled the assignment with enthusiasm, writing after just a few months, "I assure you that I see the work of God in it, and that I feel penetrated with gratitude toward those who, by their prayers, cease not to obtain for us from heaven these unexpected successes."[47] By the summer of 1839, though, things were not going so well. After little more than a year ministering to the Potawatomi people, De Smet had met discouragement that verged on despair. But deliverance soon floated down the Missouri River to reignite his "adventurous zeal." "Two Catholic Iroquois came to visit us," De Smet later wrote. "They had been for twenty-three years among the nation called the Flatheads and Pierced Noses." Father De Smet was especially impressed by their religious propensities: "I have never seen any savages so fervent in religion. By their instructions and examples they have given all that nation a great desire to have themselves baptized." He soon learned of their purpose: "The sole object of these good Iroquois was to obtain a priest to come and finish what they had so happily commenced."[48]

Pierre-Jean De Smet resolved to fulfill their wish. He soon developed a scheme to move west and serve these Indians of the mountains. The Jesuit superior in St. Louis agreed with his plan and ended De Smet's Iowa appointment, freeing him to establish a new missionary field among the Indians of Oregon Country.

The decision to send Father De Smet to the Rocky Mountains benefited from the success of Protestants. The arrival of the latest Indian delegation from the western mountains reminded Catholics of their diminishing influence among native peoples in the Americas. In his request to the father general of the Jesuits in Rome for a missionary to go west, Bishop Rosati of St. Louis explained that only four of the original two dozen Iroquois who settled among the Salish people were still living. He went on to emphasize their steadfast loyalty to the church: "Not only have they planted the faith in those wild countries, but they have besides defended it against the encroachments of the Protestant ministers. When these pretended [Protestant] missionaries presented themselves among them, our good Catholics refused to accept them."[49] The bishop thus raised the specter of religious rivalries with Protestants playing out in the mountainous regions of North America, and he insisted on sending a Jesuit envoy to bolster the spiritual resolve of the Native American Catholics to persist in their faith.

Bishop Rosati gained official support for expanding the Jesuit mission to the Rocky Mountains, and he turned to the zealous young missionary Fr. Pierre-Jean De Smet to initiate efforts among the Indigenous tribes of the region. De Smet set out for the mountains in the springtime of 1840, and by June he arrived at the American Fur Company's rendezvous on the Green River in what is now southwestern Wyoming. From there a group of Salish traders escorted the Black Robe missionary to the main camp of their people, where they were joined by the Pend d'Oreille and others in Pierre's Hole on the banks of the Green River. At that location Father De Smet performed the first Catholic mass in Wyoming. He arranged a small altar set on a low hill and decorated it with tree branches and strings of freshly cut flowers. Before him gathered the various groups of Indians; a few Canadian trappers and traders also joined them in their celebration of the Eucharist. As De Smet later recalled, "It was a spectacle truly moving to the heart of a missionary that this immense family, composed of so many different tribes, should prostrate themselves in equal humility before the Divine Host." The celebrants broke out in song, with the Canadians singing hymns in French and Latin and the Indians joining with their native languages. "All distinctions, all rivalries of peoples, were obliterated before a unanimous sentiment, that of Christian piety," exclaimed Father De Smet. "Oh! truly it was a Catholic ceremony."[50]

Father De Smet soon departed from this pious rendezvous in Wyoming, but not before baptizing two elderly head chiefs. Impressed by his warm reception, the Jesuit missionary promised his Indian hosts that a resident Black Robe would come the following year to establish a permanent mission among them.[51]

It was Father De Smet himself who fulfilled the promise when he returned west the following year, 1841. This time he brought two additional Jesuit priests, Father Nicolas Point, a French artist, architect, and former

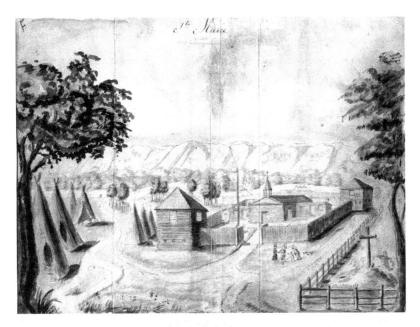

FIG. 2. Drawing of St. Mary's Mission to the Salish people in Montana by Nicolas Point. Ink on paper, ca. 1842. Jesuit Archives & Research Center, St. Louis MO.

head of a Jesuit school in New Orleans, and Father Gregory Mengarini, an Italian linguist, physician, and musician, plus three lay brothers of the Jesuit order. This intrepid missionary party set about building what De Smet imagined would be an "empire of Christian Indians" in the Northern Rockies.[52]

De Smet was convinced that the Salish, or what he called the Flatheads, would be the foundation of the empire he hoped would dominate the religious lives of Indians in the Rocky Mountains. "This nation of the Flatheads," he wrote in the fall of that first year, "appear to be a chosen people—'the elect of God.' . . . It would be easy to make this tribe a model for other tribes—the seed of 200,000 Christians."[53] With the help of their Indian allies, the Jesuits built their first mission in Montana's Bitterroot Valley and christened it "St. Mary's," the first Euro-American settlement in the region, today heralded as the place "where Montana began."[54] More missions followed as De Smet and his fellow Catholic evangelists introduced Christianity to the Salish and Coeur d'Alene people, and eventually even the Natsitapii, or "Blackfeet," who tended to be wary of Euro-Americans.

By 1846, when Father De Smet left the western mountains for the last time, the Jesuit missions were well established throughout the region that would later become Montana Territory. The Black Robes had, in their retrospective estimation, answered the pleas of Indians who had come east to St. Louis fifteen years earlier seeking priests to teach them the ways of Christianity. Despite their tardy arrival, the Jesuits had planted the seeds of a Christian kingdom loyal to the Catholic faith among the native peoples of the American wilderness.

During the years that Fr. Pierre-Jean De Smet headed the Jesuit mission enterprise in the Rocky Mountains, he came to know the places and people of the region as well as any Euro-American in the nineteenth century. But unlike his younger protégé, Francis Kuppens, De Smet never saw Yellowstone for himself: he never contemplated the brilliant colors of the Grand Canyon of the Yellowstone or the majestic drama of its falls; he never experienced the constant spectacle of the geyser basins, with their spouting fountains and boiling springs. Yet despite never having been there, De Smet knew of the place; in fact, he was one of the earliest writers to publish a description of Yellowstone's wonders. He had learned of this wonderland from his friend Jim Bridger, the renowned explorer, fur trapper, army scout, trade post entrepreneur, and notorious storyteller. In fact, Bridger made a map for Father De Smet detailing the area of the present-day national park, the most detailed cartographic representation of Yellowstone at that time.[55] De Smet concluded, based on Bridger's account and the reports of other trappers who had been there, that Yellowstone was a "most extraordinary spot" and ranked, in his estimation, as "perhaps the most marvelous of all the northern half of the continent."[56]

A Land of Many Faiths

In the early fur trapping years, religious institutions, specifically those of the Christian variety, were nearly absent from the western territories. By 1866, though, when the Jesuit missionary Francis Kuppens visited Yellowstone, Montana Territory claimed a diverse collection of Christians who would soon be building churches in their settlements. The Jesuit presence was well established by the 1860s, and as white settlers followed mining booms and built new towns, an assortment of Protestant preachers followed. Religion came west in the tracks of settlers.

Episcopalians arrived in 1867, with the first formal Episcopal worship service in Montana occurring in Virginia City in July of that year.[57] Other Protestant preachers, Methodists and Presbyterians in particular, could also be found on the streets of what was then the Montana Territory's state capital. Still, there were not enough preachers to serve the needs of everyone. Bishop Daniel S. Tuttle, who officiated at the first Episcopal service along with his associate Rev. E. N. Goddard, regularly welcomed members of other Christian sects among their Episcopalian worshippers. In fact, the bishop observed an ecumenical attitude shared by many church leaders there. Bishop Tuttle explained, "When administering the holy communion in towns where perhaps my visit was almost the only religious service of the year I did not hesitate to invite people publicly in these words: 'All Christians, by whatever name they call themselves, who will come with us in faith and penitence and charity to partake of our blessed Lord's body and blood in the holy communion this morning will be cordially and lovingly welcomed.'" His church, St. Paul's, was one of only two places of worship in Virginia City at the time (the other was the Roman Catholic church), and the bishop regularly allowed other Christians to hold services there.[58] Cooperation was the guiding principle for the pioneer preachers of Montana Territory.

Christians, though, were not the only religious people in Montana. Mining booms also brought Asian laborers, nearly all of them Chinese men, and the local papers never missed reporting what their Euro-American readers regarded as exotic religious celebrations and funerals of the so-called Celestial people. An item in a Helena paper in December 1867, for example, reported the death of a local Chinese woman whose name the paper listed only as "something almost unpronounceable, and without any particular meaning." Her death, according to the news report, resulted "from the continued effects of opium and poor whiskey." This attempt to depict the deceased woman as a derelict whose life, like her name, held no particular meaning, reflects racial animosity typical of the time. In fact, the woman appears to have been a valued member of the Chinese community in Helena; the article went on to note that her funeral was attended by "a large number of our Celestial denizens," and the observances included "the usual ceremonies of burying the deceased's clothes, offering insense [*sic*], etc." The large attendance and the formality of the ceremony belies the paper's dismissal of the woman's status in local society as insignificant.[59]

In addition to the various new religions entering Montana, including the multiple varieties of the Christian faith as well as the Asian and other religious orientations that came with immigrant laborers, native religions also persisted. The Pikuni guides who went with Father Kuppens to see the waterfalls, geysers, and spectacular scenery of Yellowstone came from just one of dozens of Native American groups who frequented the region, each with their own distinctive mythologies, ritual practices, animist orientations, and traditional regard for transcendent realities. Missionary efforts to replace these ancient traditions had mixed results at best. Many native peoples kept up the old ways even as they accepted the Christian teachings of the Black Robes and other Christians.[60]

Amid this burgeoning assortment of spiritual inclinations and religious orientations, the wonders of Yellowstone were finding their way into public imagination through a variety of voices. By the time the Jesuit missionary Francis Kuppens sat in the tents of his Native American hosts and first heard of the exquisite powers inhabiting the Yellowstone Plateau, stories of Yellowstone were circulating throughout Montana and far beyond. Kuppens's own mentor, Father De Smet, had already published impressions of the place gleaned from the mountaineer Jim Bridger. The accounts of other explorers, trappers, miners, soldiers, and occasional tourists encouraged ever more curiosity and the determination of others to experience the place for themselves. The marvelous tales of this strange landscape left little doubt that a place entirely unique, mysterious, and somewhat frightening beckoned the adventurous spirit abounding in Montana Territory.

The spirit of adventure, though, rode on the rails of development in the western territories of the United States. For the Euro-Americans establishing themselves in Montana in the 1860s, the appeal of mysterious and frightening lands was interwoven in the ethos of conquest, settlement, and the civilizing forces of a divinely sanctioned Manifest Destiny. The dominant Protestant worldview recognized the hand of God in the spectacular scenery of places like Yellowstone, and many Christian visitors viewed these magnificent sights with a reassuring confidence that God meant this land to be theirs to possess, to enjoy, and to make prosperous. America, as these pious Christians imagined it, was a nation chosen for God's glory.

2

FOR THE BENEFIT AND ENJOYMENT
OF THE PEOPLE

Jay Cooke fancied himself a fisherman. There was little in life that pleased him more than a day out on Lake Erie catching bass or plying Pennsylvania's rivers and streams for trout. As he confesses in his memoir, written in his seventies, "I was always a hunter & a fisherman."[1] This passion began as a young boy growing up in Ohio on the shores of Lake Erie. "From my earliest boyhood I have roamed the waters of Sandusky Bay & this island region, & every portion of it is most familiar to me," he explains. "I have explored every hunting and fishing ground, I have camped out for a week at a time, & on many occasions in the forests & marshes bord[er]ing the lake & bay, & upon many of the islands, I have captured every variety of game & fish."[2] Cooke's love of outdoor recreation never waned throughout his long and prosperous career, and by the end of his life, at the dawn of the twentieth century, he continued to indulge in what a close friend described as "his love of the apostolic diversion of fishing."[3]

As the nation's wealthiest citizen in the early years of America's Gilded Age, Jay Cooke could well afford the indulgence of the fisherman's recreational pleasure. A week of angling on the wild rivers and streams of Pennsylvania or methodically trolling the tempestuous waters of Lake Erie offered Cooke a welcome respite from the ambitious strivings of a banker at the center of the nation's rapid expansion and industrialization. Underlying his ambitions, though, was an unwavering devotion to a radically democratic evangelicalism that would make such leisure enjoyments available to all Americans, or at least it would greatly broaden the class of elite citizens who could indulge in the pastimes of nature's bounty. Recreational time spent outdoors coincided with his religious and patriotic values, and perhaps more than anyone else, Jay Cooke made Yellowstone National Park possible.

God's Chosen Instrument

Jay Cooke's interest in making Yellowstone known to the American public had direct benefits for his personal wealth, but it also coincided with a renewal of Manifest Destiny among the American people following the Civil War.[4] The immediate aftermath of the great armed conflict had focused the energies of northern leaders on national healing. At the same time, the conclusion of hostilities between North and South inspired an evangelical zeal to renew the Protestant promise of the nation's divine destiny.[5] For devout citizens like Cooke, building the moral institutions of a war-torn country was a first priority, but extending the benefits of a redeemed Christian society to the savage lands of the American West also ranked high. Jay Cooke aimed his reconstructionist sights on civilizing the western wilds.

Opening the U.S. West to civilized society and making places like Yellowstone accessible to civilized people fit with Cooke's own self-regard as "God's chosen instrument." He understood his life's purpose as comparable to the Old Testament patriarch Moses and to the nation's patriarch George Washington; he regarded himself, with some justification, alongside Abraham Lincoln and Ulysses Grant, as part of the American Trinity that had saved the Union. His divine destiny, he claimed, involved "the financial work of saving the Union during the greatest War that has ever been fought in the history of Man" by providing funds for Lincoln and Grant to succeed in vanquishing the Confederacy.[6] Following his great success in financing the Union cause, Cooke directed his hubris and much of his immense wealth toward efforts to redeem the nation.

Redeeming the United States following the Civil War coincided with the financial interests of Jay Cooke's banking company, especially its controlling stake in the Northern Pacific Railroad. His financial corporation, much like Cooke's own personal religious and patriotic obsessions, was built on a foundation of nationalist and evangelical Protestant zeal that was tightly woven into its corporate culture. The firm's initial partnership agreement of 1866 laid out its religious commitment in its opening paragraph by stipulating the priority of the "Old Patriarch Jacob" (opj), a separate account on the books of Jay Cooke and Company: "First, after all losses and expenses are deducted from the Profit and Loss, one-tenth of the remainder is annually appropriated to the opj fund; that is, to charitable and religious objects such as will best promote the glory of God and the extension of his kingdom."[7] Indeed, a religious tithe ranked foremost among the corporate priorities.

In addition to his company's opj fund, Jay Cooke also maintained a personal opj account. These combined funds benefited a range of religious endeavors in reconstructionist America that included rebuilding damaged and destroyed churches in the southern states after the war; direct support to clergy, especially regarding their religious education; and active long-term support of the American Sunday School Union.[8]

Jay Cooke's generosity, though, was not entirely altruistic. Much of his philanthropy coincided directly with his business ambitions. As his first biographer noted, "Wherever his financial interest carried him he followed it with subscriptions to church buildings—in the coals regions when he was a large owner in the mines of the Preston Company, in his iron towns in New York State, at South Mountain in southern Pennsylvania, at Duluth and along the line of the Northern Pacific, in Iowa where he was at one time an extensive landholder. 'opj' gave bells, steeples, organs, books for Sunday Schools, rectories, silver communion services, and eked out the modest salaries of country parsons."[9] His financial concerns along with his Christian piety constituted the singular character of a Gilded Age capitalist who regarded himself as God's chosen instrument.

The connection between Jay Cooke's sense of providential purpose and his company's financial stakes turned his attentions westward. Gaining financial control of the Northern Pacific Railroad concentrated his righteous mission on connecting the thriving eastern states with new territorial opportunities in the West. A key link in making this connection straddled the Rocky Mountains in Montana Territory. Difficult terrain and the resistance of Indigenous peoples in the region posed troublesome challenges to building a railroad that would cross the northern tier of the continent. It also offered enticing treasures to capture the U.S. public imagination. Chief among these treasures were the little-known wonders of Yellowstone.[10]

As enticing as these western wonders may have seemed to him, however, Jay Cooke did not go west until later in life. But getting the railroad built and making Yellowstone a national park required allies on the ground, and Cooke discovered the perfect ally in Nathaniel P. Langford. Originally from Minnesota, Langford had come to Montana in 1862, after his family's bank failed.[11] He arrived as the gold mines were beginning to boom, and within a couple years, his family political connections in Washington DC had arranged for his appointment as the federal collector of internal revenue for the newly established Territory of Montana. He parlayed this position into prospects for an appointment as territorial governor, but President Andrew Johnson's clash with the Senate in 1869 scuttled that opportunity.[12] In the spring of 1870 Nathaniel P. Langford found himself without a position and was available to help Jay Cooke bring public attention to Yellowstone.

Part of Cooke's plans to enhance the public's impressions of Montana Territory involved organizing an expedition to investigate the stories and rumors of the Yellowstone wonders. For this he recruited Langford to gather a group of prominent Montana citizens to explore the headwaters of the Yellowstone River. After their return, Langford then would embark on a promotional campaign to publicize the attractions of Yellowstone.

Langford's success in bringing together prominent Montana citizens to join the expedition found support in his involvement with the Masons. Freemasonry claimed a foundational role in the civilizing forces in early Montana even before churches came to most settlements.[13] The Masonic order arrived initially on the wave of gold fever, and Langford was among the first to introduce this quasi-religious tradition to the Montana gold fields.[14] By the time he was organizing an expedition to explore the headwaters of the Yellowstone River, in 1870, Langford could rely on his Masonic connections to help assemble a band of the territory's leading citizens to join in the venture.

The presence of Freemasonry in nineteenth-century Montana continued a long tradition of Masonic involvement in the settlement and colonization of North America. Indeed, the Masons had come to the English colonies long before the American Revolution. This secretive society, bound by ritual and oaths of loyalty, originated with medieval European Masons guilds, but by the 1720s the English Masons were

FIG. 3. Nathaniel P. Langford conducts the first Masonic meeting in Montana. Mural by artist Olaf Seltzer inside the Grand Lodge of Montana Library and Museum, Helena, 1937. Photo by Daniel Gardiner.

largely a social club that allowed for fraternization among middle-class gentlemen, tradesmen, and aristocrats.[15] They had arrived in the American colonies by the 1730s and grew to about one hundred Masonic lodges spread throughout the thirteen colonies at the time of the American Revolution, with membership increasing even more rapidly in the early years of the new American Republic.[16]

As their numbers expanded, the American Masons incorporated more Protestant influences, combined with Deist ideas that held sway among eighteenth-century Masons.[17] Their mixture of a biblical tone with the more rationalist orientation of Deism made Masonic lodges an effective institution for instilling notions of democratic virtue among citizens of the young nation. During the early decades of the republic, Freemasonry's ethos of democratic virtue and spiritual righteousness provided a sense of purpose and social stability in a time of rapid change for the people of the United States.[18]

Many, however, refused to embrace Freemasonry as the cornerstone of democratic society. The religious character of their practice, along with the secretive nature of the Masons' lodge meetings, invited denunciation, especially among some religious clergy, who resented the Masons' growing political influence and their criticism of evangelical Protestantism. Freemasonry stirred up public controversy in the early republic, especially in the 1820s, when a scandal in Upstate New York gave rise to an "Anti-Masonic" political party. The Masonic lodges, however, persisted through years of censure. By the 1850s they were enjoying something of a revival, although the Masons never fully recovered their earlier public influence.[19]

The expansion of Freemasonry in the middle decades of the nineteenth century followed the westward expansion of the nation's boundaries. Consequently, Masons arrived in Montana in the wake of gold fever and quickly established themselves as mainstays of civilized people in the rough-and-tumble lawlessness that characterized the early mining settlements in the region.[20] The first Masonic lodge in Montana was established in the mining town of Bannack by dispensation from the Grand Lodge of Nebraska in 1863. Actually, the Bannack lodge never fully materialized, mostly because many of the local Masons moved elsewhere in the transient nature of mining communities, but their presence had a lasting impact. Nathaniel P. Langford, who served as first master of the Bannack lodge, explains, "Masons who in the first terrible year of our history, were instant in every good word and work which had for its object the protection, improvement and purification of our little society." In fact, he recognized the Masons' role in the vigilante movement of Montana's early years when he credited the organization with "finally rid[ding] our Territory of the murderers, thieves and robbers that then infested it."[21] Their defeat, Langford concluded years later, "had its origin in principles traceable to that stalwart morality which is ever the offspring of Masonic and Religious institutions."[22]

Masons and other religiously minded folks of Montana imposed the moral principles of civilized society on the nascent settlements of the territory with their "highest purpose." Cornelius Hedges, another prominent Montana Mason, describes this highest purpose in religious terms as "the cultivation of a higher manhood, in the loving service of God and humankind. To finish up the human being to the highest point of mental and moral development, seems to be the end of the Creator in framing the Universe, and the course of his providential dealings. What higher aim can we propose to ourselves than humbly imitate his plan, and co-operate with him?"[23]

Eventually, the Masons established a visible presence in the landscape of Montana's settlements. By March 1867 an announcement in the *Montana Post* reported that Virginia City, the territorial capital, boasted of plans "to rear, here, in the heart of the Rocky Mountains, a great Masonic Temple, an enduring monument of the work of Montana Masons, and a model of modern architecture."[24] The Masons were able to dedicate their impressive temple by the end of the year, with the newly arrived Episcopal bishop, Rev. Bishop Daniel S. Tuttle, serving as chaplain. According to the news report, the new edifice was "dedicated in the name of God and the members of an Order confined to no country, creed or clime, it becomes a universal sanctuary for all Masons."[25]

The growing presence of Masonry in the Montana landscape affirmed the progress of Montanans in bringing civilized society to the region, and it helped, if only indirectly, to extend civilization to the headwaters of the Yellowstone River. Langford was serving as Most Worshipful Grand Master of Montana Masons in 1870 when he organized the expedition that would bring Yellowstone's wonders to a U.S. public hungry to manifest their divine destiny across the continent.[26] Following the explorers' return from Yellowstone that fall, Langford relinquished his title as leader of Montana's Masons to Cornelius Hedges, who had joined Langford on the expedition that would bring the region's unique attractions to the attention of eastern audiences.[27] In short, Masons helped make Yellowstone a wonderland that affirmed America's divine destiny.

An Expedition to Yellowstone

Jay Cooke had learned of Nathaniel P. Langford through William R. Marshall, an acquaintance and political ally of the Philadelphia banker who had served as governor of Minnesota. Governor Marshall had led a reconnaissance expedition into Canada in early 1870 at Cooke's behest to explore possibilities for establishing railroad connections to the north. Marshall was pleased to have his brother-in-law Langford join him on the trip into Canada, as they had undertaken together a similar reconnaissance expedition in western Minnesota the previous summer for the

Northern Pacific Railroad.[28] Following their return from Canada, Marshall sent Langford east to meet Jay Cooke with a letter of introduction that explained: "In addition to information of the country etc. of the late trip [to Canada] that may interest you, it has occurred to me that Mr. L[angford] might give you information in regard to Montana that would be of value to the NPR'R. Mr. L[angford] has been prominently identified with Montana from its first settlement."[29]

When they met that spring of 1870, Jay Cooke discovered in Nathaniel P. Langford an effective ally for his plans to promote the Northern Pacific Railroad in Montana, which included adding Yellowstone as a key attraction for prospective customers and investors that would make the railroad profitable. Their initial meeting took place at the banker's home in suburban Philadelphia. Among other topics likely discussed, they agreed that exploring Yellowstone would prove useful in promoting the westward extension of the Northern Pacific Railroad.[30] Langford left the banker's home with plans to organize an expedition to the Yellowstone Plateau and then to publicize its discoveries to a national audience.

After a brief stop in St. Paul, Minnesota, to secure a commitment from the army to provide a military escort for the Yellowstone excursion, Langford returned to Montana, where he spent the summer organizing the expedition.[31] As the territory's former collector of internal revenue and currently serving as the Most Worshipful Grand Master of Montana Masons, he was well positioned to convince a group of Montana's leading citizens to join his venture. Among them was Langford's Mason colleague Cornelius Hedges as well as Henry D. Washburn, who had served as a brevet brigadier general for Union forces in the Civil War and who had come west in 1869 to serve as surveyor general of Montana Territory. When their first choice for a leader was unable to join them, General Washburn agreed to lead the expedition.[32]

On August 22, 1870, the expedition left Fort Ellis, east of Bozeman, Montana, to set out for Yellowstone with a total of nineteen in their party, including two packers, two cooks, and a military escort of six cavalrymen.[33] As they made their way toward Yellowstone, this band of explorers, including two of Montana's most prominent Masons, brought civilization up the Yellowstone River to claim this wondrous land as a domesticated, settled, and civilized place. Armed with the Masonic confidence in a "stalwart morality" aimed at "the protection, improvement and purification of our little society," Nathaniel P. Langford and his fellow expeditioners carried a trust in providential Manifest Destiny onto the Yellowstone Plateau.[34]

The Masonic ethos to protect, improve, and purify the civilized society of Montana colored a momentous conversation of how these expeditioners might make the most of the wondrous land they encountered, at least according to a mythic tale that circulated for more than a century. It was Cornelius Hedges, the soon-to-be Most Worshipful Grand Master of Montana Masons, who urged his compatriots to put national destiny above personal ambitions, the story goes, and in so doing, he gave birth to the idea of Yellowstone as a national park. The topic came up during the last days of their adventure near where the Firehole and Gibbon Rivers converge to form the Madison River. As they relaxed by the campfire on the evening of September 19, 1870, the talk turned, according to this apocryphal tale, to the future prospects for the unusual land and its unique attractions that they had experienced in the previous weeks. After several suggestions for capitalizing on the profitable potential of this wonderland, Hedges proposed that "there ought to be no private ownership of any portion of that region, but that the whole of it ought to be set apart as a great National Park."[35] All but one of his companions readily agreed, according to Langford's retrospective account.[36] These noble and visionary men, the story implies, set aside their personal ambitions for the democratic ideal of a national park. In its later renditions, Hedges's suggestion anticipated the conservation movement that would gain momentum in the closing decades of the nineteenth century.

The campfire myth of visionary gentlemen acceding to the more honorable option of preserving Yellowstone makes a great tale, but historians have identified less noble and more complicated origins of the national park idea that made Yellowstone the world's first federal parkland.[37] Most park historians now recognize that the beginnings of national parks arose predictably from numerous cultural forces at play in postbellum America. Foremost among the formative factors that made Yellowstone National Park possible were the interests behind the Northern Pacific Railroad, specifically the financial stakes of the railroad's chief underwriter, Jay Cooke and Company.[38] Moreover, these economic factors were closely bound to a religious vision that comported with American imperial ambitions.

Uncovering the Nakedness of the Sleeping Yellowstone Beauty

Even as it brought civilization to Yellowstone, the Washburn expedition brought Yellowstone to civilization. The most important result of the group's "discovery" was revealing the Yellowstone wonders to the broader American public. As one of Jay Cooke's correspondents reported shortly after the Washburn party returned home: "The villains in Helena [Montana] are wholly uncovering the nakedness of our sleeping Yellowstone Beauty. It breaks my heart."[39] But it did not break Cooke's pious heart. Waking the Yellowstone Beauty was exactly what he hoped for in sponsoring and encouraging the expedition.

The "villains in Helena" were the members of the Washburn party recently returned from Yellowstone, most prominently Nathaniel P. Langford, who got busy preparing lectures about their adventure for a tour of the eastern United States sponsored by Jay Cooke and Company. He planned to generate helpful publicity for the Northern Pacific Railroad by presenting his Yellowstone lecture in several major cities. After only two lectures, though, a throat ailment prevented any further speaking engagements. Newspaper coverage of his initial talks, however, had the desired effect of arousing a hint of public interest in Yellowstone's wonders.[40]

Following his foreshortened winter tour of East Coast cities, Langford penned a pair of articles for the popular magazine *Scribner's Monthly*.[41] For much of the American public, these sketches of the Washburn party's adventures in wonderland were the first exposure to this remarkable place high in the western mountains. The wide reach of the *Scribner's* readership added to the growing public fascination with Yellowstone pushed along by the publicity machine of Jay Cooke and Company. By the time *Scribner's Monthly* featured the pair of Langford's descriptive essays in the late spring of 1871, Yellowstone was well on its way to achieving its iconic status as a wonderland of the American West.

The popularity of Langford's *Scribner's* articles relied to a large extent on religious attitudes toward nature held by many Americans in the nineteenth century. His tale reads as part adventure story, part promotional boosterism touting the beneficial attractions of Montana Territory, and part guidebook for subsequent travelers. Implicit in this narrative was a well-established American aesthetic and scientific curiosity germinated in the Calvinism that Puritans had brought to America in the seventeenth century and which their cultural heirs had further cultivated in the nineteenth century.[42] This convergence of aesthetic and sciential perspectives in the *Scribner's* articles of Yellowstone conveyed a certain reverent exuberance that drew upon widespread literary conventions that had grown from these religious roots.

Langford opens his first essay with a "great curiosity to see the wonders of the upper valley of the Yellowstone" aroused by the "strange and marvelous" tales of trappers and mountaineers.[43] He tells how the explorers entered "the wildest imaginable scenery of river, rock, and mountain" in the first days of their journey.[44] In recounting their movement southward along the Yellowstone River, Langford turns to specifically religious imagery to describe the first major attraction they encountered, a geological oddity of "two parallel vertical walls of rock, projecting from the side of a mountain to the height of 125 feet, traversing the mountain from base to summit, a distance of 1500 feet." They designated it "Devil's Slide," a name that remains today for this attraction that lies just north of the Yellowstone park boundary.[45] Langford rationalizes somewhat apologetically this turn to demonic imagery in the precedent of "the old mountaineers and trappers" who "had been peculiarly lavish in the use of the infernal vocabulary," a tradition that Langford and his compatriots would perpetuate as they encountered other Yellowstone attractions reminiscent of the "infernal regions."[46]

At the same time, Langford's descriptions of Yellowstone's wonders relied on more romantic interpretations of nature that Transcendentalist writers had made popular. At the Grand Canyon of the Yellowstone, he writes, "The brain reels as we gaze into this profound and solemn solitude" of the canyon's chasm. He continues: "The sense of danger with which it impresses you is harrowing in the extreme. You feel the absence of sound, the oppression of absolute silence," but, he concludes, "you thank God that he had permitted you to gaze, unharmed, upon this majestic display of natural architecture." On viewing the magnificent Lower Falls, Langford exclaims, "A grander scene than the lower cataract of the Yellowstone was never witnessed by mortal eyes."[47]

His romantic vision of Yellowstone's grandness was not limited to the scenery alone, but it also included Langford's view of Indians. In the second of his two 1871 articles, Langford speculates about the religious significance of Yellowstone's mountains for local Indigenous people. Among the Blackfeet people, in particular, he explains, "there is a fable that he who attains its summit catches a view of the land of souls, and beholds the happy hunting-grounds spread out below him, brightening with the abodes of the free and generous spirits."[48] He does not reveal how he knows this "fable," nor does their belief in "free and generous spirits" compromise his general ambivalence toward Indians. In fact, this romanticized view of the Indigenous people and their myths, regarded somewhat dismissively as quaint fables, appears in contrast to the nervousness Langford relates upon actually encountering American Indians. His company became alarmed to discover early in the expedition a small group of mounted Indians across the river and more watching them from behind a butte. "Our camp was guarded that night," Langford recalls, "with more than ordinary vigilance."[49] On the other hand, Indians also added to the pleasure of their sightseeing. In Langford's estimation, a group of six Indians seen along the shores of Yellowstone Lake were "one of the curiosities of the expedition."[50] Even the human presence in Yellowstone inspired these visitors' wonder.

The greatest of wonders, though, were to be found in the geyser basins along the Firehole River. Their initial impression was nothing short of astonishment, "to see in the clear sunlight, at no great distance, an immense volume of clear, sparkling water projected into the air to the height of one hundred and twenty-five feet." This first of the geysers repeated its spectacle regularly, earning from members of the Washburn expedition the name "Old Faithful."[51]

Other spectacles were just as impressive as the expeditioners made their way down the Firehole River, delighting in the geysers, boiling springs, and "architectural features of the silicious sinter" surrounding many of the thermal attractions. Langford describes for the *Scribner's* readers the "grand eruption" of the geyser they named "the Giantess": they stood

on the side of the geyser nearest the sun, the gleams of which filled the sparkling column of water and spray with myriads of rainbows, whose arches were constantly changing—dipping and fluttering hither and thither, and disappearing only to be succeeded by others, again and again, amid the aqueous column, while the minute globules into which the spent jets were diffused when falling sparkled like a shower of diamonds, and around every shadow which the denser clouds of vapor, interrupting the sun's rays, cast upon the column, could be seen a luminous circle radiant with all the colors of the prism, and resembling the halo of glory represented in paintings as encircling the head of Divinity. All that we had previously witnessed seemed tame in comparison with the perfect grandeur and beauty of this display.[52]

Langford strains to convey the experience he felt in witnessing the effusions of the Giantess. He resorts to the two intertwined strands of a U.S. Protestant aesthetic to find words that best express his experience: on the one hand, he uses traditional biblical imagery that paints "the halo of glory . . . encircling the head of Divinity," and on the other, he turns to a romantic nature aesthetic that frames the aqueous column of the geyser as a picture of "perfect grandeur and beauty."

Langford's allusions to religious imagery circulating in postbellum U.S. culture conformed to the nationalist sentiments of Manifest Destiny.[53] The Calvinist notion of God's word revealed in nature affirmed for patriotic nineteenth-century Americans the providential aim of their crusade "to overspread and to possess the whole continent."[54] The scenic wonders of the American West were prime evidence for faithful Protestants of God's intentions for the destiny of the United States as a Christian nation.

Bringing attention to places like Yellowstone also supported the evangelical and entrepreneurial intentions of Jay Cooke. Langford concludes his two-article series in *Scribner's* with a promotional word for Cooke's railroad enterprise: "By means of the Northern Pacific Railroad, which will doubtless be completed within the next three years, the traveler will be able to make the trip to Montana from the Atlantic seaboard in three days, and thousands of tourists will be attracted to both Montana and Wyoming in order to behold with their own eyes the wonders here described."[55] Though his predictions that trains would be bringing passengers to Montana "within the next three years" proved wildly optimistic, Langford reveals the underlying motive of his enthusiasm for exploring

Yellowstone and sharing his experiences of its marvels. His efforts were part of a grand plan to connect Montana directly to the rest of the United States by the steel rails overspreading the North American continent.[56]

The World's First National Park

This grand plan of railroad development included a calculated effort to present the Yellowstone wonders to the U.S. public. Langford's revelations of the Yellowstone landscape to the *Scribner's Monthly* readership followed his promotional lecture tour of eastern states sponsored by the railroad's chief financier at the precise moment of a major push to sell Northern Pacific Railroad bonds.[57] And it paid off handsomely, at least in the short term. As *Scribner's Monthly* readers enjoyed a first inkling of Yellowstone's fantastical attractions in Langford's essays, another expedition that would bring even greater recognition of the region as a treasure of the American West was in the making. The esteemed geologist and explorer Dr. Ferdinand V. Hayden, who attended Langford's first lecture in Washington DC, had submitted to Congress a proposal for a formal geological survey of the headwaters of the Yellowstone River.[58]

Dr. Hayden had attempted to reach Yellowstone more than a decade earlier with the aborted expedition of 1859–60 led by Capt. William F. Raynolds. Since then, Hayden had harbored ambitions to reach the source of the Yellowstone River.[59] The time seemed right to gain support for his proposal when publicity about Yellowstone's wonders from Langford and others had whetted enthusiasm among members of Congress.

Hayden's plans to explore Yellowstone also benefited from support from Jay Cooke. Cooke's engineering of the Washburn expedition and his promotional campaign that enticed public curiosity about Yellowstone created a favorable political atmosphere for Hayden's proposal. Additionally, Cooke may have contributed funds directly to Hayden. On the eve of his departure up the Yellowstone River, the geologist admitted to a reporter for the *Helena Daily Herald* that his surveying work was in part "at the instigation of J. Cooke & Co., who contemplate running a branch road through this [Two Ocean] Pass to connect with the Central Pacific, if practicable."[60] Ostensibly working for the U.S. government, it appears that Hayden also may have been working for Cooke.

Hayden gained funding support from Congress and probably had financial backing from Cooke and Company, but he needed to gain the public's confidence as well. He realized that carefully drawn maps, scientific observations, and the collection of geological specimens were not enough to capture public imagination and gain funding for subsequent expeditions. He needed to bring something of the experience of surveyed lands to the American people. With three other major survey enterprises vying for congressional sponsorship, Hayden needed more than scientific reports to inspire enthusiasm for his future initiatives. He needed artists.[61]

Hayden's first expedition to the region initiated what would become by far the most ubiquitous activity in Yellowstone: photography. Still a relatively new technology, photographic documentation had already made its claim on the geological surveys. Hayden had taken photographer William Henry Jackson on an expedition the previous year, which led to Jackson's appointment as official survey photographer with offices and a darkroom in Washington DC.[62] His photographs on Hayden's 1871 survey would be indispensable to documenting and promoting the wonders that lay at the headwaters of the Yellowstone River.

Besides Jackson, another photographer, J. Crissman of Bozeman, Montana, joined the troop, and the expedition also included Henry Wood Elliott, the official survey artist who had worked with Hayden the previous two years.[63] In addition, a representative of Jay Cooke's company requested from Hayden that artist Thomas Moran—a late figure in the Hudson River School of landscape painters—be allowed to join the expedition, and although the survey was already underway, Hayden accepted Moran as a "guest artist."[64] This would be Moran's first trip into the western wilds, and he hurriedly made arrangements to join Hayden, already in Montana. A personal loan from Jay Cooke gave him the needed funds, and Thomas Moran soon was off on the greatest adventure in his budding artistic career.[65]

Yellowstone would come to define Moran's life and career in significant ways. His daughter later observed, "Every artist of genius experiences during his life a great spiritual upheaval," and her father's great inspirational moment came in Yellowstone. "To him," Ruth Moran maintained, "it was all grandeur, beauty, color and light—nothing of man at all, but nature, virgin, unspoiled and lovely. In Yellowstone country he found fairy-like color and form that his dreams could not rival."[66] But traveling to Yellowstone in 1871 was not an obvious choice for Thomas Moran. Although he had established a reputation as a landscape painter, he had little experience as an outdoorsman. In fact, before reaching Montana, Moran had never even ridden a horse.[67] But he quickly adapted to the rough life of an expeditioner, and he was soon tramping around the Yellowstone country, often only in the company of photographer William Henry Jackson.[68] Together they produced photographs and drawings that would have an immeasurable impact on the future of Yellowstone.

The Hayden expedition of 1871 set out to provide scientific evidence of Yellowstone's unique geological features, but the images produced by the photographer Jackson and the painter Moran captured the attention of congressional representatives in Washington and secured Yellowstone as a place of divine wonder in the public imagination.[69] A letter awaited Hayden when he returned from Yellowstone to his office in Washington DC. It was from A. B. Nettleton, Jay Cooke's envoy, urging the geologist to include a recommendation in his official report of the survey. Specifically, Nettleton suggested, "let Congress pass a bill reserving the Great Geyser Basin as a public park forever."[70] Thus, the idea specifically to make Yellowstone a national park came initially from Cooke's organization, and its considerable lobbying leverage went to work over the winter months of 1871–72 to implement the plan. The firm enlisted the influential efforts of both Dr. Hayden and Nathaniel P. Langford as well as the Montana congressional delegation and other political allies of the Northern Pacific Railroad in generating support for the park idea.

Among the most persuasive elements in the lobbying effort to make Yellowstone a national park were Langford's essays in *Scribner's Monthly*. Every congressman received a personal copy of his articles along with the official report of the 1870 Washburn expedition. In addition, Dr. Hayden arranged for an exhibit in the U.S. Capitol rotunda of geological specimens from his 1871 Yellowstone survey interspersed with a display of Moran paintings and Jackson photographs highlighting the wonders of Yellowstone.[71] Enticed by such evidence of Yellowstone's unique character and urged by the lobbying efforts of Cooke's people, the House and Senate took up consideration of legislation "to consecrate for public use this country for a public park."[72] Objections were few, and when the congressmen were assured that no funds would be appropriated for the new park "for several years at least," the Yellowstone Act passed easily. On March 1, 1872, President Ulysses Grant added his signature to the bill, creating the world's first national park.[73]

Picturing Yellowstone

Soon after finalizing the legislation to make Yellowstone a national park, artist Thomas Moran unveiled his magnificent painting of the *Grand Cañon of the Yellowstone* at a gala reception in New York City. Perhaps more than any other rendering of Yellowstone, pictorial, literary, or otherwise, Moran's master work fixed the park as an iconic destination in the minds of many in the United States.[74] Jay Cooke himself had arranged for the highly publicized single-painting exhibition of Moran's grand landscape, and although he was unable to attend the opening reception, the banker's brother Pitt Cooke as well as the directors of the Northern Pacific Railroad were all present.[75] Railroad officials who had viewed the painting prior to its official unveiling were "decidedly enthusiastic about it."[76]

Their praise anticipated the enthusiastic public reception of Moran's monumental painting. Color intrigued Thomas Moran, and the critics who viewed his "Great Picture" nearly all mentioned the vivid palette that burst from the canvas.[77] Unspoken in the reviews, however, or in any subsequent discussion of Moran's work were the racial messages implicit in the painting. Despite his masterful depiction of the canyon's colors in his masterpiece, Moran painted Yellowstone as a white place. His artistic rendering of the canyon, perhaps the single most influential work in establishing Yellowstone's iconic reputation, affirmed the white Protestant values of Manifest Destiny that justified securing this large tract of Indian lands as a treasured place of the American nation.[78]

This view of Manifest Destiny as a Protestant ideology of whiteness is most apparent in the imperialist intentions of the United States in the nineteenth century, specifically in the conquest, displacement, confinement, and systematic destruction of the numerous Indigenous communities spread across the American West. In this regard Thomas Moran's famous painting of the Yellowstone canyon conformed to the dominant religious sentiments in U.S. society by painting an iconic space of whiteness. Mo-

FIG. 4. *Grand Cañon of the Yellowstone*, Thomas Moran, 1872, oil on canvas mounted on aluminum, 84 x 104¼ in. U.S. Department of the Interior Museum, Washington DC, INTR 03001.

ran includes in the foreground miniscule human figures dwarfed by the immensity of the canyon, with Dr. Hayden and the figure of an Indian shown on an outcropping high above the gleaming blue rapids of the river at the canyon's bottom. Others in their party wait with their horses off to the side, while Hayden and the Indian stand as lone silhouettes outlined by the radiant gold of the canyon walls. The white geologist points toward the river, while the Indian faces away from the canyon with his head turned back in the direction of Hayden's gesture.[79] A large tree frames the left edge of the scene, and dark pines in a line stand along the canyon sides like pious devotees in solemn reverence to the divine sanctuary. Towering cathedral spires rise toward the right, while the view focuses on the distant falls in the left center of the painting. On the plateau in the background can be seen pillars of steam rising from far-off hot springs, and the snow-peaked range of the Teton Mountains are faintly visible in the far distance.[80]

Moran's framing of the scene invites viewers to join the figures at the bottom in gazing on a redemptive space that not only symbolically but literally highlights a story of white salvation. The majestic waterfall that captures the viewer's attention echoes what may be the most powerful theme in Protestant Christianity, the Fall, the epic story of humankind's lapse and the source of the human condition under the spell of original sin. Meanwhile, the white "discoverer" of Yellowstone, Dr. Hayden, directs the Indian's view of the canyon in a metaphor of conquest and progress, with the native figure turned away from the scene.[81] Moran positions the white geologist looking toward the light-filled future, while the Indian figure is turned toward the shadowed past, suggesting to Moran and his white contemporaries "the end of the 'savage state' and the arrival of 'civilization.'"[82] The positioning of the two figures also symbolizes, according to cultural geographer Gareth John, the imperialist relationship of U.S. explorers and Native Americans, "as if the latter were conceding the territory in its pristine natural condition to the former."[83]

Moran's depiction of the canyon's vivid coloration amplifies the imperialist theme by privileging white as the color of uplift, as the symbol of a redemptive whiteness rising toward a heavenly paradise above this wild terrestrial paradise. A cloud of white mist shrouds the falls and rises all the way to the upper edge of the canvas, where it spreads out as it enters the celestial realm. White columns also rise from steam vents along the canyon wall and from hot springs on the distant plain. The colorful walls of the canyon bleach white as they reach their highest point in the upper-right corner of the painting, and the white peaks of the distant Teton Mountains stretch along the rear of the scene.

Like the other Hudson River School painters before him, Moran infused his masterpiece with Christian themes that affirm the American landscape as a place of white Protestant conquest claimed in the beneficence of divine providence.[84] The New York City unveiling of *Grand Cañon of the Yellowstone* revealed the newly established national park as a place of sublime beauty that confirmed the providential claims of Manifest Destiny overspreading the American continent with the hubris of white Protestant righteousness.[85] The painting very quickly became a symbol of American progress and domination in the western territories, and the U.S. Congress agreed to purchase the canvas to be the first work of landscape art to hang in the U.S. Capitol.[86] The painting also became familiar to the nation's schoolchildren, with reproductions of Moran's masterpiece soon hanging in nearly every classroom across the country.[87]

Moran's epic rendering of the Yellowstone canyon and falls perfectly suited Jay Cooke's intentions when he arranged for the artist to join the Hayden expedition. The Protestant evangelical fervor that combined Cooke's religious devotion with his business pursuits found aesthetic expression in Moran's painting. Viewers recognized in the skillful artistry on the canvas the providential redemption of God's chosen nation in the glorious Yellowstone landscape. At the same time, by affirming the evangelical logic of Manifest Destiny, the painting also helped to sell railroad bonds. It must have seemed to Cooke that he had made a profitable investment in Moran's talents that paid dividends both financial and spiritual.

A Park for America

When President Ulysses S. Grant added his signature to the Yellowstone Act on March 1, 1872, the first-ever national park became a reality, a park created specifically "for the benefit and enjoyment of the people." Enactment of the legislation effectively transformed the unclaimed space of the Yellowstone "wilderness" into a "civilized" place of parkland, "from Wilderness to Wonderland."[88] Of course, with no budget appropriations to go with it and no plan for managing the new federally designated parkland, the legislation was largely symbolic. Yet it initiated a tradition of federal parks that would become arguably the most treasured sites in U.S. civic culture.

The new national park was a product of Manifest Destiny. Rather than the campfire story invented long afterward about forward-thinking conservationists adamant on preserving a sacred land, Yellowstone was a consequence of eastern capital extending its reach westward, spearheaded by the wealthiest of U.S. capitalists, Jay Cooke.[89] This expansionist mindset of eastern capital that converted Yellowstone into a national park gained its moral authority and justification in the essentially religious discourse of Manifest Destiny, with religion, specifically Protestant Christianity, as a fundamental element in nationalist ambitions "to overspread and to possess the whole continent."[90] A Calvinist notion of God's word revealed in nature affirmed for many patriotic nineteenth-century Americans the providential aim of their crusade to conquer and settle the American West in the postbellum era. Accordingly, the scenic wonders of western lands were prime evidence for these believers of God's intentions for the destiny of the United States as a Christian nation.[91]

Recognizing signs of God's providence in the American landscape contributed to the popularity of nineteenth-century landscape painters.[92] From Thomas Cole to Thomas Moran, from Frederic Church to Albert Bierstadt, the providential meanings of American scenery were given pictorial reality. These and other artists, illustrators, and photographers translated the nation's divine sanction into aesthetic forms, giving a sacred character to places like Niagara Falls; the Catskills, Adirondacks, and White Mountains; and later the stunning vistas of the American West, and especially places like Yosemite in California, the Grand Canyon in Arizona, and Yellowstone in Wyoming. Their iconic images helped define a shared sacred heritage for the people of the United States.[93]

At the same time, the message of Manifest Destiny also emphasized the Christian obligation to settle, civilize, and develop these wildlands, and this, too, was apparent in the art of the era. Two 1872 paintings in particular reveal the dominant sentiments of Manifest Destiny shared by many in the United States. On the one hand, Moran's monumental *Grand Cañon of the Yellowstone* highlights the aesthetic power of western landscapes as the diminutive figures stand before the immense and powerful sublimity of the canyon and falls. In contrast, another painting of the same year, though comparatively much smaller in size but equally influential in its public impact, insists on the providential inevitability of overspreading Christian civilization from sea to shining sea. John Gast created *American Progress, or Manifest Destiny* for publisher George A. Croffutt to promote the travel book *New Overland Tourist and Pacific Coast Guide*, thus linking the nationalist rhetoric of Manifest Destiny to tourist excursions in the American West.[94] The Croffutt travel guides had a readership of over two million by 1871, thus guaranteeing substantial circulation for Gast's illustration.[95]

Gast's painting portrays an epic imaginary of Manifest Destiny, with Indigenous tribes and herds of bison fleeing the onslaught of inevitable conquest as modern civilization sweeps westward across the American landscape.[96] The artist personifies Progress itself in racialized, gendered, and sexualized terms that emphasize the purity and innocence of the divinely sanctioned advance of the United States.[97] A youthful white woman dominates the center of the painting, barefoot and scantily clad in a diaphanous gown that flows seductively from her unblemished body

FIG. 5. Artist John Gast's painting *American Progress, or Manifest Destiny* first appeared in 1872 in the book *New Overland Tourist and Pacific Coast Guide*. Oil on canvas, 11½ x 15¾ in. Autry Museum of the American West, Los Angeles, object ID 92.126.1.

as she moves steadily westward, leaving a trail of cities, newly cultivated ground, and railroads in her wake. She carries a "School Book" pressed to her bosom in her right hand, while her left hand strings telegraph lines across the plains. Ms. Progress floats westward with easy determination as an image of white feminine purity, the epitome of innocence that transforms the darkness of the savage West with the light of civilization borne on the twin foundations of the modern civilized world: education and technology.[98]

These two paintings, Moran's *Grand Cañon of the Yellowstone* and Gast's *American Progress, or Manifest Destiny*, both burst onto the U.S. cultural scene in the same year that Yellowstone became a national park. When set beside each other, they reinforce a common message in different ways: civilization will triumph in the wild territories of the American West. This message shouts unabashedly from Gast's painting, but it also underlies the aesthetic power of the Moran artwork. Moran claims the Yellowstone landscape as an aesthetic attraction that affirms Gast's message of inevitable progress. The awe-inspiring Yellowstone canyon is America, a destination for the people of the United States to visit and experience for themselves. Those who are unable to travel to the national park can claim the wondrous land for themselves by viewing Moran's artistry. His massive painting allows viewers to enter the scene as they stand with the artist beside the figures at the edge of the canyon to experience the sublimity of its grandeur.

Neither painting displays obvious indications of a religious presence. No churches, Bibles, preachers, or missionaries appear in either one, but the message of both relies on implicit religious understandings of national purpose. The providential logic of Manifest Destiny afforded an interpretive frame for U.S. viewers to find nationalist meanings in these artworks. They also conveyed clear racial messages as well. In both paintings the artists' palettes give special attention to whiteness. In Gast, the racial message appears in explicit form, as a white woman dressed in an all-white gown brings light, civilization, education, and modernization to the darker elements of the continent. The hardworking settlers and pioneers are all white as they bring order and prosperity to the enlightened land, while the Indians and animals fleeing in fear present a chaotic scene of dark figures, savage in their wild and disorderly state, including a bare-breasted Indian woman looking back as she leads a horse away from the onslaught of white progress. The only white in the darker portion of the canvas are the snowy peaks of distant mountains pointing heavenward. Like Moran's *Grand Cañon of the Yellowstone*, Gast's *American Progress, or Manifest Destiny* affirms the whiteness of God's divine favor in the manifested destinies of the American people.

Thomas Moran's paintings portrayed Yellowstone as a sacred site in this tale of white civilization's providential triumph. Congress had transformed this special landscape "from Wilderness to Wonderland," claiming it as an extension of the modern, civilized nation.[99] No longer a wild place, an unproductive land with the constant threat of hostile Indians, the Yellowstone Act created something new, a national park for the edification and sublime affirmation of white civilized Christian people. Like the urban parks that were being built in many U.S. cities, Yellowstone became a place where beleaguered citizens of the industrial world could find rejuvenation and spiritual uplift.[100]

Almost none of those city dwellers could actually visit the new park, but travel reports, photographs, and artworks brought Yellowstone to the U.S. public. In particular, Thomas Moran's paintings offered the aesthetic experiences of Yellowstone's wonders, allowing viewers to stand, if only imaginatively, before God's creation at the Grand Canyon of the Yellowstone or to witness the sublime power of the geysers' steaming waters erupting into the mountain air. For many in the United States, the mysterious and remote land of Yellowstone became a fulfillment of the white Christian hope of God's promise for the nation's destiny.

3

PILGRIMAGE TO WONDERLAND

Sitting in the dawn light on the rim of the Grand Canyon of the Yellowstone in the early 1890s, Olin Wheeler thrilled at the scene before him. "Grand and glorious pageant," he wrote;

> Vision mighty and eternal; for unnumbered aeons thou hast been slowly, through the attritive powers given thee by Nature's God, working out thy destiny. With a perseverance sublime, by the power of torrent and beat of wave, the rush of the avalanche, the grinding of the glacier, the hot breath of the geyser, the subtle uplifting of the frost, the downpouring from the clouds; by all the powers of earth and sky, the wind and hail, the lightning's glare, the thunder's crash, hast thou worked onward, channeling the mountains, sculpturing the hills, painting the cliffs, that man, the noblest of God's creations, might stand before thee in awe and rapture, and feel himself uplifted to that spirit land from whence he came.[1]

For Wheeler, Yellowstone displayed the drama of creation in its landscapes. The geological sciences may have diminished somewhat the authority of biblical Scripture as a literal account of creation, but the enthralling scene before Wheeler impressed even more keenly the creative genius of the Christian God. As he contemplated the "unnumbered aeons" of patient channeling, sculpting, and painting that had fashioned the canyon's "vision mighty and eternal," Wheeler the tourist became the reverent pilgrim who stood before his god "in awe and rapture."[2]

Olin Wheeler was not unusual in experiencing spiritual uplift on the rim of the Grand Canyon of the Yellowstone. The feeling of deep spiritual connection upon viewing the mountain vistas or witnessing the grace and power of erupting geysers has been a common theme for many visitors. Numerous travelers before and since have arrived in Yellowstone with a tourist's curiosity only to find themselves swept up by an aesthetic rapture in their experiences of the park's attractions. Like Wheeler, a good many tourists became humble pilgrims in the transformative landscapes of the Yellowstone sacred wonderland.[3]

The transformative appeal of inspirational experiences in a wildland made Yellowstone an attractive destination for well-heeled tourist pilgrims of the nineteenth century. The resulting financial windfalls for purveyors of tourist services, especially the railroads, encouraged development of infrastructure and visitor accommodations during the first decades of the park.[4] As access improved along with the availability of lodging, dining, transportation, and tour guide services, visitation gradually increased. And with more people coming to Yellowstone, conventional itineraries tended to ritualize the experiences that visitors had of the park.[5]

A Pilgrimage Destination

Following the creation of Yellowstone National Park in 1872, it remained for the most part a wild, undeveloped land. Civilizing Yellowstone was mostly an imaginative act. Congress had not appropriated any funds for the management and operation of the park, and even the first park superintendent, Nathanial P. Langford, served without pay.[6] Accordingly, accommodations were virtually nonexistent in the early years of the park; in fact, even basic infrastructure such as roads and sanitation were lacking. As a consequence, tourist traffic through the park amounted to little more than a slow trickle in the first years. A few bold entrepreneurial spirits tried to develop attractions to take advantage of a potential tourist trade, but Yellowstone's wonders were too remote. Lacking convenient transportation lines coupled with the entire absence of adequate lodging and dining accommodations, only the hardiest of adventurers made their way to the park. It would be nearly a decade before the national park could generate sufficient tourist revenue to support the enterprises that would cater to visitors' needs and comfort as they enjoyed the delights of Yellowstone.

Yet despite the difficulties and hardships of visiting Yellowstone in the first years of the national park, people came, and for some of them the journey's hardships heightened the rewards. Extending into the modern world a long tradition of religious travel that stretched back to ancient times, pious souls made pilgrimages to the sacred wonderland of the national park.

The piety that visitors brought to Yellowstone in its early years as a national park and that many visitors have continued to experience over the ensuing decades has rarely been "religious" in terms of recognizable devotional traditions. More commonly, sightseers' and other tourists' experiences of Yellowstone have elicited profound emotional responses often framed in devotional sensibilities and expressed with imagery couched in the familiar language of religions.

For many of the nineteenth-century Yellowstone tourists, most of whom came from Christian, usually Protestant, backgrounds, the strange and frightening power of the geysers and other thermal features often elicited diabolic imagery. For instance, Harry J. Norton, who had joined a "Geyser Exploring Party" from Virginia City, Montana, in early September 1872, entered the geyser basins along the Firehole River with much trepidation. "One brief hour," he wrote, "has sufficed to change our quiet, love-inspiring, soul-entrancing scenery into that of a land of awe and wonder. The natural king has faded from our vision, and the supernatural monarch has ascended the throne with glittering crown, and with magic wand is ever directing our footsteps through his mystic domain. . . . One hour! and the Queen of Quiet has lain down her sceptre of loving order, and the King of Confusion and Passion reigns supreme."[7] This chaotic scene, Norton and his companions surmised, boiled up from a sinister underworld. The hot springs, geysers, fumaroles, and other thermal features of the region, they decided, must share a single subterranean water source, "creating a common sympathy and a common diabolism. Indeed, there is good reason for this theory, if not for the one that the whole underground-area of the Geyser region is an immense boiling lake (of 'fire and brimstone'), without other vent or outlet than the fissures apparent on the ground surface."[8] They trod cautiously on the fragile coverings of hell itself.

At night in the Upper Geyser Basin, surrounded by the boiling, hissing sounds of geysers, hot springs, and fumaroles, Norton's dreams took him into the inferno of the underworld. Similar to Dante's purgatorial tours, an enchanting creature guided the slumbering explorer and revealed to him, "This repulsive region is the source and cause of the so-called mysteries in your admired Geyser-land, and the steam and heat and groans of the Giantess, Giant, and Castle geysers are produced by the burning of souls and bodies such as yours; and you mortals, while gazing at the mysteries of that country, are indirectly witnessing the everlasting punishment of friends and relatives."[9] Upon awakening, a relieved Norton returned to the terrestrial wonders of the geyser basin.

Though his Christian imagination related Yellowstone's thermal features to the hellish imagery of the underworld, Norton more frequently found aesthetic delight in the park's attractions. Even his initial fear of geysers subsided as he eventually perceived them more in terms of the celestial realm than the severe agonies of the underworld. In describing an eruption of the Giantess Geyser, Norton remarks, "Playing hither and thither in the mellow sunlit mist, miniature rainbows are seen, and the air glistens with the falling water-beads as if a shower of diamonds was being poured from the golden gates of the Eternal City."[10]

As his party toured the new national park, the pilgrims' experiences led them time and again through heavenly gates into novel wonders that escaped words. The Grand Canyon of the Yellowstone, in particular, left Norton dumbstruck: "To say that we can *describe* (literally) their grandeur and marvellous beauty, would be to assume to correctly portray the illuminated heavens, or carve out of poor, weak words the glories of the Heavenly City itself. The subject is beyond the conception of the most vivid imagination—language is inadequate to express the unapproachable picture presented—the eye only can photograph the gorgeous scene." But like so many writers, he attempts to reduce such ineffable beauty to words. "The bright sunlight pours over the immense barrier with all its dazzling rays against the imprisoning walls, and reflecting from side to side, is melted into an amber flood of mellow light; while the beautiful surroundings, canopied o'er by the soft blue dome of an autumnal sky, give forth Nature's warmest, kindliest smile to her ardently worshipping children."[11] The whole scene of the canyon, Norton concludes, its vibrant walls and the majesty of its waterfalls, "is clothed with a splendor that speaks of Divinity."[12] This divine nature of Yellowstone, in Norton's esti-

PREACHING PULPIT TERRACES.

FIG. 6. Preaching from "Pulpit Terraces" at Mammoth Hot Springs, from a booklet of engravings titled *Yellowstone National Park: The World's Wonderland*, arranged by W. C. Riley, ca. 1890. University of Delaware Library Special Collections, Newark.

mation, reveals the park's inherent religious significance: "With the single exception of the fall of Adam," he asserts, "Yellowstone furnishes more food for thought than any other we have knowledge of."[13]

The following summer another park visitor also found much food for spiritually uplifting thought in Yellowstone as a place of religious signif- icance. Rev. Edwin J. Stanley, a Methodist preacher serving in Montana Territory, joined a party of tourists going to Yellowstone in August 1873. Finding themselves at Mammoth Hot Springs on the Sabbath, Reverend Stanley felt compelled to offer his companions a worship service. His account, though, suggests that the communicants showed little enthusiasm for attending church while on vacation. He hints at ministerial frustration in relating: "I preached on Sunday to a clever and very attentive audience who seemed to appreciate the services. However, pleasure-resorts are not the most favorable places to make religious impressions."[14]

Favorable religious impressions, though, were abundant in the scenery and attractions of the national park. Like Norton and other early visitors to Yellowstone, Reverend Stanley resorted to the imagery and language of his Christian faith in relating his experiences of the park's attractions. He contemplated divine mysteries revealed in the terraces at Mammoth Hot Springs: "Where the vast amount of material comes from, how it is decomposed, brought hither and arranged in the ten thousand wonderful forms it has taken, and how long this work has been in progress, are questions that arise in the mind, but which we leave for others to discuss. . . . Known unto the Great Architect, and to him only, are all his works. His ways are past finding out."[15] Similarly at Tower Falls, the party's next stop after Mammoth Hot Springs, Reverend Stanley "lingered long in that retired chamber alone, meditating on the wonderful works of Nature." There beside Tower Creek, where the falls crash into the narrow gorge, Stanley recalls, "as I watched the water descending in jets and crystal showers, and listened to its hushed murmur, subdued to softness by the overhanging cliffs and towering pines, I could but admire the modestly beautiful little cataract hid away in this lonely yet lovely solitude." Afterward, "I returned to camp feeling myself a better man, and meditating upon the greatness, wisdom, and goodness of Nature's God."[16]

God's greatness, though, was absent from other park features, some of which suggested a more diabolic presence. Much like Norton and other early visitors, Reverend Stanley suspected ominous treachery awaited them in the hellish stench of Yellowstone's hot springs, geysers, and other thermal features. Not wanting to face the devil himself, Stanley stayed behind when his party went to view Hell-Broth Springs. Its description repulsed him. "The greenish-yellow, paint-like fluid, and the sulphurous slime, the noisy ebullition, the sickening, suffocating fumes emitted, and the desolate and unearthly appearance of the place" seemed to him to justify the underworld imagery in the name that early explorers had bestowed upon the hot springs.[17] Likewise, when they later arrived at the steaming basins of the Firehole River, the satanic presence could be felt at every turn. The boiling lakes of the Lower Geyser Basin recalled the harrowing scenes of Christian literature. "One is vividly reminded of the scenes in Dante's 'Inferno,'" Reverend Stanley explained. "Could we but have heard the cries of the tormented, Bunyan's picture of the pit in the side of the hill which the pilgrims were shown by the shepherds on their way to the Celestial City, where they 'looked in and saw that it was very dark and smoky'; thought that they 'heard a rumbling noise as of fire, and a cry of some tormented, and that they smelt the fumes of brimstone,' would have been complete."[18]

Yellowstone may have suggested the fiery imagery of a satanic underworld, but Reverend Stanley also experienced profound inspiration in uplifting, spiritual encounters with the park's scenic wonders. Like Norton the previous year, he found himself at a loss for words while standing at the rim of the Grand Canyon of the Yellowstone. "This place is of great interest to the tourist, where he will be tempted to tarry long amid the wondrous grandeur and beauty of scenes which even the finest linguist must ever fail to describe and the most skillful artist despair of painting, the eye being the only medium through which a just conception of the surpassing beauty and sublimity of the place can be obtained."[19] Later he clambered down to the bottom of the canyon, where he was overtaken by "the strangely bewitching beauty and sublimity of this scene, the overpowering sense of the presence of Deity which it gives." The incredible beauty of the place left Stanley and his companions

> awed into silence and reverence, feeling that we were in the very antechamber of the great God of Nature, and that he was talking to us and teaching us lessons of his greatness, his grandeur, and his glory, that human language must ever fail to express. A sense of the awful pervades the mind, and we almost felt that we were trespassing upon sacred ground. I felt like baring the head and bowing the knee to One who could pile up rocks in such stupendous majesty, and carve and paint them in such matchless splendor, "who cutteth out rivers among the rocks"; "who holdeth the waters in the hollow of his hand," and spreadeth them out in such grandeur and beauty. "Great

and marvelous are thy works, Lord God Almighty. Heaven and earth are full of thy glory."[20]

Reverend Stanley also was overcome by the spectacle of God's glory as his party camped along the shore of Yellowstone Lake, where "the beholder is filled with admiring wonder, and in the midst of such awe-inspiring influences is tempted to bow the knee and worship at Nature's shrine."[21] He gazed reverently at the distant peaks of the Absaroka Mountains "melting away in the clouds as if uniting terrestrial with celestial glory, clothing things earthly with the tapestry of the heavenly world. Who is not inspired when amid the mountains?"[22]

The inspirational treasure of Yellowstone's mountain scenery also accompanied Stanley into the geyser basins of the Firehole River, where, much like Norton, Stanley put aside his initial fears as the thermal features gained aesthetic appeal that overcame their devilish associations. In fact, while touring the Upper Geyser Basin, Stanley predicted a time when "the philosophers and tourists, and the lovers of the sublime and the wonderful in Nature, will gather from all countries and climes to make investigation, to behold and wonder, and even worship at Nature's shrine" in this park, where visitors "are ushered into a land of marvelous wonders and mysterious, soul-entrancing, indescribable beauties, where everything is life and animation; and the beholder is soon lost to the dangers and vexations of the way, rapt in delightful bewilderment, and carried away with the enchantments of this mystic region."[23] For Reverend Stanley as well as for generations of visitors who have followed in the century and half since he traveled there to behold its enchanting treasures, Yellowstone opens a window into the mystic regions of wonder.

The Yellowstone Sublime

Rev. Edwin Stanley's prediction of a time when "the lovers of the sublime and the wonderful in Nature" would flock to Yellowstone reflects the aesthetic value of the first national park in a time when genteel classes of the United States were popularizing travel to "the sublime and the picturesque" places of the natural world.[24] The circulation of artworks and literature featuring the wonders of the American West inspired people to visit these places with expectations of transformative spiritual experiences. Travel accounts in newspapers, periodicals, and books, along with the popularity of paintings by Hudson River School artists like Thomas Moran, brought attention to the wonders of natural landscapes of the American nation. Yellowstone quickly joined the ranks of iconic images of Yosemite, Niagara Falls, the Hudson River Valley, the Adirondacks, and White Mountains to entice a burgeoning leisure class in Gilded Age America.[25] By the end of the century, art and literature had made the wonders of Yellowstone familiar in U.S. culture. *Harper's* editor Charles Dudley observed in 1897 that "all the world knows, from the pens of a thousand descriptive writers and from the photographs, the details of these marvels."[26]

Travel to these places promised emotionally powerful and spiritually moving experiences. But many visitors who had endured the hardships of nineteenth-century travel to places like Yellowstone soon found, much like Harry J. Norton and Reverend Stanley, that words to describe their experiences were hard to find.[27] Time and again, visitors expressed their frustration at finding language adequate to their experiences of Yellowstone.[28] Nevertheless, often with no hint of irony, these travelers translated their ineffable experiences into words. Yellowstone quickly became a popular topic in the burgeoning popular literary genre of travel writing.[29]

Much of what these earlier visitors found so difficult to express about Yellowstone involved an existential confrontation with profound realities that combined emotional, psychological, aesthetic, and spiritual elements. They imagined themselves facing the raw reality of their very being. Many of them, seeking an adequate language to share the profundity of their experiences, resorted to religious language to describe what they saw and felt in Yellowstone.

This religious language took several forms. Christian writers (who have been the overwhelming majority of white Americans who visited Yellowstone, then and now) often resorted to conventional biblical language, imagery, and themes in relating their experiences of the park. The frightening sights, sounds, and stench of gurgling hot springs and bubbling mud pots evoked Christian images of the hellish underworld, while the uplifting and emotionally moving mountain scenery and waterfalls sometimes elicited angelic references to the celestial paradise.

While some visitors shared Reverend Stanley's reticence in avoiding the hellish features of the park's thermal attractions, others, as Joel Daehnke points out, "seemed intent on confrontation with the landscape as a corrective to moral backsliding." For instance, when British writer Rudyard Kipling visited the park in 1889, his touring party included an "old lady" from Chicago. According to Kipling's report, she reminded her traveling companions "that the Lord has ordained a Hell for such as disbelieve his gracious works," and she surmised, as Kipling wrote, "if we find a thing so dreffel as all that steam and sulphur allowed on the face of the earth, mustn't we believe that there is something ten-thousand times more terrible below prepared un*toe* our destruction?" Daehnke concludes that for nineteenth-century American tourists, "recreation maintained its ties to Christian values; outdoor pastimes and sightseeing in parks such as Yellowstone continued to elicit responses in the form of openly religious experiences."[30]

Besides more conventional, biblically derived imagery and moral lessons for describing recreational encounters of Yellowstone, the distinctly romantic language of Transcendentalist literature also influenced how white Americans responded to the sights, sounds, smells, and experiences of the national park. Ralph Waldo Emerson's essays and lectures, in particular his 1836 essay *Nature*, had introduced a more aesthetically robust religious language for thinking about the natural world. Emerson had shifted the Christian perspective from regarding nature as an object separate from and inimical to human experience to one of subjective immersion in nature, concluding, "Therefore, that spirit, that is, the Supreme Being, does not build up nature around us, but puts it forth through us."[31] The growing popularity of other Transcendentalist writers spread these romanticized religious perspectives more widely in American culture. Henry David Thoreau's book *Walden; or, Life in the Woods*, arriving in 1854 to mixed reviews, was finding a wider audience in the post–Civil War period. His admonitions for simple living and personal growth in connection with nature encouraged attention to the outdoors. "We need the tonic of wildness," Thoreau counseled. "We can never have enough of nature."[32] Similarly, Walt Whitman's poetry, with its romanticized images of the United States as "essentially the greatest poem," influenced readers to "travel it for yourself."[33]

The growing influence of a romantic aesthetics introduced by Emerson and his literary heirs coincided with the American embrace of the sublime. In fact, the desire to encounter numinous experiences in landscapes where one could "glimpse the face of God" ranked high in the appeal of Yellowstone for early tourists.[34] Harry Norton sought this sort of experience when he climbed to the terrifying brink of the Lower Falls of the Yellowstone River in 1872: "Never did mortal eye behold a sight of more sublime magnificence, as within three paces of the roaring cataract we peered into the abyss below."[35]

This notion of sublime experience had originated with eighteenth-century British philosopher Edmund Burke and was later elaborated by German philosopher Immanuel Kant as a paradoxical sensation of both terror and awe in confronting nature. Sublime landscapes in places like Yellowstone elicit profound dread while also inciting an irresistible awe and wonder. In this manner, according to Kant's analysis, the sublime makes possible a regard for wild nature as "aesthetically agreeable."[36] For nineteenth-century U.S. travelers, this notion of the sublime encounter with nature provided an explanation for their visceral responses to wild scenery and also a vocabulary for expressing their experiences.[37]

By the time Yellowstone became a national park, the sublime operated as a cliché of travelers' experiences in impressive landscapes. In tourist accounts of the American West, including the newly established national park, *sublime* served as the conventional adjective for one's ineffable, aesthetically powerful experience of scenic wonders and interactions with the natural world. As a typical example, one Yellowstone visitor in the 1890s remarked about the "sublime chasm" of the Grand Canyon of the Yellowstone that it "is not the grandest on earth, yet there is none more beautiful in the world." More than beautiful, though, the canyon elicited something more profound, more frightening, and more glorious, a nearly ineffable sublimity: "You look on stillness, solemn as midnight, profound as death. The mighty distance lays the fingers of silence on its white and fearful lips. The opulence of color throughout this canyon is magnificent and fascinating; the whole gorge flames; it is as though rainbows had fallen out of the sky and hung themselves there like glorious banners. . . . It is as if the most glorious sunset had been caught and held resplendent over that awful gorge."[38]

FIG. 7. This cover image of a Northern Pacific Railroad promotional brochure from 1885 highlights "Alice's Adventures in the New Wonderland: The Yellowstone National Park." University of Delaware Library Special Collections, Newark.

The promise of these sorts of sublime experiences in the wilds of the Yellowstone wonderland made the park a desirable pilgrimage goal for many travelers in the late decades of the nineteenth century. Its appeal inspired some of these visitors to spread the good news of the place that the railroads promoted as the "New Wonderland," capitalizing on the popularity of Lewis Carroll's fantasy novel *Alice's Adventures in Wonderland*.[39]

In reflecting on his experiences in Yellowstone in 1873, Rev. Edwin Stanley surmises, "When civilization advances sufficiently in the West, and visitors come in numbers to justify the building of hotels, and other improvements, such as making parks for the game, and preparing otherwise for the pleasure and entertainment of the tourist, this will be a wonderful resort for pleasure-seekers in the summer." He continues by predicting that "the time is coming when it will be the great central resort for the lovers of the grand, the wonderful, the beautiful, and the sublime in Nature, from all parts of the inhabited world."[40]

That time, however, was more than a decade away. Besides the few crude structures serving travelers in the early years, better tourist accommodations would not begin to appear until the Northern Pacific Railroad began service to Yellowstone National Park in 1883.[41] The earliest visitors to venture into Yellowstone National Park found it much like it had been when Nathaniel Langford organized the Washburn expedition in 1870.

By the end of the century, though, Yellowstone had become a popular stop for travelers touring the American West. More convenient and comfortable transportation, grand hotels, eating establishments, and a conventional itinerary that ritualized the pilgrimage experience made the park a premier destination among the U.S. traveling class as well as for foreign visitors. Most of them came prepared for what they would see and experience, having read travelers' accounts such as those published by Harry Norton and Rev. Edwin Stanley. They arrived in the park armed with guidebooks and promotional literature put out by the railroads. An ever-increasing crowd of pilgrim tourists made their way to Yellowstone to see for themselves a place "unrivaled in wild and weird wonders" that beckoned "the lover of the marvelous in Nature."[42]

The Wonderland Itinerary

Pursuing the "unrivaled in wild and weird wonders" of Yellowstone connected "the lover of the marvelous in Nature" with an ancient human compulsion for religious travel. Virtually every known culture in the history of humanity has in one way or another employed an innate penchant for travel in seeking out auspicious places of transcendent forces. From the time of the earliest surviving cultural traces painted on rough walls deep in the bowels of dark caves to the ornately baroque constructions of elaborate shrines, humans have been journeying to sites they regard as special—places where they can leave the mundane concerns of their ordinary lives and encounter an alternate reality of transcendent powers.[43]

In spite of its ubiquity, or perhaps because of it, religious travel encompasses a wide range of traditions, practices, and destinations, making the category of "pilgrimage" difficult to pin down to a clear definition. Among the most commonly known pilgrimage traditions are the Hajj, the annual pilgrimage to Mecca, in Saudi Arabia, that is one of the Five Pillars of Islam; devotional travel to Christian shrines such as Lourdes in France, Compostela in Spain, and Tepeyac near Mexico City in Mexico; journeys to Hindu temples where ancient tales of the gods come alive for devotees at the places of mythical events that mark the sacred landscape of India; and travel to venerable Buddhist sites that commemorate the life of Gautama, the historical Buddha. Each of these and hundreds of other pilgrim traditions have their own unique histories and conventional practices of honor and devotion. But all display at least a few common elements, most obviously the element of travel for devotional or spiritual purposes.[44]

The conventional practices and interpretations of pilgrimage traditions also relate closely to modern tourism, which is usually regarded as a secular activity but is historically derived from religious pilgrimage. The origins of tourism as a cultural practice reveal it as a close cousin of religious travel, if not itself a modern form of pilgrimage, as anthropologists Victor and Edith Turner recognize in their observation that "a tourist is half a pilgrim, if a pilgrim is half a tourist."[45] In Western Europe tourism as we know it today first developed in the contexts of the Renaissance, Reformation, and Enlightenment movements that are the historical foundations of modernity. By the nineteenth century leisure excursions to distant destinations became more common with advances in travel, especially new modes of transportation introduced with the steam engine, encouraging an elite class of Americans to indulge in the growing popularity of extended tours both abroad and in America.[46]

The rapid growth of tourism in the United States in the nineteenth century, largely driven by the construction of an extensive network of railroad lines crisscrossing the continent, made possible new pilgrimage destinations. An "American Grand Tour" of resort destinations in the northeastern portion of the country had become popular by the 1830s.[47] With the completion of transcontinental railroads following the Civil War, the natural wonders of the western United States offered new destinations for tourist visitors. In fact, the immense popularity of places like Yellowstone and Yosemite relied to a large extent on their accessibility afforded by railroads and related accommodations designed to entice pleasure travelers.[48]

With regular train service to the park boundary beginning in 1883, a conventional itinerary became the most common way to experience Yellowstone.[49] Arriving by train from the north along the Yellowstone River through Montana's Paradise Valley, visitors would disembark at the town of Cinnabar, three miles from the park boundary.[50] Their ritual tour of the park would then begin with horse-drawn coaches to carry them up to the National Hotel, which opened by the end of the 1883 tourist season at Mammoth Hot Springs. There they would settle in relative comfort while exploring the northern park's main attraction, the terraced hot springs.[51]

After a night or two at Mammoth Hot Springs, according to a promotional publication of the era from the Northern Pacific Railroad, the tourists would pile into a stagecoach for their extended circuit of park highlights. They made sightseeing stops at Rustic Falls, Obsidian Cliff, Lake of the Woods, Norris Geyser Basin, Paint Pots, Monument Geyser Basin, Gibbon Canyon, Gibbon Falls, the Lower Geyser Basin, "and the last, the crowning point of all wonders, the Upper Geyser Basin." From there the tourists were taken to Yellowstone Lake, where, according to the railroad's promotional account, they would experience "a sense of relief at getting away from the odor and sight of so much hot water." After a brief respite in the relative serenity of the lake, the tour would continue to "the great Falls and Grand Cañon. Here the sensation is that of *quiet* wonder and amazement, while at the Geysers it is that of *excited* wonder and *delight*."[52]

Not all visitors experienced wonder, amazement, and delight in every aspect of their Yellowstone travels. Though most surviving accounts indicate their strong impressions of the natural features, many were gravely disappointed by the lodging and dining available to tourists in the early decades of the park. Margaret Cruickshank, for example, found the accommodations in the park woefully lacking when she made a weeklong tour in August 1883. Her distress came in part from ill timing in that first season of railroad service that brought visitors to the park boundary: her tour coincided with the arrival of VIPs hosted by the railroad for promotional purposes and also at the exact time of President Chester Arthur's highly publicized trip as the first U.S. president to visit Yellowstone. The few operators offering lodging and food in the park were ill prepared for the sudden crush of visitors, and ordinary tourists like Cruickshank were given little consideration as the entrepreneurs gave priority to the president and the other high-profile tourists. At the "Forks of the Firehole" in the Lower Geyser Basin, Cruickshank's party stayed at Marshall's "house of entertainment." With only three of them to keep up with the unanticipated crowds, Marshall and his two helpers were "all overworked and all cross. Not being forethoughted or forehanded as to providing and not having very high standards I cannot praise their results," wrote Cruickshank.[53]

This sort of disappointment in the conditions and accommodations for travel made tours of Yellowstone a challenging experience that only the hardiest of souls could enjoy. Margaret Cruickshank warns that the park is "no place for the delicate." Traveling in a "light, strongly made two-seated vehicle, with an outside seat for the driver," pulled by a team of "two strong horses, mountain-born and mountain-bred," the passengers had to get out and walk on the steepest segments of the rough roads. "Then began our sufferings," Cruickshank complains, as they labored alongside the carriage: "The dirt was almost ankle deep and the heat and clarity of the air made it a serious business." Moreover, she continues, "wherever you go there are streams to ford, corduroy to fall over, sagebrush plains to crawl along, and mountains to cross."[54]

Even as accommodations became more available and more attuned to a fastidious class of well-heeled visitors, travel in the park remained somewhat of an ordeal. Besides the unbearable dust on the roads, Carter Harrison complained in 1890 that overcrowding at the hotels sometimes meant that "one is compelled to take a bed in a room with several others and may even be forced to crowd two in a bed. That happened once to our party. But none of the travelers had the small pox or itch, so no great harm resulted. By hugging the outer rail of a bed, instead of the bed fellow, the necessity of tumbling two in a bed is not altogether a catastrophe."[55] He also was annoyed by the entertainment at the Mammoth Hot Springs hotel, where "they will insist on a brass band's tooting a good part of the time. The noise it made was execrable."[56]

Although accommodations gradually became more comfortable and acceptable for most travelers, the roads in Yellowstone had not improved markedly by the last decade of the nineteenth century. Like many travelers of the time, Harrison comments on the dust, which at times "is very deep, causing passengers in some of the vehicles to be choked and rendered very uncomfortable," though rains helped control the dust clouds during his visit.[57] Another park visitor in the early 1890s, Charles J. Gillis, remarks that his Yellowstone adventure "would have been far more comfortable if there had been less dust, fewer mosquitoes, and better roads."[58]

But the discomforts of choking dust and clouds of mosquitoes, the unsavory meals, inadequate lodging, only enhanced the allure of Yellowstone. Like religious pilgrims in all eras and travelers everywhere, the challenges and distress of the journey only heightened the value of the destination.[59] When it comes to pilgrimage, including its modern touristic modes, the more challenging the effort and the higher the cost, the greater the reward.

Among the most prized rewards for travelers everywhere in all ages has been the acquisition of material objects to preserve the memories of places visited. Obtaining a memento of the sacred journey has been an essential practice throughout the history of religious pilgrimage, a tradition that persists in modern tourism with travelers' compulsion to acquire souvenirs of their travel experiences.[60] Visitors to Yellowstone have perpetuated this tradition; the temptation to carry away a Wonderland relic has been a standard part of Yellowstone pilgrimage from the earliest days.

Philetus W. Norris, who would later serve as the park's second superintendent, could not resist the impulse to gather souvenirs of the Yellowstone wonderland when he visited in 1875. He tells how he and his guide, "vandal-like, anxious to secure wonders, even by defacing nature's temple," crawled to the edge of a geyser cone in the Soda Butte Valley region, and there at "the very verge with knife and hatchet detaching the crystal stalactite and enamel ornament beneath. Though most of them were dashed to atoms many hundreds of feet below, some were secured, one of which, a double hollow opal triangle, is perhaps older than Solomon's ancient masonic emblem."[61] Norris's "vandal-like" efforts were made in the name of science, as he was collecting specimens for the Smithsonian Institution in Washington DC.[62] However, early travel accounts and Yellowstone guidebooks sometimes encouraged the common tourist to indulge in such vandalistic behavior. Rev. Edwin J. Stanley, the Methodist minister who toured the park in 1873, in describing a geyser cone in the Upper Geyser Basin, remarks that the elegant patterns and bright colors show "the handiwork of a Master-Artist, and, though so delicate in appearance, so solid that a hatchet is often necessary to obtain a choice piece for your cabinet."[63] For these early Yellowstone tourists, a relic of divine handiwork was a treasured prize, despite the damage it may cause the "Master-Artist's" creation.

The willful destruction of Yellowstone's precious attractions gained public attention and became a common refrain in criticisms of the growing numbers of heedless souvenir-seeking marauders touring the park. In the same year that Reverend Stanley toured Yellowstone, citizens of Bozeman, Montana, petitioned the U.S. secretary of the Interior for improvements to the park and greater protection of its attractions. Among their complaints was "the vandalism that is rapidly denuding the park of its curiosities."[64] Capt. William Ludlow of the Corps of Engineers, who briefly surveyed Yellowstone in 1875, became indignant witnessing park tourists wantonly "with shovel and axe, chopping and hacking and prying up great pieces of the most ornamental work they could find." He reported, "Men and women alike joining in the barbarous pastime."[65] It was a pastime that also appears in the reports of Gen. Philip H. Sheridan's expeditions through Yellowstone in 1881 and 1882. The general was particularly aggrieved by damage to the park's most famous attraction; the 1882 expedition report notes, "The vandalism which I commented on in my report of last year has since been continuing until the whole top of the crater of the most wonderful of all the geysers, Old Faithful, has been broken down almost out of all recognition."[66]

Tourists, though, were not the only vandals hacking away at Yellowstone's delicate features. According to his 1879 superintendent's report, Philetus Norris undertook the contradictory strategy of protecting Yellowstone's wonders by "breaking them off with ax and crowbar, and shipping them by the carload to Washington and elsewhere."[67] Such heedless destruction by the park's highest official did nothing to discourage the destructive habits of pilgrims to Yellowstone who continued to carry away their relics of Wonderland. A visitor in 1880 remarked that the Mammoth Hot Springs "must have been of great beauty before the tourist tramped it."[68]

By the end of the nineteenth century, severe penalties had been instituted for removing relics, but threats of punishment did not abate the compulsion to obtain a piece of the park. S. B. Stonerook, who toured Yellowstone in the 1890s, found a notice posted at the park's entrance warning about "carrying specimens out of the park." He reports, "The penalty for removing any relics, defacing the park, and molesting any of the animals is $2,000 fine, and two years in penitentiary." Such threats, however, did not deter the intrepid pilgrim; Stonerook brags, "I got a fine specimen of soda-stone from an extinct Geyser, adjoining this was a fine soda spring, where I filled a beer bottle to take along to Iowa."[69] Like religious pilgrims have done for millennia around the globe, Yellowstone's visitors have returned to their homes in Iowa and elsewhere with material mementos of their destination.

Visitors' desire to carry away souvenirs of their Yellowstone experiences translated to lucrative opportunities for park concessionaires. Selling Yellowstone made the park an attractive destination, and selling mementos captured even more of the pilgrims' dollars. The visual arts, including the photographs of William H. Jackson, had initially inspired the public's affection for Yellowstone, and photographic images proved a popular item for visitors' purchase. Among the earliest and most successful to capitalize on this lucrative market was F. Jay Haynes. He first came to Yellowstone in 1881 as "Official Photographer" for the Northern Pacific Railroad, and by 1883 Haynes held that title for both the park and the Yellowstone Park Improvement Company, the main enterprise providing accommodations inside the park.[70]

Haynes's images not only became a prized souvenir for visitors of the park; they also shaped much of the public perception of Yellowstone through the final decades of the nineteenth century and into the early part of the twentieth. His association with the Northern Pacific Railroad provided much of the visual imagery that went into the railroad's promotional efforts, especially its campaigns to promote the "Wonderland" of Yellowstone. For many in the United States, familiarity with the park and

FIG. 8. F. Jay Haynes photograph of tourist party on the Mammoth Hot Springs terraces, Yellowstone National Park, 1888. Montana Historical Society Research Center Photograph Archives, Helena, catalog #H-01946.

its attractions arrived by way of railroad advertisements and publications, much of it adorned with Haynes's photographs of the park's wondrous features. Of course, this also heightened the demand for his images, as the tourist pilgrims to Yellowstone wished to carry home with them a Haynes print purchased in one of his two stores operating in the park.[71]

F. Jay Haynes gained iconic stature in Yellowstone, evidenced today by Mount Haynes, an 8,235-foot peak in Madison Canyon near the west entrance of the park that commemorates his legacy.[72] The photographer's fame and fortune came in no small part from his association with the Northern Pacific Railroad, which as the sole provider of rail transportation to the park in the nineteenth century, made Yellowstone an attractive and profitable destination. The railroad worked hard to make the scenic wonderland an attractive and profitable commodity, and its efforts relied to a large extent on the artistry of photographers, painters, and writers who enticed the public imagination with their imagery of Yellowstone's attractions.[73]

The publicity and artistic renditions enticed pilgrims to Yellowstone, but they did not all go there for the same purposes. Some of the park's earliest visitors came to find relief for bodily infirmities, much like pilgrims who had traveled to holy shrines of saints seeking miracles to heal their broken and ailing bodies. Even before it was set aside as the world's first national park, there were plans for health spa resorts on the Boiling River (or Hot River) and at the Mammoth Hot Springs.[74] These entrepreneurial efforts were attracting a clientele soon after the park opened. When Rev. Edwin Stanley toured the new national park in 1873, he found at Mammoth Hot Springs "scores of invalids already flocking here to be healed of their maladies." He goes on to report, "Some remarkable cures have been effected here, mostly of diseases of the skin, and rheumatism," although he maintained a skeptical attitude about such claims and instead attributed the visitors' improved conditions to "the invigorating mountain-air and the healthful influence of camp-life."[75] Nevertheless, a belief in the curative powers of the Yellowstone hot springs persisted to the end of the nineteenth century. During his visit in 1890, Carter Harrison contemplated the healing potential of Yellowstone's hot springs, concluding that "there will be found many of them of great hygienic value, and sanitariums will be established to make the park a blessing to the afflicted of the country."[76]

The "invalids" seeking cures for their ailments, though, were far outnumbered by pilgrims seeking aesthetic inspiration and uplift in the magnificent scenery and unique features of the Yellowstone landscape. The vast majority of travelers entering the national park in the nineteenth century set out, as one tourist pilgrim exclaimed in 1896, "for a famous journey to the wonderland of the ages, the celebrated Yellowstone National Park."[77]

A Wonderland of American Destiny

The sublime spiritual experiences that many visitors found in the Yellowstone wonderland encompassed more than their own individual encounters with the park's scenery and attractions. They relied to a large extent on perceptions of racial differences and a triumphant confidence in the divinely sanctioned destiny of U.S. nationhood. For most nineteenth-century tourist pilgrims, experiencing Yellowstone elicited the aesthetic affirmation of entitlement for white Protestant America.

The racial imagination of Yellowstone figured prominently in some of the earliest accounts of pilgrimage to the park. On his way into the park in 1873, Rev. Edwin J. Stanley pondered the fate of the Yellowstone Valley through which he passed, "this vast stretch of rich country, which during ages past has been the undisputed abode of the wild red-man; these streams, on the banks of which he was born, and by the side of which he was reared; these plains, over which he roamed at will with the wild beasts that he loved to chase—all must soon come under the influence of civilization, and yield to the scepter of the irrepressible white man."[78] Reverend Stanley himself benefited from the irrepressible advance of white civilization in visiting the new national park even as he lamented the consequences for the area's original inhabitants. But although he reveals a degree of sympathy for native peoples, especially in regard to their mistreatment at the hands of corrupt whites, Reverend Stanley resorts to racial stereotypes that condemn the Indigenous residents of the region. He acknowledges that they have suffered under the schemes of unscrupulous white intruders, but, he argues, "this does not account for all their misdeeds. They are savages by nature, and delight in war and bloodshed."[79] With this in mind, the Methodist preacher justifies genocide as the inevitable fate of recalcitrant Indians. "They must be subdued," Stanley insists. Native peoples, he argues, "must be made to feel the strong arm of the Government, and fear it, before they will respect 'the powers that be,' or before any progress can be made toward their civilization. Let there be a mild but firm government exercised over them. Faithfully observe every treaty, and punish them for every misdemeanor. Then will we have peace throughout our borders, and the Indian will be civilized as far as the possibilities of his nature will permit."[80]

Reverend Stanley's ambivalence that mixes sympathy and condemnation of native peoples of the Yellowstone region typifies much of nineteenth-century U.S. public opinion regarding the "Indian problem."[81] It also suggests Yellowstone's place in the genocide of Indigenous people and their cultures, which can be seen clearly in the sentiments of such characters as the park's second superintendent, Philetus W. Norris.

A Civil War veteran and successful land speculator and developer in the Detroit, Michigan, area, Norris first traveled west in 1870 and became enchanted with Yellowstone's charm. He manipulated a degree of political influence to gain appointment as the national park's second superintendent in 1877, replacing the erstwhile superintendent Nathaniel P. Langford, whose management of the park had suffered much criticism. The year before his appointment, Norris published an opinion piece on "The Indian War," insisting that extermination of Plains Indians would bring benefits to the nation. "The halo mid the gloom," Norris concludes, "is that though this Sioux war may be long, expensive and bloody, it must be sure and final, opening up the mines for development, and the great national highway to the Wonder Land of the upper Yellowstone evermore be trod in peace. Cheering hope. God speed the day."[82] As he maneuvered for the superintendency of the national park, Norris reiterated that fulfilling American destiny, which for him included opening the highway to Yellowstone for pilgrims to the "Wonder Land," necessitated triumph in the "expensive and bloody" war against the Indigenous inhabitants of western territories.

Norris came to Yellowstone with a genocidal regard for native peoples typical of white Americans of his day. As park superintendent, though, he sought to reassure the public that Indian hostilities did not threaten visitors. During the first season of his official position at the helm of the park, a band of Nez Perce passed through Yellowstone, fleeing the U.S. Army. They encountered several tourist parties and others in the park, resulting in numerous casualties, including the killing of two park visitors.[83] But Norris downplayed the incident as an aberration by partially Christianized Indians. In his official 1877 report, he resorts to the widely accepted myth that American Indians feared Yellowstone. The Nez Perce willingness to enter the park, in Norris's estimation, indicates that they "have acquired sufficient civilization and Christianity to at least overpower their pagan superstitious fear of earthly Fire Hole Basins and Brimstone Pits." He goes on to assure the public that Indians in the park are a rarity: "Owing to the isolation of the Park, deep amid snowy mountains, and the superstitious awe of the roaring cataracts, sulfur pools and spouting geysers over the surrounding pagan Indians, they seldom visit it, and only a harmless Sheep Eater hermits, armed with bows and arrows, ever resided there and even they have now vanished."[84]

In fact, though, Indians had not vanished from Yellowstone. The following year Norris reports that a road building crew in the Upper Geyser Basin had a near encounter with what he interpreted as hostile Bannock Indians. But the danger, Norris insists, was short-lived, as "General Miles met and in a sharp conflict nearly exterminated the Bannocks."[85] As park superintendent, Norris highlighted the near extermination of Indians as a necessary accomplishment in making Yellowstone accessible and safe for the benefit and enjoyment of the people.

Norris's insistence that ridding the region of Indians so that "the great national highway to the Wonder Land of the upper Yellowstone evermore be trod in peace" was more than the reassuring rhetoric of a government official charged with facilitating visitation to the park. Like many in the United States during the Gilded Age years, Norris held a fervent faith in the divine purpose of the nation. This foremost meant "civilizing" the continent and its Indigenous inhabitants. In an address to the Detroit Scientific Association, Norris spoke of the need to clear the Yellowstone Valley region north of the park of Indians, making it safe for settlement, agriculture, and mining. He remarked:

> Let the government of this mighty people firmly say to these painted vagabonds, this great Yellowstone Valley is now in the pathway of civilization, embrace it and remain, accept a reasonable remuneration for your quit claim and depart to the mountains or the plains in peace, or tarry and be exterminated by a power that will not falter in opening up a free National highway to the great National Park, and the numerous and valuable mines and valleys around it. Then will the over tasked business man and the weary and worn seekers of health and pleasure turn . . . to nature's crowning temple in this peerless lava and snow-encircled Wonder Land, and here in this masterpiece of His power and beauty look reverently from nature up to nature's God, who created it for His own wise purpose, preserves it for our enjoyment and benefit, and which He doubtless will in His own chosen time destroy.[86]

Although he ends with a hint of an apocalyptic destiny for the region, Norris affirms for the Christian people of the United States their righteous claim to Yellowstone and all the other treasures of the American continent as a matter of divine providence.

Philetus Norris situates Yellowstone as "nature's crowning temple" within the larger national narrative of Manifest Destiny that demanded Indigenous peoples to accept modern civilization or "be exterminated by a power that will not falter," a choice that had become official U.S. policy in the years following the Civil War. President Ulysses Grant explained in his 1871 State of the Union address, delivered just months before signing the Yellowstone Act that created the world's first national park, that "many tribes of Indians have been induced to settle upon reservations, to cultivate the soil, to perform productive labor of various kinds, and to partially accept civilization. They are being cared for in such a way, it is hoped, as to induce those still pursuing their old habits of life to embrace the only opportunity which is left them to avoid extermination."[87] This genocidal policy of condemning native societies to either accept and conform to the white world's standards of "productive labor" and acceptance of "civilization" or face "extermination" found its moral justification in the Christian ideal of Manifest Destiny. It also found confirmation in the establishment of Yellowstone and the other national parks. Their preservation of God's sublime handiwork indicated the triumph of the divine providence guiding the nation in transforming untamed territories of savage wilderness into civilized refuges where pilgrims could witness the Creator's supreme scenic accomplishments in "Edenic" landscapes.[88] For many in the United States, such awe-inspiring landscapes confirmed the nation's destiny to embody the divine virtues of freedom, democracy, and opportunity.[89]

This confirmation of the divinely ordained destiny of the United States gave religious purpose to conquest and settlement, and by the end of the nineteenth century, the subjugation of Indigenous cultures was nearly complete. Though native peoples had been frequenting the region for millennia, at the turn of the twentieth century their presence in Yellowstone amounted to nothing more than the imaginative ponderings of tourists. But their imagination of Indians continued to bolster white visitors' self-esteem as a racially superior people, evidenced in the notion that native superstitions about Yellowstone's thermal attractions kept Indians out of the park. Carter Harrison, for instance, remarks in his 1891 book, "No wonder the Indians have given this section of the country a wide berth, for well might they believe it the home of the evil spirit."[90] Harrison acknowledges that the steaming landscape inspired dread in white Christian tourists as well: "A good white man, who flatters himself that he is a child of God and believes in sovereign reigning grace, is struck by it with awe akin to terror." But elements of the volcanic landscape affirm a Protestant puritanical ethos of order and regularity, as with the Old Faithful geyser that Harrison notes "becomes familiar to the civilized tourist and seems to win from him a sort of affection, because of his conscientious behavior. His very regularity, however, would strike the more terror into the heart of the untutored red man."[91] At the end of the nineteenth century, it was religion that explained the absence of Indians in Yellowstone in the white imagination, not the genocidal policies and actions of the U.S. government. The sublime terror that faithful Christians might confront in the hellish lands was overcome by their rational and civilized confidence in a savior God, while the "untutored red man" remained overcome by terror of a pervasive evil among the boiling waters and steaming fountains.[92]

As the United States entered the twentieth century, any threat that native peoples may have posed to Yellowstone visitors was a distant memory. The transformation of Yellowstone from frightening wilderness to civilized park was complete, a monument to Manifest Destiny. This sacred wonderland had become an appealing destination for tourist pilgrims, a place where "man, the noblest of God's creations, might stand before thee in awe and rapture, and feel himself uplifted to that spirit land from whence he came."[93]

4

SACRED NATURE AND
THE WHITE RACE

Theodore Roosevelt stepped forward on the makeshift platform at the entrance to Yellowstone National Park in Gardiner, Montana, on April 24, 1903. He was the chief attraction for the crowd gathered to witness a Masonic ceremony of dedication. As a Freemason himself, Roosevelt had been invited to participate in the ritual laying of the cornerstone to the massive arch being built at the park's main entrance.[1] Some of the onlookers were curious about the Masonic dedication rites, but most had come to see and hear the president of the United States. He had galloped into town that afternoon on horseback following two weeks of camping, sightseeing, and rest in Yellowstone, a much-needed respite from the grueling pace of his "Great Loop" tour of the American West. Roosevelt rode into Gardiner ready to serve as the guest of honor in the religious ceremony at the gateway to the world's first national park.

Roosevelt's vacation retreat in Yellowstone coincided with efforts to make the entrance to the park more appealing to visitors by building a great stone arch up the hill from the new railroad depot being constructed in Gardiner. Hiram Martin Chittenden, an influential Corps of Engineers officer working in Yellowstone, felt that the rather arid and relatively drab landscape at the park's busiest entrance needed a more bold and inspiring feature to create excitement for railroad passengers.[2] Under his supervision, work began in early 1903 on a towering arch built of native stone; when finished, it would stand some five stories tall, a fitting monument to greet the crowds of tourists entering America's Wonderland.

As work began on the new arch, the Freemasons of Montana planned for a formal ceremony of dedication to lay the cornerstone of the arch. The Masons had been an influential force in the early history of Montana, with prominent leaders at the forefront of local efforts to create Yellowstone National Park. An exploration of the Yellowstone Plateau in 1869 by two Masons, Charles Cook and David Folsom, set in motion the subsequent expeditions that culminated with legislation establishing the park. Another Mason, Nathaniel Langford, had organized the Washburn expedition of 1870 at the behest of financier Jay Cooke. He also served as the new national park's first superintendent. Cornelius Hedges, another participant on the Washburn expedition to Yellowstone, had been grand master of the Montana Masons, having succeeded Langford in that role. Hedges subsequently served thirty-five years as grand secretary of the Grand Lodge of Montana. His presence at the dedication of the new arch lent an air of historical consequence to the ceremony.

It was Roosevelt's participation, however, that made the ceremony itself a historical event. To the delight of nearly four thousand cheering spectators gathered to witness the ritual laying of the cornerstone and dedication of the arch, the president arrived galloping into town on horseback. He worked his way through the adoring crowd to where the heavy cornerstone hung suspended "on heavy block and tackle from a large bunting-bedecked derrick of two wooden poles, each topped with an American flag."[3] Once the dignitaries and Masonic leaders had assumed their positions, "the ritualistic ceremonies of the order" commenced.[4]

The formalities began with a "canister" placed in a hollowed-out "depository" in the foundation where the arch's cornerstone was to be laid; in it were a number of items relating to local Freemasonry and to the park as well as a 1903 world atlas and a "Holy Bible."[5] Next Masonic grand master Frank E. Smith handed a trowel to the president, who "spread the mortar on the bed that was to receive the stone," and when all was ready, "the huge block of basalt was lowered into place." The Masons sanctified the newly placed cornerstone with corn, wine, and oil, these being the Masonic "elements of consecration," as explained to the audience. They then ceremoniously inspected the cornerstone with "the implements of Masonry," before pronouncing it "well-formed, truly laid and correctly proved.'"[6]

Once the cornerstone was in place, President Roosevelt followed the other dignitaries onto the makeshift speakers' platform. When Roosevelt stood to speak, "a prolonged cheer" greeted him.[7] As the applause quieted, the president began his remarks by thanking the crowd. He then launched into his prepared speech, exclaiming, "Nowhere else in any civilized country is there to be found such a tract of veritable wonderland made accessible to all visitors, where at the same time not only the scenery of the wilderness, but the wild creatures of the Park are scrupulously preserved, as they were the only change being that these same wild creatures have been so carefully protected as to show a literally astonishing tameness." He continued by emphasizing the democratic virtues of the national park as a land "preserved with wise foresight," which in Roosevelt's estimation "is noteworthy in its essential democracy." In this regard Yellowstone National Park "was created, and is now administered for the benefit and enjoyment of the people." Yet citizens cannot be complacent in assuming that places like Yellowstone are not threatened by those who would profit from their attractions. Roosevelt warned, "The only way that the people as a whole can secure to themselves and their children the enjoyment in perpetuity of what the Yellowstone Park has to give, is by assuming the ownership in the name of the nation and jealously safeguarding and preserving the scenery, the forests, and the wild creatures." He concluded by reiterating that national parks are not solely for the benefit of the privileged classes, but "the essential features of the present management of the Yellowstone Park, as in all similar places, is its essential democracy—it is the preservation of the scenery, of the forests[,] of the wilderness life and the wilderness game for the people as a whole instead of leaving the enjoyment thereof to be confined to the very rich who can control private preserves."[8]

Following his speech, Roosevelt mounted his horse to ride through the throngs of well-wishers three miles to the railroad terminus in Cinnabar. There he boarded the presidential train and departed, never to return to Yellowstone or to see the finished arch that bears his name.[9]

Theodore Roosevelt's participation in the Masonic ceremony consecrating and dedicating what in later decades would be known as the Roosevelt Arch marks a symbolic pivot in the significance of Yellowstone and all national parks. On the one hand, the arch served as a monumental entranceway at the terminus of the railroad line that brought passengers to the park. Conceived to heighten the excitement and anticipation of visitors, and thereby increase profits for investors who controlled transportation, accommodations, and retail outlets within the park, the arch

FIG. 9. President Theodore Roosevelt addresses the crowd at the Masonic ceremony to dedicate the stone arch at the northern entrance of Yellowstone National Park on April 24, 1903. Library of Congress, Washington DC, #2010647485.

itself commemorated the capitalist victory over the wild and savage lands of the American West. On the other hand, Roosevelt's advocacy of a conservationist agenda grounded in the rhetoric of democratic values marks a new emphasis for U.S. national parks. As one visitor remarked upon viewing the newly completed arch, "One wishes that no others save those who love Nature in all her moods, might ever pass through the massive stone archway marking the entrance to the Nation's fairyland, 'For the Benefit and Enjoyment of the People.'"[10] Yellowstone's monumental entrance welcomed all nature-loving visitors to the fairyland preserved and protected for their benefit and enjoyment.

In this regard Yellowstone stood at the center of changing attitudes about nature and the religious regard that many felt for wild places in the United States that were quickly disappearing by the beginning of the twentieth century. The national park initially had been devised as a promotional feature for the Northern Pacific Railroad and for boosters of the Montana Territory to bring more attention, settlement, and investment to the American West.[11] By the end of the nineteenth century, however, this wonderland had become a sacred preserve, a hallowed place of wildness.

The evolving regard for nature as a sacrosanct resource for national prosperity coincided with changing religious, racial, and gender attitudes among the dominant sectors of U.S. society. By the turn of the twentieth century, religion, race, and gender were tightly bound together in a nationalist ideology that regarded a democratically conceived "people" in very particular, privileged terms. Perhaps no one better articulated the rhetoric of this ideological perspective than Theodore Roosevelt, who both contributed decisively to these evolving attitudes but also benefited politically and financially as their embodiment.

A Religious Regard for Wildlands

His two-week sojourn in Yellowstone in 1903 was scheduled as an interlude of rest and recreation for Theodore Roosevelt away from the grueling itinerary of his Great Loop tour, which covered fourteen thousand miles by train, with stops in nearly 150 cities and towns, where the president delivered roughly two hundred speeches in the eight weeks of travel.[12] Escaping the spotlight for a vacation in the national park allowed the president to enjoy a degree of relative seclusion before continuing on to the West Coast.

Initially, Roosevelt had hoped to hunt cougars while in Yellowstone, careful not to shoot any inside the park but to track them beyond the park's boundary. The potential for political scandal, though, changed his mind—his opponents would certainly make much of the conservationist president hunting big cats in the national park. But ever the consummate hunter, the president did capture a field mouse while in the park, which he then killed, skinned, and prepared the pelt, according to a member of his entourage, "as neatly as a professed taxidermist." He sent it off to the National Museum of the United States (the Smithsonian), hoping he had discovered a new species (which he had not). As it turned out, the mouse was the only game that Roosevelt killed during his 1903 Yellowstone outing.[13]

Accompanying Roosevelt "camping and tramping" in Yellowstone was the popular naturalist, essayist, and poet John Burroughs.[14] Early in his writing career, he had been a protégé of the poet Walt Whitman, who had taught the young Burroughs that natural history writing should be much like poetry, based on an inspired vision of nature, and that purely objective scientific observation was insufficient for conveying the truth of nature.[15] Having rejected the religion of his Baptist upbringing, Burroughs adopted an inspired vision of nature with a distinctly spiritual element; his poetic affinity for nature contrasted to the vain amassing of wealth that dominated the values of the elite class in Gilded Age America. In the woods, he repeatedly suggested, one could seek a deeper, more meaningful apprehension of one's own divine nature. "Saints and devotees," he wrote, "have gone into the wilderness to find God. Of course, they took God with them, and the silence and detachment enabled them to hear the still, small voice of their own souls."[16]

John Burroughs's career as a writer revealed an evangelical zeal for what his biographer characterizes as "a new church of the woodlands" built upon a sacrament of "baptism in nature" to heal the debilitating effects of urban life. As industrializing impulses were rapidly transforming America by pushing more people into the squalor and tense anxieties of city life, Burroughs insisted that harried citizens could find liberation in the calm of the woods.[17]

Theodore Roosevelt lavished praise on "Oom John" (the pet name that the president bestowed upon Burroughs during their western trip together, *oom* meaning "uncle" in Dutch) as "foremost of all American writers on outdoor life."[18] But his admiration also had an element of political expediency. Roosevelt purposely brought Burroughs on his Yellowstone excursion to burnish the president's public image and to deflect political criticism. In a private letter, Roosevelt wrote that taking Burroughs with him to Yellowstone was like "the town's prize burglar attended by the

Methodist parson," suggesting that the poet's unblemished reputation might lend some moral cover for the president's compromised ethical standing in the press.[19] Burroughs for his part tended toward hero worship of Roosevelt, much like he had revered Walt Whitman early in his career. Blunting criticism of the president was a role that Burroughs welcomed and embraced.[20]

Burroughs's popularity as the nation's leading nature writer in the closing decades of the nineteenth century was soon overshadowed by another writer, the self-described "poetico-trampo-geologist-bot[anist] and ornith-natural, etc!" John Muir, whose advocacy of wilderness preservation was saturated with religious sentiment and a language that merged nineteenth-century U.S. Protestantism with the Romanticist religion of nature.[21] In contrast to Burroughs, Muir espoused a more hardline, less accommodating attitude toward preserving nature, especially wilderness mountains and wild forestlands. Like other nineteenth-century conservationists, Muir had been thoroughly convinced by the warnings of the proto-environmentalist George Perkins Marsh that the rapid expansion of industry and increasing human populations made it urgent to recognize wilderness as an inherent good that must be preserved. Burroughs, however, never accepted this more radical vision of the need to protect nature. He was more inclined to tame nature than to preserve its feral character. In short, Burroughs preferred more a garden than a wilderness.[22]

The two nature writers had become acquainted in the 1880s, when they first met in the home of magazine editor Richard Watson Gilder. When Muir was again in the northeastern United States in 1896, Burroughs invited him to visit at his rustic Hudson Valley cabin Slabsides. Their friendship deepened three years later during an extensive exploration of Alaska sponsored by railroad magnate E. H. Harriman. On this expedition Burroughs became enamored of Muir's fascination with glaciers. Similar to Muir, he recognized a divine hand in the spectacular drama of the immense sheets of ice calving into the sea on the Gustavus Peninsula (now part of Glacier Bay National Park); as Burroughs wrote in his journal, "Here with this violence, is how God builds his world."[23] Yet despite his affinity with Muir's interests, Burroughs was enchanted as well by the attentions of rich and powerful men such as Harriman and Roosevelt.

He was unwilling to cross swords with anyone who would jeopardize his access to the parlors of East Coast wealth and power.[24] This may explain Burroughs's reluctance to criticize too harshly capitalist interests that threatened the pristine nature of wildlands.

John Muir, on the other hand, whose eminence and influence eventually eclipsed John Burroughs, had no such qualms. His willingness to do battle with more powerful interests that threatened wilderness lands with the ravages of industrialization has made him a quasi-mythical figure among his many devoted partisans, who regard him as the founder of the modern environmental movement. Eulogized in 1912 as "the most rapt of all prophets of our out-of-door gospel," Muir enjoyed during his lifetime a hard-earned reputation as a fierce and relentless advocate of preserving wildlands. He also was known as the leading defender and promoter of national parks. In the estimation of environmental historian Roderick Nash, "As a publicizer of the American wilderness Muir had no equal."[25]

Muir's widespread popularity rested to a great extent on his religious sensibility that combined the romanticism of the Transcendentalists with the biblical imagery of evangelical Protestantism, a combination that has made him an enduring prophet of environmentalism and wilderness for more than a century.[26] The biblical influence came from his upbringing as the eldest son of an overbearing and zealously devout Scottish father, who imposed a strict religious discipline on his children, including mandatory study and memorization of the King James Bible.[27]

John Muir's father, Daniel, had left the Calvinist Presbyterians of Scotland when he encountered the teachings of a fellow Scot, Alexander Campbell, during Campbell's speaking tour of Scotland in 1847. Son of a Scotch-Irish minister, Campbell had been ordained in his father's church and with him made a stir on the frontier of the expanding American nation. The Campbells espoused an egalitarian Christianity, free of a clergy that could exert power and control over a congregation. Alexander Campbell also found divine inspiration in the forests of his adopted country, remarking that "the voice of nature will never contradict the voice of revelation." Nevertheless, for Campbell the only true and reliable voice of God was the Protestant Bible.[28] For Campbellites like Daniel Muir, the Bible became the central element of their lives and the prism of their knowing.

Enthralled by Campbell's religious message and the opportunities that could be found in America, Daniel Muir took his family to the United States in 1849, when John was only eleven years old, eventually settling in Wisconsin. Despite the constant labor of farm life interspersed with his father's religious demands, young John Muir found himself charmed by what he later described as a "sudden plash in pure wildness, [this] baptism into Nature's warm heart—how utterly happy it made us. . . . Oh, that glorious Wisconsin wilderness!"[29]

When he arrived at the University of Wisconsin, John Muir discovered a curriculum that "taught science as the study of God's creation," instilling in him a lifelong passion for botany and geology as a religious exploration of the works of God.[30] The sole science professor at the university when Muir attended was Dr. Ezra Carr, who had declared that science taught students to learn the "plan and purposes of God as expressed in the natural world."[31] This mixing of science and religion—or more accurately, science as religiously informed investigations of creation—led Muir, like many other young Protestants who would lead the nascent U.S. environmental movement, "away from orthodoxy toward a spiritual (and not merely scientific) relationship to nature."[32]

Besides his childhood biblical indoctrination and the religiously oriented science curriculum of his university years, Muir's forging of his religious regard for wilderness relied as well on a Romanticist reinterpretation of nature and its significance. Perhaps no single thinker did more to romanticize the popular appreciation of nature in the United States than the American philosopher, essayist, poet, and celebrated Lyceum speaker Ralph Waldo Emerson. His early book-length essay *Nature* initiated a conversation about the spiritual value of the natural world that played a foundational role in the literary, philosophical, and spiritually oriented aesthetic movement known as Transcendentalism.[33] Significantly for the scores of subsequent authors, poets, artists, pundits, and activists following in Emerson's path—including the likes of Henry David Thoreau, Walt Whitman, John Burroughs, as well as John Muir—nature became the means for experiencing an authentic spiritual reality unburdened of religious tradition, ritual, and formal church community.

In 1871 Emerson traveled to the U.S. West Coast, where he met Muir in California's Yosemite Valley.[34] Though their visit together was brief, with Emerson declining Muir's invitation to spend "a month's worship with Nature in the high temples of the great Sierra crown," they established a bond that lasted the remainder of Emerson's life.[35] Their meeting inspired Muir's interest in Emerson's writings, complementing his previous absorption in the works of another Transcendentalist author, Henry David Thoreau, whom Muir subsequently emulated both in lifestyle and as a writer.[36]

These various influences—his father's Campbellite biblical religion, the religiously tinted science of his university studies, the Transcendentalist writings of Emerson and Thoreau—cultivated in the young John Muir a spiritual regard for nature. According to his interpretation, nature's beauty in all of its complexity and constant wonder revealed the ever-present reality of God. He would write in the journal of his first summer in Yosemite: "Oh, these vast, calm, measureless mountain days, inciting at once to work and rest! Days in whose light everything seems equally divine, opening a thousand windows to show us God."[37] Even the massive, ancient trees of the Sierra Nevada preached God's word: "Sequoias, kings of their race, growing close together like grass in a meadow, poised their brave domes and spires in the sky, three hundred feet above the ferns and lilies that enameled the ground; towering serene through the long centuries, preaching God's forestry fresh from heaven."[38]

Reverence of nature, though, came for John Muir most notably in solitude, in the absence of humans in wild places. While on a long autumn trek through the mountains, Muir paused in a meadow where "every tree seemed religious and conscious of the presence of God. A free man revels in a scene like this and time goes by unmeasured. I stood fixed in silent wonder or sauntered about shifting my points of view, . . . giving free expression to my joy, exulting in Nature's wild immortal vigor and beauty, never dreaming any other human being was near." But then his reverie was interrupted by the sudden appearance of "a man and a horse [who] came in sight at the farther end of the meadow, where they seemed sadly out of place."[39] Claiming this meadow for himself alone, Muir's enjoyment of wilderness worship required complete solitude for the worshipper to perceive God's presence "in Nature's wild immortal vigor and beauty." In short, Muir's romanticized ideal regarded wilderness as an unpeopled reserve.

These sorts of sentiments made John Muir, by the turn of the twentieth century, the leading voice in the United States extolling the virtues of unpeopled wilderness. In part based on Emerson's encouragement, Muir had embarked on a writing career that would establish him as a renowned literary figure in his own day and whose works still remain foundational in the canon of American environmental writing. A good deal of his popularity and enduring legacy derives from his advocacy of wilderness preservation and his related promotion of U.S. national parks. Most often associated with Yosemite in California, his spiritual home for most of his adult life, Muir also brought national attention to other parks, including Yellowstone.[40]

Already an acclaimed naturalist and essayist with a national reputation, Muir visited Yellowstone National Park in August 1885.[41] His short tour of the park was not particularly enjoyable, owing to unpleasant weather and a persistent stomach problem, but he nevertheless celebrated the wildness, scenery, wildlife, and thermal features in a hastily written article for a San Francisco newspaper.[42] He especially highlighted Yellowstone's importance as headwaters of three great river systems, the Yellowstone and Missouri Rivers, the Green River, and the Snake River, but he also included an emphasis on the spiritual value of the park in an essay he later penned for the *Atlantic Monthly* that eventually became the second chapter of his 1901 book, *Our National Parks*. In it he exclaims: "A thousand Yellowstone wonders are calling, 'Look up and down and round about you!' And a multitude of still, small voices may be heard directing you to look through all this transient, shifting show of things called 'substantial' into the truly substantial, spiritual world whose forms flesh and wood, rock and water, air and sunshine, only veil and conceal, and to learn that here is heaven and the dwelling-place of angels."[43]

This image of Yellowstone as a worldly expression of a transcendent "truly substantial, spiritual world" reveals the religious influences that shaped U.S. aesthetic views of nature by the beginning of the twentieth century. Muir's success as an author relied to a large extent on his eloquent incorporation of this religiously inflected aesthetics in popularizing wilderness preservation. His writings portray Yellowstone and all national parks not merely as playgrounds for recreational pleasures but as inherently sacred lands demonstrating the perfection of God's creation.[44] They also demonstrate discernible social attitudes of the day, especially regarding racial differences. Besides transforming parklands and other wild places into sacred ground, Muir's influence also contributed to the persistence of national parks as "icons of whiteness."[45]

Conserving Nature and Whiteness

Muir's racial views were not a consistently prominent aspect of his advocacy for preserving wild nature and promoting national parks. However, his attitudes toward African Americans, Native Americans, and other nonwhite peoples appear clearly at various points in his body of work and were fundamental to his advocacy of unpeopled wilderness. In 1867, before going west, the young John Muir left his midwestern roots and set out on a "thousand-mile walk" that took him into the heart of the American South during Reconstruction, an epic journey that elicited his racial ambivalence.[46] Having avoided the military draft during the Civil War by fleeing to Canada, Muir was no abolitionist willing to fight for racial justice.[47] Despite what his biographer describes as having met southern Blacks "more or less as equals" and on occasion sharing "the intimacy of their homes to an extent that few white northerners, or white southerners, ever did," Muir's observations of the southern United States were rife with demeaning racial attitudes.[48] He later recalled his observations in Georgia that "the Negroes are very lazy [revised to *easy-going* in the published version] and merry. . . . One energetic white man, working with a will, would easily pick as much cotton as half a dozen sambos and sallies."[49]

Initially intending to continue his long walk all the way to South America, a bout with malaria in Florida redirected Muir's sights westward. His arrival in California in March 1868 began his long romance with the state's landscapes, especially its mountains. He was not enamored, though, of the Indigenous people who had inhabited those landscapes for generations. Not unlike his impressions of African Americans during his southern sojourn, Muir adopted an ambivalent view of Native Americans. In describing an elderly native woman, for instance, whom he encountered his first summer in Yosemite, Muir contrasts her unfavorably to "Nature's neat well-dressed animals," lamenting "that mankind alone is dirty."[50] More damaging, however, than his repulsion of their dirtiness was the total erasure of Indigenous inhabitants' presence in Muir's vision of the American landscape.[51] A pervasive disregard on the part of the United States of Native American relationships with their traditional homelands has resulted in a history of cultural genocide, and John Muir's reverent characterization of wilderness as an unpeopled paradise has contributed to this legacy. The popularity of his writings at the turn of the twentieth century following the U.S. conquest and confinement of American Indian nations helped to erase Native Americans' long-held attachments to the land.

Muir's erasure of Native American presence in the story of the nation's wildlands was a widely shared sentiment among U.S. citizens of the day, as it remains even now. Among the loudest voices expressing this view was that of the president of the United States, Theodore Roosevelt. When he met Muir in California in 1903, following the president's visit to Yellowstone, their common interests immediately cemented a personal bond. Sharing a passion for outdoor life, they quickly abandoned the pomp and adulation that accompanied Roosevelt everywhere he traveled and went off alone (except for two guides, two packers, and three mules) to spend three nights camping in the Yosemite wilderness.[52] Roosevelt had insisted on having Muir serve as his host, and Muir in turn relished the opportunity to command the president's attention on urgent needs for wilderness preservation.[53] As the foremost advocate for national parks as protected reservations of pristine wilderness and a recognized conservationist with a profound intimacy with the natural world, John Muir was an ideal companion for Roosevelt's visit to Yosemite.

The deepening of the mutual admiration and personal bond between John Muir and Theodore Roosevelt during their time together in Yosemite revealed a shared environmental ethic that superseded their differences. Those differences, however, were significant and had a strongly gendered quality. Much of Roosevelt's public image had been built upon his insistence on big game hunting as the quintessential masculine activity that had implications for the well-being of the nation—he wrote of the "peculiar charm" of the wilderness hunter: "The chase is among the best of all national pastimes; it cultivates that vigorous manliness for the lack of which in a nation, as in an individual, the possession of no other qualities can possibly atone."[54] The hunting of wild animals in Roosevelt's estimation not only affirmed the virility of "vigorous manliness"; it also ensured the strength of the nation. Muir, on the other hand, strongly disagreed. He repeatedly condemned the "murder business" of hunting, and he even wrote that boys should be taught to grow out of "natural hunting blood-loving savagery into natural sympathy with all our fellow mortals—plants and animals as well as men." In contrast to the masculine ideal of Roosevelt's hunting mentality, Muir envisioned a "glimmering recognition of the rights of animals & their kinship to ourselves."[55]

Yet despite their differences, both Roosevelt and Muir were passionately committed to preserving nature. But even here, philosophical disagreements divided them. While Muir envisioned the sacred purity of nature absent of a human presence (other than the recreational enjoyment of nature by a privileged class of travelers), Roosevelt tended toward a more pragmatic ethos. More often than not, the president sided with his chief forester, Gifford Pinchot, a leading advocate of the "utilitarian" approach to conservation, famously summed up as "the greatest good, for the greatest number, for the longest run."[56] This view of rational management of natural resources for the good of society, which became a pillar of Progressive ideology and politics, motivated Roosevelt's unprecedented accomplishments in setting aside federal lands for protection and sustainable management. During his presidency, he was able to establish 130 million acres of federal forest reserves, more than fifty wildlife sanctuaries, and five new national parks. He also signed into law the Antiquities Act, allowing him to designate eighteen areas as national monuments.[57]

Theodore Roosevelt's legacy of "launching conservation as a national political movement" also entailed a racial dimension.[58] Along with a concern about the wasteful depletion of the nation's resources was the perception of threats to the undisputed dominance of the white race. Conserving natural resources demanded rational, scientific management principles, and likewise, averting "race suicide" required the scientific application of eugenic policies.

Roosevelt's background as a lifelong Presbyterian steered him toward a thoroughgoing embrace of Darwinist principles, based in part on the influence of Alexander von Humboldt and his "noticeable Calvinistic moralism." Darwin's book *On the Origin of Species*, according to environmental historian Mark Stoll, derived in part from Humboldt's observations of the interconnectedness of nature in a harmonious whole of a dynamic cosmos. Stoll writes, "It was a natural theology without a creator."[59] Roosevelt, like many of his generation, fully embraced the Darwinian evolutionary paradigm. It not only defined how he viewed the natural nonhuman world, but it also provided a scientific justification for his advocacy of eugenics. He and other early-twentieth-century Progressives embraced eugenics as the rational response to the threat of race suicide evident in the declining birth rates of white Protestants. He wrote in 1914: "I wish very much that the wrong people could be prevented entirely from breeding. . . . Criminals should be sterilized, and feebleminded persons forbidden to leave offspring behind them. But as yet there is no way possible to devise which could prevent all undesirable people from breeding. The emphasis should be laid on getting desirable people to breed."[60]

Though his commitment to eugenics was a single element in Roosevelt's complicated, inconsistent, and often paradoxical racial politics, it became a foundational pillar in the Progressive movement that was not distinct from his monumental achievements in the conservation of natural resources and the preservation of wilderness lands.[61] The entanglement of wilderness preservation with the preservation of the white race can be seen perhaps most clearly in one of the last initiatives of Roosevelt's presidency, the three-volume National Conservation Commission report, compiled by the commission's executive chairman, Gifford Pinchot, the president's closest and most trusted adviser on environmental issues. When he brought it to Congress in 1909, Roosevelt declared the report as "one of the most fundamentally important documents ever laid before the American people."[62] On appointing the commission in 1908, Roosevelt had stipulated that its work was "conditioned upon keeping ever in mind the great fact that the life of the Nation depends absolutely on the material resources, which have already made the Nation great. Our object is to conserve the foundations of our prosperity."[63] Conserving prosperity, though, had a racial element. The final report's volume on "National Vitality, Its Waste and Conservation" addressed key issues of Progressive politics with ten far-reaching recommendations that ranged from public health to labor regulation to the elimination of poverty and crime. This broad range of social issues all pointed toward its tenth recommendation, which advocated "eugenics, or hygiene for future generations," including forced sterilization and marriage prohibition for "degenerates generally" while establishing social norms to encourage eugenically preferable marriages. The report explicitly connected these eugenic policies to environmental concerns, concluding that "the problem of the conservation of our natural resources is therefore not a series of independent problems, but a coherent, all-embracing whole. If our nation cares to make any provision for its grandchildren and its grandchildren's grandchildren, this provision must include conservation in all its branches—but above all, the conservation of the racial stock itself."[64]

Though Congress took little interest in the lame-duck president's National Conservation Commission report, the linkage between protecting natural resources and conserving the white racial stock of the nation persisted as cornerstones of Progressive politics. One of the more influential champions of this Progressive agenda for preserving nature and saving the white race was Madison Grant, a close associate of Theodore Roosevelt who gained fame and notoriety for his popular treatise advocating eugenic solutions to the nation's problems. Many of his contemporaries knew Grant as an indefatigable warrior for wilderness preservation; he had collaborated with Roosevelt in the 1890s to found the New York Zoological Society with the intent of breeding captive bison to repopulate the Great Plains and Rocky Mountain regions, and he was involved in a variety of other conservation initiatives. Grant earned enduring infamy, however, as the author of what was perhaps the most influential book on eugenics, *The Passing of the Great Race*, a racist tome that even Adolf Hitler described as "my Bible."[65] The popularity of Grant's book exposed an underlying terror among members of the white mainstream of U.S. society who felt threatened by "the specter of deterioration and degeneration of the human species—race suicide on the cultural level and an environmental wasteland on the other."[66] The solution to both, in the Progressive worldview, was rational, scientifically informed management to protect our most cherished resources, both racial and natural.

The Progressive efforts to preserve both nature and the white race, led by Theodore Roosevelt and his allies such as Gifford Pinchot and Madison Grant, were not in any way contradictory or paradoxical for many Americans, with eugenics and environmentalism, in the words of historian Garland E. Allen, becoming "intimately connected in the minds of many during the first half of the twentieth century."[67] Allen points out that the ideologies undergirding the social and political programs of both eugenics and environmentalism "were not only compatible, but for those who adhered to them, mutually reinforcing."[68] For Theodore Roosevelt and his Progressive followers, preserving nature and the unique lands of the American nation was inextricably linked to perpetuating the dominance of the white race. In their imagination of the United States, the hallowed grounds of Yellowstone and other national parks were exemplary sites of white supremacy.

With God in Yellowstone

For some U.S. citizens, places like Yellowstone provided occasions for promoting the confluence of religion and white supremacy. One such person was Bishop Alma White, who in 1901 had founded the Pentecostal Union, commonly known as the Pillar of Fire.[69] She came to Yellowstone in 1919, and similar to John Muir and Theodore Roosevelt before her, she spent a very limited time in the park, with only four days for her visit.[70] Like Muir, Bishop White also discovered God in Yellowstone, although unlike the deity that Muir was accustomed to experiencing in wild mountainous terrains, Alma White's God was a stern, judgmental, white Pentecostal god.[71]

Bishop White built her career on interpreting every event—small or large, good fortune and bad, illnesses of her own and others, relationships, places, and virtually all experiences—through the lens of providential, moralizing significance. In her world all things had divine meaning, which could be elucidated through biblical interpretation. In typical fashion, for instance, she wrote that the tragedy of the *Titanic* ocean liner in 1912 foretold "the doom of those who are given to greed and pleasure in a world cursed by sin. The inspired Book foretells these things and men have only to read and understand, but alas how few do so."[72]

While in Yellowstone, Bishop White spent much of her brief tour passing judgment on other visitors and drawing moral conclusions about the scenery, wildlife, and thermal features.[73] At one point in the book that she wrote of her experience in the national park, *With God in Yellowstone*, she expresses disapproval of the driver's attentions toward two young ladies in her touring party. She remarks, "It was not very pleasant to ride behind a driver with so much responsibility, who was carrying on a flirtation." She then explains, "Human nature has been so weakened through the fall that there is not much dependence to be put in one where a play by the opposite sex is being made on the heartstrings. Samson was shorn of his strength by the fair-faced Delilah, and made to grind without eyes in the mills of the Philistines, after he had rent a lion, carried off the gates of Gaza, and defied all enemies of Israel."[74]

With God in Yellowstone sermonizes the religious significance of the park, which White viewed primarily as "an object lesson . . . to convince people of the infallibility of God's word."[75] In the preface to the book, she explains that her intent is "not simply to give a brief account of a recent trip to Yellowstone National Park and to describe some of Nature's grandeurs, but to elucidate spiritual truths that were demonstrated in this place of many 'wonders' in a thousand miracles before my eyes. . . . In the canyons, rivers, and waterfalls, in the lakes, springs, and pools, specimens of Eden have been preserved on the outside of a thin crust, covering the sulphurous flames of the regions below, where the rumblings of God's wrath are heard threatening the world with judgments."[76] For her, God was a real presence in the Yellowstone landscape.

Most impressive of Yellowstone's wonders for Alma White, as for many visitors before her and after, was the Grand Canyon of the Yellowstone. "I have been many times through the Rocky Mountain regions, passed through the Royal Gorge, and have seen most of the places of interest that the mountain passes, fastnesses, and peaks afford, but nothing had ever so charmed, awed, inspired, and bewildered me as did the first glimpse of the Grand Canyon of the Yellowstone." White then proceeds to interpret the canyon theologically: "Solomon's kingdom symbolizes the second work of grace taught in the Scriptures, an experience which no one can understand unless he is in possession of it. Experience is necessary to enjoy it in its fulness; and so with nature's grandeur and magnificence on such a tremendous scale as in the Grand Canyon of the Yellowstone." She remarks on the ineffability of such experiences: "One must see with the eyes what the mind fails to grasp with the hearing of the ear. Language, with its adaptability to the uses of mortal man, is inadequate. Word-pictures, though drawn by the most visionary and

FIG. 10. Upper Falls of the Yellowstone River, where Alma White "spent one of the most profitable hours of my life," May 16, 2015. Photo by T. S. Bremer.

gifted, fail to convey except in a slight degree the grandeur of nature's activities and exhibitions in this the most inspiring and picturesque spot on the globe."[77]

A pair of quasi-mystical moments typify Bishop White's experiences at the Grand Canyon of the Yellowstone. The first came as a realization of the sublime nature of her initial encounter with the canyon: "After I was again seated in the car, for a few moments my eyes were closed to all the world about me, and in a new sense I began to realize the infinite depths of divine power and wisdom, and how small is the creature when compared with the Creator."[78] Then, on her last day at the canyon, White was overcome with the aesthetics of Christian suffering when she went alone to the Upper Falls, an impressive 109-foot cascade roughly a half-mile upriver from the more spectacular Lower Falls: "Here, with no one present but the unseen host, I spent one of the most profitable hours of my life.... For a short time, surrounded by nature, with all of its primitive beauty and grandeur, I seemed to forget my burdens, and had a foretaste of what it will be when the cross is laid down and the crown is won. But to be an overcomer, I knew there must be no shrinking from duty until the last battle is fought."[79]

This sort of emphasis on reading the wonders of nature to discern religious lessons continued throughout White's prolific career as an author. An obvious example is her book *The Voice of Nature*, a collection of poems published a decade after her Yellowstone book. In one poem she instructs that for "those who know the Lord, / Who love and trust Him every day," the key to reading "the Book of Nature" is to be found in "His holy word."[80] In this poem and throughout much of her literary output, White counsels that all interpretations of the natural world must conform to God's holy word in the canonized text of Protestant Christianity.

White characterized herself as an "ultra-fundamentalist" Christian, but as at least one scholar has puzzled over, White was also a committed feminist, "almost terrifying in her intense earnestness" in advocating for "equality between the sexes," a somewhat paradoxical conviction for a fundamentalist Christian.[81] Her intensely religious commitment to women's equality, however, did not extend to racial equality. White publicly supported the Ku Klux Klan, and she wrote three books praising the hate group's efforts. Her portraits of the Klan regard them in narrowly Christian, specifically Protestant terms.[82] Most of her praise details their nativist patriotism, especially their anti-Catholic campaigns, while ignoring their culture of violence.[83] In addition to her religious emphasis, though, White makes clear her white supremacist adulation of the Klan. As she explains in her book *The Ku Klux Klan in Prophecy*:

> The Klan stand for the supremacy of the white race, which is perfectly legitimate and in accordance with the teachings of Holy Writ, and anything that has been decreed by the all-wise God should not work a hardship on the colored race. . . . For the best interests of all concerned, the black race should occupy the place intended for it by the Creator. It is within the rights of civilization for the white race to hold the supremacy; and it is no injustice to the colored man. The white men of this country poured out their blood to liberate the colored people from the chains of slavery, and the sacrifice should be appreciated.[84]

Her Yellowstone book also hints at a white supremacist attitude toward Native Americans, for instance when she learned that the bison in the park were rapidly going extinct. "It seems," she surmises, "that the buffalo and the Indian go together, and thrive only where civilization has not yet come," thus suggesting that Indians, as a sort of subhuman animal closer to buffalo than to modern white people, are not capable of being civilized.[85]

Alma White's racialized religious interpretations of Yellowstone National Park reflect a contentious history of race relations and bigoted attitudes that have been endemic to the United States from long before its eighteenth-century founding. Bringing such attitudes to Yellowstone, however, relies in no small part on the influence of John Muir and Theodore Roosevelt, who made the park and other places of scenic wonder into sacred sites of white America. Muir envisioned preserving wilderness as an unpeopled domain. These wilderness reserves, though, and the national parks in particular, were for white visitors. As he assured readers in his popular book *Our National Parks*: "The Indians are dead now. . . . Arrows, bullets, scalping-knives, need no longer be feared; and all the wilderness is peacefully open."[86] Absent of Indians, the wilderness had been made open for the white man to find his deity in the mountains and among the trees. Going beyond Muir's reassurances, Roosevelt and the Progressive movement that he led regarded racial differences as an essential element in the preservation of wild places and the scientific management of natural resources. Linking conservation with eugenics, Roosevelt and his associates made the logic of white supremacy fundamental to the American love of nature. For Alma White this meant equating her appreciation of nature and her experiences of the Yellowstone wonders with the word of her Christian God, who ordained "the supremacy of the white race."

A Wonderland of Whiteness

Like Muir, Theodore Roosevelt has often been mistakenly identified as a founding figure of U.S. national parks. Neither one played any part in the beginnings of the national park movement—Yellowstone had been established long before either of them had any significant influence in conservation initiatives, more than thirty years before they went camping together in 1903. However, their contributions in the closing decades of the nineteenth century and the early years of the twentieth century were enormously influential in defining how many people would come to regard national parks as sacred treasures of the American landscape.

Their influence relied largely on emerging concerns at the turn of the twentieth century about the conservation and management of the nation's natural resources. Three distinct views of managing public lands had come into focus to counter the unrestrained, rapacious extraction of natural resources that fueled the rapid expansion of the industrial revolution. The most radical approach was that of John Muir, whose religious devotion to nature as a direct expression of God's word committed him to relentlessly advocate for wilderness preservation completely free of any sort of improvements or human presence. Though he opposed both the development of wildlands and any manner of permanent human occupancy on those lands, Muir allowed for visitors, like himself, who sought to escape "the stupefying effects of the vice of over-industry and the deadly apathy of luxury" by "getting in touch with the nerves of Mother Earth; jumping from rock to rock, feeling the life of them, learning the songs of them, panting in whole-souled exercise, and rejoicing in the deep, long-drawn breaths of pure wildness."[87]

John Burroughs, however, did not join Muir in resisting human intrusions on wildlands. Instead, he adopted a more genteel, pastoral "garden aesthetic" for valuing nature. In contrast to Muir's praise of nature's inherent wildness, Burroughs preferred taming natural areas as domesticated spaces of romanticized, inspired retreat. As a haven for escaping the pressures of overcrowded, dirty, and profane urban life, the calm of nature's gardens allowed modern citizens "to hear the still, small voice of their own souls." The restless spirits of Gilded Age America, in Burroughs's poetic vision, could experience a new "baptism in nature" in his imagined "church of the woodlands."[88]

Gifford Pinchot had little patience for either Muir's religious devotion to wildness for its own sake or Burroughs's aesthetic of nature's gardens. He regarded public lands as sources of national prosperity to be scientifically managed. "Wise use" for him meant "the greatest good, for the greatest number, for the longest run" in his "utilitarian" philosophy of natural resource management.[89] In his infamous battle with John Muir over Yosemite's Hetch Hetchy Valley, Pinchot ultimately prevailed in the prolonged struggle that pitted the preservation of a treasured portion of the national park against the future needs of San Francisco for a reliable water supply following the 1906 earthquake. In what would become a seminal moment that galvanized resistance from the fledgling environmental movement, Pinchot criticized those who would preserve the valley "untouched for the benefit of the very small number of comparatively well to do to whom it will be accessible. The intermittent aesthetic enjoyment of less than one per cent is being balanced against the daily comfort and welfare of 99 per cent."[90] In the end this utilitarian argument won the day, and the picturesque Hetch Hetchy Valley disappeared under reservoir waters.

Theodore Roosevelt kept all three of these public figures in his orbit, but he relied on them in different ways. Although he expressed great admiration and praise for John Muir and especially "Oom" John Burroughs, Gifford Pinchot exerted more direct influence on Roosevelt's policies and conservation legacy. As the head of forestry in Roosevelt's administration and his closest advisor on conservation issues, Pinchot commanded the course of the Progressive agenda for public lands and natural resources.

Gifford Pinchot also provided the link between conserving nature and conserving the racial stock of white America. An outspoken eugenicist whose utilitarian approach to land management coincided with the logic of scientifically managed reproductive policies, Pinchot made explicit the need for "conservation in all its branches" to guarantee the nation's continued prosperity. For him this meant not only the conservation of natural resources "but above all, the conservation of the racial stock itself."[91]

This confluence of conserving nature and conserving the white race made possible the popularity of later public figures like Alma White. Her theological interpretations that glorified the natural world as God's precious creation while celebrating white supremacy and the racist activities of the Ku Klux Klan fed on the legacies of Progressive leaders such as Theodore Roosevelt, Gifford Pinchot, and Madison Grant. Their rhetoric linking conservation and eugenics gave White's interpretations a legitimacy readily accepted by many in the United States during the interwar years.

None of these individuals spent any great amount of time in Yellowstone, but their enduring importance has formed the image that many people have about national parks generally. Probably most influential has been John Muir's regard for wilderness lands as sacred reserves where one can experience divine presence. His beloved Yosemite epitomized wild precincts where visitors could enjoy days "in whose light everything seems equally divine, opening a thousand windows to show us God."[92] Through these windows opening to the deity of nature's holiness, a new vision of national parks emerged. In Muir's pious regard for the sanctity of wild-lands and in the growing public appreciation for preserving what was left of wilderness at the turn of the twentieth century, places like Yellowstone gradually changed from appealing tourist destinations to become sacred wonderlands deserving of reverence. But for many visitors in the first half of the twentieth century and enduring in less obvious ways to the present, Yellowstone remained a wonderland of whiteness.

5

EVANGELIZING WONDERLAND

Christian churches came late to the Upper Yellowstone River region. Methodists erected the first permanent place of worship in 1898 at a settlement known as Pine Creek in the valley north of the national park.[1] Before then, and for a good many years after, the religious needs of Christians in that part of the world relied mostly on the peripatetic ministrations of circuit riders and other mobile clergy.

Besides the Methodists, an Episcopalian may have been the most recognizable of Christian clergy associated with Yellowstone and surrounding communities to the north of the park in the first years of the twentieth century. The Reverend John Pritchard had settled sometime around the turn of the twentieth century on a ranch near Fridley, Montana (today the town of Emigrant, located in the Paradise Valley on the highway between the park and the city of Livingston). His willingness to accept a drink whenever offered earned him the moniker "Whiskey Ike," but he was widely respected as a tireless pastor ministering to the religious and spiritual needs of a far-flung district. From his home base he traveled under all sorts of conditions to settlements throughout the valley and into the park, where he served as chaplain for the U.S. Army at Fort Yellowstone.[2] This military installation, located at Mammoth Hot Springs, housed troops that had been assigned in 1886 to protect the park from poachers, wildfires, illegal commercial enterprises, and damage to the thermal features by tourists. By the time Reverend Pritchard began providing pastoral support, Fort Yellowstone had become a permanent post and headquarters for administering the national park.[3]

Reverend Pritchard covered his sprawling territory with the help of the trains carrying tourists and other travelers between Livingston and Gardiner, at the north entrance of Yellowstone National Park. Although he had to travel seven long miles to the nearest station in Fridley, the tracks passed just a half-mile from his ranch, and the engineers obliged him by stopping to give him a ride whenever he flagged them down. He was able to get to the remote corners of his district on relatively short notice as well as make it to his regular preaching appointments with the help of these generous railroad workers.[4]

Reverend Pritchard's passage on the local trains was usually welcome, though on one occasion he met with a cold reception. On this particular day, he hurried to catch the train to Gardiner, tearing his coat as he went through a barbed wire fence to wave it down. The train stopped and allowed him to board, but he quickly learned the ride wasn't what he was expecting. "After he got on the train," his daughter recalled years later, "he found out it was a Special with some high officials on board. They gave him a good bawling out," presumably for interrupting their specially arranged passage to the Yellowstone wonderland. They did not put him out, though, since he was on his way to hold a worship service in the park.[5]

The scarcity of clergy in the region made Reverend Pritchard ecumenical by necessity. When the citizens of Gardiner, Montana, for example, undertook building a Union church in their community that would be available for "all ministers of all faiths," they turned to Reverend Pritchard to help with planning and fundraising for the place of worship. He graciously agreed, and when the church was finished, in 1905, the community showed its appreciation by giving ownership for the new building to the Episcopal Diocese of Montana, with the stipulation that it would remain available for use by all Christian denominations.[6]

Reverend Pritchard's ecumenical approach allowed him to marry couples of various Protestant traditions; baptize babies; bury the departed; preach regularly in the few houses of worship available in the region; console the grieving, the ill, and the frightened; and likely bring at least a few wayward souls to Jesus over the course of his career serving worshippers in Yellowstone National Park and parts north. He also initiated the tradition of regular religious services in the park in his role as chaplain for the soldiers stationed at Fort Yellowstone. This tradition continues today, though not in the way that Reverend Pritchard practiced his calling in the first decades of the twentieth century. Worship services had been available, though quite infrequently, in and near Yellowstone going back to the earliest years of the park. Even though most leisure travelers have no interest in formal worship while vacationing, as the Methodist tourist Rev. Edwin Stanley observed during his 1873 visit to the park, that has not deterred earnest Christian evangelists from capitalizing on the crowds who descend on Yellowstone every year.[7] Most significant has been an evangelical Protestant parachurch organization that originated in Yellowstone and became ubiquitous in U.S. national parks and other recreational destinations across the country in the second half of the twentieth century.

Christian Worship in Yellowstone

Rev. John Pritchard's service to the U.S. Army as chaplain at Fort Yellowstone involved conducting worship services in a troop mess hall. At least a few of the faithful found this arrangement unsatisfactory, so in 1905 Reverend Pritchard joined with the commanding officer of the Yellowstone post, Capt. John Pitcher, and the United States commissioner for the park, Judge John W. Meldrum, to get approval and funding to build a chapel for the soldiers stationed there. This required substantial political maneuverings, but after several setbacks, in 1911 the U.S. Congress finally approved authorization to build a chapel in Yellowstone National Park that included an appropriation "not to exceed $25,000."[8] With the legislation and money in hand, officials began planning for the chapel right away. They settled on a traditional Gothic cruciform structure that would seat 250 people, and in keeping with the precedent of other buildings in the park, the chapel would be constructed of materials that blended with the local landscape.[9]

Construction on the new chapel at Fort Yellowstone was completed in January 1913, and worshippers gathered for a service of consecration in June of that year. It was an ecumenical affair, with the Episcopal bishop of Wyoming performing the consecration and clergy from Lutheran, Presbyterian, and Congregational denominations participating in the celebration. News reports emphasized that the chapel was for everyone of all faiths, "not only for soldiers, but for everyone in the Park. Both Catholic and Protestant denominations have the use of the building."[10]

FIG. 11. Originally built to serve soldiers at Fort Yellowstone, the Yellowstone National Park Chapel at Mammoth Hot Springs was consecrated in 1913 and is still used for worship services, weddings, and other events. August 1, 2006. Photo by T. S. Bremer.

The chapel remained an army facility until October 1916, when the newly formed National Park Service, an agency within the U.S. Department of the Interior, took over management of Yellowstone. Reverend Pritchard stayed on after the army left, holding worship services once or twice every month until he left in 1919 for an appointment in Olympia, Washington.[11] Others made use of the chapel as well, including Catholics, Mormons, and occasionally clergy visiting the park.[12] Worshippers kept the chapel active with regular services, sometimes more than one, every Sunday through the busy summer months, with less frequent gatherings during the winter. With so many different groups wanting to use the space, the park administration found it necessary by the 1930s to appoint a "Church Committee" to sort out the various requests for reserving the building and to manage its upkeep.[13]

Like most recreational destinations, Yellowstone experienced a precipitous drop in visitors during World War II, and the scarcity of tires and fuel for automobiles made it an insurmountable hardship for clergy from nearby towns to travel to the park for worship services. Consequently, only two services were held in the chapel through all of the war years and only two more in 1946.[14]

In the period of greater prosperity following the war, with a growing U.S. middle class whose members enjoyed more leisure time with regular paid vacations, visitation to Yellowstone National Park gradually increased. Moreover, as the nation plunged headlong into the midcentury decades of the Cold War, religion became a defining element of national identity like it never had before—many citizens, including a good number of the nation's leaders, emphasized the religious character of the United States in contrast to the godless enemy in the Soviet Union.[15] The time was ripe for the melding of religion and the national parks, and a young seminarian working in Yellowstone was well positioned to capitalize on the moment.

Warren W. Ost had first come to Yellowstone in 1946 from his hometown of Minneapolis, Minnesota, to spend the summer working in the national park. He returned for a total of four summers as a bellman at the Old Faithful Inn while he pursued a ministerial degree at Princeton Theological Seminary in New Jersey. These were happy and fulfilling summer jaunts for Ost; according to his own testimony, "While I was involved in no formal ministry in the four years as a bellman, there were singing groups, hiking groups, prayer groups organized among the employees and talent shows every night."[16] An aptitude for organizing, coupled with the evangelical enthusiasm of a pastor-in-training, turned his Yellowstone experience into the genesis of a national ministry that he envisioned for national parks throughout America and eventually for the entire world. Though he would never fulfill his global ambitions, Ost's ministry impacted thousands of young (and a good number of not-so-young) evangelists serving the religious needs of national park visitors, employees, and local residents.[17]

A Christian Ministry

As he neared the end of his seminary studies, Warren Ost sought opportunities to continue working in Yellowstone. David de L. Condon, Yellowstone's chief park naturalist who served as chair of the superintendent's

Church Committee at the time, approached Ost about contacting seminaries to ask for students to lead worship in Yellowstone. Condon asked him if he would draft a letter of inquiry to send to the major seminaries, and Ost obliged. The letters went out under Condon's name, and when one arrived at Princeton Theological Seminary, where Ost was a student, the director of field education asked him what he thought of it. Ost explained what they had in mind, and the director was pleased with the idea and asked him if he could draft a reply. So Ost began his career as a national park pastor by writing the reply to a request that he had written.[18]

Their plan was not the first time that using seminary students to provide worship services in Yellowstone National Park had been suggested, but fortuitous timing, along with key relationships that Ost had cultivated during his four summers working there, made him an obvious candidate for the position.[19] Condon, as chair of the Church Committee, had been working with local ministerial associations to supply various clergy for worship services, but the relationship had become strained in recent years. The local ministers wanted a more adequate share of the collections to justify the time and expense involved in traveling to the park for worship with a transient congregation.[20] Condon and others on the Church Committee were familiar with Warren Ost and impressed by his enthusiasm for organizing musical events and leading worship in the park. The young seminarian seemed a convenient alternative to the less-than-ideal relationships with local ministers from nearby communities.

For his part Ost jumped at the opportunity. He arranged a series of meetings in early 1952, beginning with a conference between representatives of Princeton Theological Seminary and National Park Service officials in Washington DC. This first consultation concluded with the government indicating "its general approval of a national ministry if it could be properly sponsored interdenominationally." Next came a meeting between the seminary representatives and the newly formed National Council of Churches (NCC). These efforts resulted in "unanimous judgment in the meeting that this was a new area of evangelism which merited serious consideration." Ost then arranged a conference between the executive director of the Joint Department of Evangelism of the NCC and representatives of both the National Park Service and the Department of Interior. Ost and the NCC official found the government people "enthusiastic about the possibility of eventually carrying on a religious program, not only in Yellowstone, but in all the national parks. They promised to cooperate." Based on this promise, the NCC submitted a formal proposal to the Park Service, which the director of the National Park Service, Conrad L. Wirth, officially approved. By May 1952 NCC's Joint Department of Evangelism had assumed administrative responsibility for A Christian Ministry in the National Parks (ACMNP), with Warren Ost as the director. The NCC appointed a national committee for the ministry, which oversaw its development in the 1950s.[21]

Part of Ost's success in getting approval from the National Park Service was his emphasis on enhancing visitors' appreciation of the nation's natural treasures. According to training materials from the ministry's early years, its mission involved giving "spiritual and moral content to the awe that the miracles of God's creation inspire in the visitors and employees in our National Parks." Of course, the "spiritual and moral content" they provided had a distinctly Protestant evangelical flavor. The training manual goes on to explain: "As Christians, Jesus Christ gives us the clue to the ultimate meaning of creation. The Ministry in the National Parks emphasizes the vital link between God the Creator of natural wonders and God the Re-Creator of men's lives through Jesus Christ. The ultimate glory of God's Creation is Jesus Christ."[22] For a certain segment of Christian travelers seeking spiritual edification in the wonder of God's creation, Ost's ministers had much to offer.

Warren Ost's ministry also had the full blessings of some powerful supporters outside the government. Businessman Horace Albright's involvement in the creation of the National Park Service in 1916 and his subsequent leadership positions within the agency had made him legendary in Park Service circles. He introduced the work of ACMNP to his good friend John D. Rockefeller Jr. Trusting Albright's enthusiasm about Ost's ministry, the philanthropist agreed in 1957 to a gift of fifty thousand dollars to be given over three years.[23] The sudden boost of funds allowed unprecedented growth, helping to establish ACMNP as a major presence in protected areas from the Virgin Islands to Washington's Olympic Peninsula.[24]

The success of the ministry and its long-term financial viability relied on park concessionaires to employ ACMNP "worker-witnesses" in the hotels, restaurants, stores, and automobile service stations operating in the park. Using his own experience as a bellhop, Ost developed a model of "bi-vocational ministry" that involved students working secular jobs with concessionaires and sometimes with the Park Service and then organizing and conducting religious activities after their regular working hours. This arrangement served well the evangelizing goals of the ministry, providing "unlimited opportunities for Christian witness and pastoral care among fellow employees, many of whom were young people."[25] In short, the worker-witnesses exploited their roles as workers to deliver their religious message in "witnessing" to the captive audience of coworkers.

Ost describes this model in his 1960 sabbatical report as "the Ministry's peculiar genius."[26] It began, he readily acknowledges, out of economic necessity as "a useful technique for expanding the program rapidly without great cost." The ministry's leaders, however, soon came to realize that its benefits were more than merely financial; they eventually regarded the worker-witnesses "as the very center of our concept of the Ministry." Chief among its advantages were the trusting relationships it cultivated that positioned the ministry volunteers as community leaders. "Largely because of this concept," Ost writes, "the resident park community does not regard the Ministry as imposed by the churches from without, but rather as growing up within the park community." He used his own experience in Yellowstone as the best example, recalling, "My leadership was possible, largely if not entirely, because of my identification with the people, not so much as a minister but as a bell-hop. . . . I feel sure that I could not have done my work as effectively without the background and acceptance which came from the four summers at Old Faithful as a bell-hop."[27]

Reverend Ost characterizes his notion of worker-witness as a well-worn tradition in U.S. Christianity, claiming that every Protestant denomination at some point in its history utilized a "worker-minister technique." "Particularly in the West," he notes, "it was necessary for the frontier preacher to have a job to support himself and his family." Some traditions, Ost writes, continue this approach, the Church of Jesus Christ of Latter-day Saints as a prominent example. Importantly, the ACMNP model emphasizes a core tenet of Protestant doctrine, the "priesthood of all believers," in its requirement for volunteers to work closely with others of different

FIG. 12. Worshippers in the Yellowstone National Park Chapel at a Sunday morning service with a Christian Ministry in the National Parks, August 1, 2006. Photo by T. S. Bremer.

traditions. This can bring tensions and disagreements, but their common goals teach the young worker-witnesses about doctrinal flexibility and ecumenical cooperation. They are reminded in such circumstances, in Ost's words, "that the traditional character of each ecclesiastical system somehow had to be judged by the Gospel and its insistence on the 'priesthood of all believers.'"[28]

Across the United States in the latter half of the twentieth century, visitors encountered these enthusiastic worker-witnesses doing God's work in the national parks, where they spread their gospel message to coworkers and park visitors. ACMNP established itself as a fixture in America's parklands, and its numbers continued to grow over the decades. By 1961 these ministries could be found in thirty-three National Park Service units, filling 146 summer positions and another 10 winter placements.[29]

A Christian Ministry in the National Parks reached its peak years by the middle of the 1970s, when it had placements in fifty-seven park, forest, monument, and resort locations, plus interns at its headquarters in New York City, a total of 273 positions.[30] By then ACMNP was an autonomous ministry, having parted ways with the National Council of Churches in the early 1970s. A decade later its impact had diminished somewhat, in part due to changing requirements for seminarians but also because of the changing hiring practices of park concessionaires, which meant fewer jobs set aside for volunteer ministers. Another concern being voiced in some quarters were "issues related to the separation of Church and State."[31] As the ministry adjusted to a changing social environment, ACMNP was already beginning to scale back some of its operations.

Largely because of ACMNP, faithful Protestants visiting Yellowstone have consistently been able to find Sunday worship in the park since the 1950s, at least during the busiest months of the summer tourist season. Not everyone, though, agreed that the religious offerings in Yellowstone suited the needs of all devout visitors. A handwritten complaint in 1968 to the park superintendent from Mrs. Irving E. Blecher of New Jersey chastised what seemed to her as the park's apparent prejudice against non-Christian traditions. She wrote, "I would be very much interested to know why, if you make provision for any religious observance at Yellowstone at all, you are not aware that you have left out one of the oldest religions, that of the Jewish people, many of whom have enjoyed the wonders of Yellowstone." In reply, Stanley Canter, then serving as chair of the superintendent's Church Committee, emphasized that although he regretted "that there are no Jewish services within the Park," it is not up to the Park Service to provide religious services, which are arranged by the various denominations.[32] Canter's reply deflects responsibility for the absence of Jewish worship in the park while ignoring, or perhaps concealing, the privileged relationships that A Christian Ministry in the National Parks enjoyed with the National Park Service both locally as well as at the highest levels. The experience of a Jewish couple in another park, however, would forever change those relationships.

A Breach in the Wall of Separation

The event that changed business as usual for A Christian Ministry in the National Parks struck in 1993. The organization was already past its prime, with the aging Warren Ost only a few years from relinquishing his leadership. An unfortunate incident with one of the worker-witness volunteers far to the south of Yellowstone, in Big Bend National Park in Texas, put the ministry in an unfavorable spotlight after being named in a federal lawsuit. Although A Christian Ministry in the National Parks and the other affected parties denied that the outcome changed anything about how ACMNP operated, it marked a clear turning point that forever changed the cozy Cold War relationships and privileges the ministry had enjoyed in the first forty years of its work in national parks.

Rita and Karl Girshman had just returned from a long morning hike in March 1992. They had traveled from their home in Maryland outside of Washington DC for a week of hiking and exploring with friends in Big Bend National Park. Happily exhausted, they showered and looked forward to a quiet rest in their room at the Chisos Mountains Lodge. They lay on the bed unclothed and relaxed, letting the cool air soothe their naked bodies.

Perhaps they had dozed off when a light tap on their locked door startled them. They roused a bit, puzzled who it might be. They weren't expecting visitors. As they began to rise from the bed, a key turned in the doorknob, the door swung open wide, and a young man bolted into their room. Rita Girshman shrieked in shock while her husband shouted a curse at the intruder. Before them stood a tall young man, a boy really, not much beyond adolescence with a shock of bright-red hair. He seemed nearly as startled as the alarmed occupants of the room. He stammered: "Uh, Oh. I didn't mean to disturb you." The young man stepped farther into the room. "I just wanted to give you this," he said, tossing a salmon-colored flyer onto the floor. Then without hesitating, he left as suddenly as he had arrived.[33]

Karl Girshman scrambled into a pair of shorts and took off after the intruder. As he chased after the young man fleeing down the walkway, he shouted a battery of questions in rapid fire: Who are you? What right do you have entering our room uninvited? Where did you get a key to our room?

The lanky intruder paused and faced the irate Mr. Girshman. He hurriedly stammered an explanation—that he was an employee of the lodge, that he worked in the housekeeping department. Then without offering excuses or an apology for the disruption of their quiet afternoon, he turned to enter other guests' rooms before disappearing down the stairs.

Meanwhile, Rita Girshman picked up the flyer the young man had dropped on their floor, and when Karl returned, they examined it together. Their eyes fell on the familiar arrowhead logo of the National Park Service, but they noticed right away something strange about it: inside the logo were the words *A Christian Ministry in the National Parks*, and below them in bold print, the flyer read:

A Christian Ministry
In Big Bend National Park
invites you to join in worshipping
our Lord and Savior
Sundays

10:00 am—Basin Amphitheater
5:30 pm—Rio Grande Village
Amphitheater

Interdenominational Services
Everyone welcome!
Come as you are!

A storm of swirling emotions swept through the room. The Girshmans' initial embarrassment turned quickly to rage. Not only had their privacy been violated, but the intrusion seemed to them a clear assault on their Jewish faith. At the same time, a bit of humor tempered their outrage. They could not help chuckling at the invitation to come as they were—would a retired Jewish couple be welcomed naked to an evangelical Christian event?

The insulting invasion of their room had been staged, somewhat unintentionally, by the local ACMNP volunteers. The Girshmans were astounded to discover that for forty years, young Christian evangelists had been given considerable latitude for proselytizing among national park workers and visitors. In their minds the young intruder had violated more than their privacy when he entered their room that day. He had crashed through the sacrosanct wall of separation that defines religious freedom in the United States, brashly disregarding two centuries of tradition and legal edifice that kept religion safely out of government-controlled public spaces. As they learned more about the young man and his activities, and especially about the organization that had brought him to Big Bend, their incredulity turned to anger. A gaping hole, it seemed to them, had opened in the U.S. wall of separation between church and state. They determined to repair it.

The next morning, even before he could file a formal complaint about the incident, Karl Girshman received an apology from the director of operations for National Park Concessions, Inc., the private company that operated the Chisos Mountains Lodge. The operations manager assured him that this sort of incident would not happen again. Karl was not satisfied, and he went to discuss the matter with National Park Service officials. The ranger who oversaw concession relations in the park explained that the young man who had entered their room worked for the park concessionaire, but he was in the park as a student minister affiliated with a national ministry approved by the National Park Service, an arrangement that this particular ranger was not too enthusiastic about, according to Rita Girshman's impressions.[34] The Girshmans made a formal criminal complaint against the intruder, but they also lodged a more general complaint about the National Park Service's complicity in sponsoring religious activities in Big Bend National Park. When they returned home to Washington DC, they got busy pressing their First Amendment concerns. A year after their harrowing encounter with the young evangelist from A Christian Ministry in the National Parks, the Girshmans filed a lawsuit in federal court that named, among others, the director of the National Park Service as well as the secretary of the United States Department of the Interior.

The Girshmans had uncovered what to them were several unsettling aspects of the relationship between the National Park Service, park concessionaires, and A Christian Ministry in the National Parks. Park concessionaires reserved jobs for student ministers—a referral by the ministry guaranteed a job for an applicant. Although ministry activities ostensibly occurred during employees' free time, the student minister who entered the Girshmans' room was assigned to distribute ministry announcements as part of his paid employment with the concessionaire. Apparently, the rules were sometimes (maybe often) disregarded in actual practice. In some parks, resident ministers enjoyed reduced-cost housing provided by concessionaires and sometimes by the National Park Service, and various parks hosted national conferences and other meetings of ACMNP.[35] This especially cozy relationship that the evangelical group had with concessionaires and Park Service officials troubled the Girshmans.

In response to their complaint in federal court, a Park Service representative in Washington DC defended the presence of the worker-witnesses laboring in the national parks. He explained: "The ministry's activities in park areas are conducted pursuant to that organization's exercise of rights guaranteed by the First Amendment. Public assemblies, religious services and other First Amendment activities that take place in park areas are regulated by individual park superintendents pursuant to a permit issued in accordance with the provisions of the regulation." In other words, within the bounds of constitutionally guaranteed free exercise of religion, local superintendents had considerable discretion in regulating the ministry's activities. There was great variability, however, among the nearly seventy individual park units where ACMNP was operating in the 1990s. In fact, some park superintendents, the Girshmans were dismayed to learn, actually served on the local ACMNP committees that oversaw the placement of student ministers in their parks.

Karl and Rita Girshman set out to repair what they regarded as an unconscionable breach in the church-state wall of separation. Their legal action in the U.S. District Court in Washington DC charged the director of the National Park Service and the secretary of the Interior with violating the First Amendment prohibition of government sponsorship of religion. As one partisan observer remarked at the time: "There's a terrible entanglement of church and state going on in our national parks. People don't realize their national parks are being used to promote Christianity."[36] But Rev. Warren Ost, still at the helm of A Christian Ministry in the National Parks, responded with an emphatic "Baloney." He went on to explain: "No government money is involved. Besides, the Constitution bars government's establishment of religion, not the expression of it. These complaints are from people who don't have religions and are busy condemning and damning anyone who has."[37] For the aging evangelist, charges of improprieties by his ministry were more evidence of the nation's anti-religion element. Ironically, the plaintiffs in this action were lifelong

Jews who were esteemed members of their congregation. Reverend Ost's response reveals a rather narrow evangelical Protestant view of "people who don't have religions."

The government for its part was not about to go to court in defense of narrow views of religion. Officials acknowledged that their oversight of religious activities in national parks needed clarification, and they agreed to a settlement of the Girshmans' lawsuit. First on the list of grievances was the use of the National Park Service arrowhead logo. The settlement states unequivocally, "Insofar as a Christian Ministry in the National Parks is currently using the arrowhead symbol on its stationery and other materials, such use is not authorized pursuant to this regulation and, accordingly, is prohibited." The agreement reiterates the "current general practice, where it now exists, of posting a disclaimer on National Park bulletin boards (or wherever notices are posted) informing the public that different persons and groups engage in religious activities in the parks but that the Park Service does not endorse any group or message." Moreover, the settlement states the Park Service policy of not offering special housing arrangements or any sort of subsidies, direct or indirect, to religious groups or their agents unless the same arrangements or subsidies are available to all others on an equal basis. Letters went out to all park superintendents and concessionaires holding contracts to provide goods and services in national park units: no more special treatment for ACMNP or any other religious organization. Superintendents were reminded of illegal conflicts of interest that might arise from membership on local ministry committees.[38]

The Girshmans' anger about their impolite treatment in Big Bend National Park fundamentally changed the special relationship that ACMNP had enjoyed with the National Park Service and park concessionaires. The ministry replaced its arrowhead logo with a pyramidal design sporting a grizzly bear silhouetted against the outline of a mountain. Student ministers in each park were required to apply for permits each time they wanted to use park facilities for religious purposes, and all permit applications were to be considered on a first come, first served basis—reserving a space for an entire season was no longer allowed. Disclaimers now accompanied all announcements of devotional activities, making clear the neutrality of the National Park Service in all things religious. And the ACMNP worker-witnesses could no longer count on a guaranteed job—park concession-aires were forbidden to set aside jobs specifically for student ministers.[39] Whatever special privileges that the ministry had previously enjoyed in its relationship with the Park Service and concession operators had vanished under the legal scrutiny instigated by Karl and Rita Girshman.

The Christ Concession in Yellowstone

Abiding by the settlement agreement resulting from the Girshmans' law-suit did not occasion any significant changes in ACMNP's mission. The ministry continues even today to recruit young Christian evangelists to spend their summers in a national park. As of 2024, according to the ministry's website, they place "roughly 150–200 ministry team members into 75 locations in 45 national parks from Alaska to the Virgin Islands."[40] Even without the help of privileged status, ACMNP evangelizing remains in the U.S. parks.

The ministry in Yellowstone continued uninterrupted following the Girshmans' lawsuit. When I sat down in 2006 with the ACMNP resident minister Rev. Dr. Bill Young, who had served in that position since 1983, he told me that little had changed. One procedural difference had to do with the permit system. When he started in the 1980s, they were able to secure permits for the entire year, but beginning in the 1990s, religious groups wanting to practice in the park had to get a special use permit every week, which required going to park headquarters in Mammoth Hot Springs. Since Reverend Young actually lived in government housing in Mammoth, he would sign for everyone as a matter of courtesy, not just for the various ACMNP locations in the park but for all of the religious groups, including Mormons, Catholics, Seventh-Day Adventists, and others.[41]

Reverend Young also explained how housing arrangements had changed. The Park Service previously reserved housing for the resident minister to rent, but the agency eliminated that privilege in the 1990s. He said that he was able to continue living in the government housing at Mammoth Hot Springs only because his wife was a National Park Service employee.[42]

Overall, Young told me, relations with the National Park Service have been quite good. Since A Christian Ministry in the National Parks is very much like a park concessionaire, he explained, any tensions the ministry has with park officials are similar to the kinds of tensions that concessionaires encounter, primarily over the use of facilities in the park. On the other hand, having a resident minister there has benefited the Park Service. It would occasionally ask him to serve in an official capacity, such as helping with park dedications by giving an invocation or dedicatory prayer, or on occasion, when hosting VIPs who asked for religious services, park officials would call on Reverend Young. He mentioned that he once performed an outdoor service for the U.S. secretary of the Interior and his entourage when they were touring the park. More often, the Park Service would call him to help with a crisis, such as a sudden illness or accident. He often found himself ministering to total strangers, especially when a park visitor would die. On those occasions his ministry was more like a chaplaincy than a pastoral appointment.[43]

For most of the seasonal worker-witnesses, though, their appointments remained more pastoral as they went about organizing worship services and other religious activities, preaching, and evangelizing. Not all of them conformed to Reverend Ost's ideal of the worker-witness who established strong and trusting relationships with coworkers. For instance, I worked with one of them at Canyon Village in Yellowstone during my summer employment at the service station in 1978. His name was Chuck, and he didn't quite fit the model. He was a tall Southern Baptist with a booming voice, very much matching my largely naive and uninformed stereotype of a southern preacher with a pronounced southern drawl, the Elvis hair, and a Bible always in hand. In my recollection, he was somewhat aloof, not really socializing with the other employees, a bit arrogant and too busy with his ministry work to spend any time with the rest of us. Chuck certainly did not do much to cultivate trust or leadership, at least not with me. In fact, I can't remember ever having a single conversation with him, although that likely was as much from my own negligible social skills as it was from any reluctance on his part. He definitely never attempted to witness his faith message to me.

Chuck probably knew, like most ACMNP volunteers, that his work was not for everyone. The worker-witnesses in Yellowstone and other parks are there for those in need of their brand of religion, whether it be for Sunday worship while vacationing or for support and consolation in times of crisis. Those are the people they focus on by necessity, whether they be coworkers in a seasonal job, year-round park residents, or tourists visiting for a few days. On occasion they can be offensive, as the Girshmans found out in Big Bend. But for the most part, they hardly register in the visitor experience. To the vast majority of vacationers in Yellowstone, the ACMNP remains mostly invisible or at best an amusing oddity in the park's cultural landscape.

Though many may still question the appropriateness of evangelical Protestant missionaries operating in the U.S. national parks and other federal and state facilities, A Christian Ministry in the National Parks has adapted to changing contexts over the course of its seventy-year history. At the outset the ministry was very much a product of its times, a reflection of the nation's religious anxieties in a Cold War climate. The unfortunate incident with the Girshmans in Big Bend National Park forced ACMNP to acknowledge that the decades of Cold War had come to an end and the privileges it had enjoyed in its early years had vanished. ACMNP no longer had a monopoly on religion in the national parks. Still, it continues to provide much-needed services for a variety of religious people.

Certainly, ACMNP ministers and volunteers were not the first Christian evangelists to view Yellowstone as fertile ground for their missionary efforts or to interpret the park as the special province of God's people. In fact, Christians of various sects have proffered religious interpretations of Yellowstone since before the establishment of the national park. These have included a broad spectrum of Christian and Christian-derived traditions that have used Yellowstone to further their faith, from the moderate Protestantism of mainline denominations and parachurch organizations like A Christian Ministry in the National Parks to the reactionary fundamentalism of evangelists like Alma White. Additionally, eclectic New Age religious innovators have also reinterpreted the meanings of Yellowstone as they incorporated the park into their own distinct sacred geographies. Some of these unconventional religionists have been quite inventive in their mythic tales of Yellowstone and surrounding regions.

6

NEW AGE YELLOWSTONE

The human race did not begin in the Garden of Eden, according to the teachings of the Church Universal and Triumphant (CUT). The church's adherents believe that humanity originated at the Grand Teton Mountain in Wyoming and that followers of their faith ultimately will find their destiny there. A church official explained to me: "The Garden of Eden isn't the beginning of mankind's history on earth. Our understanding is that the first, mankind's beginning on earth, was actually at the Tetons. . . . So it's kind of like that this is the beginning, and this is where people can return to the heaven world."[1]

CUT inherited this view of humankind's origins and destiny from a precursor tradition, the "I AM Religious Activity," a new religious movement that flourished in the 1930s. Its religious teachings about the Grand Teton also include Yellowstone to the north of the Teton Mountains. Deep beneath Yellowstone's forested lands, in the lore of the I AM tradition, two secret underground caverns protect a cache of sacred stones of extraordinary powers. In the waning centuries of the Poseidonis civilization fourteen thousand years ago, as followers of this tradition understand it, the Yellowstone Plateau in the Rocky Mountains was the location of "the richest gold mine the world has ever known." In that ancient lost civilization, claimed their Ascended Master Saint Germain, the quarry "belonged to the government and much of its wealth was used for experimental and research purposes in chemistry, invention, and science." The Ascended Master explained this history to his disciple Godfré Ray King, the pseudonym of Guy Ballard, founder of I AM, when they toured this underground site in 1930. Saint Germain went on to reveal to Ballard that also in Yellowstone, only thirty-seven miles from the gold mine, was a diamond mine that produced "the most beautiful yellow diamonds that have ever been found." In addition, the mine produced "a few rare stones of very remarkable beauty and perfection. If properly cut, they showed a tiny blue flame at the center that looked like liquid Light." When worn by certain individuals, this blue flame rose an inch above the surface of the stone. These remarkable yellow diamonds are the source of the name Yellowstone, according to Saint Germain, and sixteen of them are still held in sacred trust by the Great White Brotherhood at the Royal Teton Retreat, a complex of elegant rooms, storage vaults, and secret tunnels deep beneath the steep summits of Grand Teton National Park just south of Yellowstone.[2]

The sacred stones, including those remaining inside the hidden mineral works beneath Yellowstone, have enormous beneficial powers, according to Guy Ballard's account of his time with the spirit being Saint Germain. When put to wrong uses, however, they have potential for catastrophic consequences. For this reason, the secret mines of Yellowstone remain sealed and their entrances invisible to protect their treasures until a time when humanity is prepared to utilize their powers for beneficial purposes. As Ballard explains, the "marvelous beauty" of the national park "veils its ancient mysteries and wonders from our present American civilization."[3] Consequently, millions of visitors tramp through Yellowstone each year entirely unaware of the mighty spiritual powers that lie below the surface. Only the properly initiated devotees of the Ascended Masters have any idea of Yellowstone's true potential, according to the heirs of the I AM tradition.

A number of these devotees have made their home with the Church Universal and Triumphant, whose Montana property abuts the north-western boundary of Yellowstone National Park. The church's location puts them close to the secret mines of Yellowstone and in proximity to the Royal Teton Retreat in the Teton Mountains roughly one hundred miles south of their ranch. Moreover, their Montana location has its own significance in the sacred geography of CUT. Besides serving as the church's world headquarters, their Royal Teton Ranch marks the site of world redemption, a place where another Ascended Master, Gautama Buddha, established his "Western Shamballa." While his "yang" presence remains in the Eastern Shamballa over China's Gobi Desert, Gautama's "yin" presence resides over the Heart of the Inner Retreat on CUT's ranch property, "a cathedral of nature bordering on Yellowstone Park." This Western Shamballa, Gautama Buddha promised, "is indeed the place where all shall return to the cause and core of the Dharma ([i.e.,] the Teaching) and the Sangha [holy community]."[4] According to CUT teachings, the future wellbeing of humanity, in fact of the earth itself, relies on this return of Dharma and Sangha.

In recent years a serene calm encircles the high valley of the Heart of the Inner Retreat at the foot of what the church calls Maitreya Mountain on the CUT property. When I visited in 2016, the Heart locale was quiet and empty of any human activity, belying the intense spiritual energies of Gautama Buddha's Western Shamballa or the site's history as a refuge from impending nuclear holocaust. Yet underneath the deceptive beauty of spectacular scenery in the mountainous terrain sloping downward from the Yellowstone Plateau, storms of spiritual passions roiled.

I AM

The devotional passions that would come to rest on the boundary of Yellowstone National Park have their origins in the tumultuous spiritual awakenings of nineteenth-century America far from Yellowstone. In the decades following the Civil War, numerous movements vied for recognition and for devotees in the marketplace of U.S. religions. Most of these new spiritual orientations drew on earlier religious perspectives. Two in particular, New Thought and Theosophy, both offspring of the nineteenth-century excitement over Spiritualism, had relevance for the people who would identify in the 1970s as the Church Universal and Triumphant.

The Spiritualist craze that swept across the U.S. cultural landscape in the middle decades of the nineteenth century began with ominous rappings on the walls and furniture of a house in the hamlet of Hydesville, New York. Two young sisters living in the house, Margaret and Kate Fox, interpreted these rappings as communications from spirits. Their ability to decipher the spirits' messages quickly attracted public fascination, and the two girls, later joined by their older sister, Ann Leah Fox, soon gained national and international fame. They further inspired others to cultivate the occult arts of communicating with the dead, and séances became a regular event on the American cultural scene, both as earnest efforts to commune with the departed and as popular entertainments of the era.[5]

The appeal of Spiritualism joined other developments in the nineteenth-century U.S. spiritual marketplace to establish novel metaphysical traditions that gained varying degrees of popularity. In one notable example, Phineas Parkhurst Quimby of Portland, Maine, influenced by "mesmerism," Spiritualism, and other nineteenth-century traditions of healing and spirituality circulating in the United States, enjoyed a considerable reputation as a "mental healer." He based his success on the premise that one's erroneous beliefs cause physical maladies and that by substituting new, healthful beliefs, the body would return to its naturally healthful state.[6] Among Quimby's followers seeking to heal ailing bodies was Mary Patterson, widely known by her later married name, Mary Baker Eddy. She had traveled to Maine in 1862 for an extended visit to receive Quimby's treatments. He succeeded in providing the relief that she had long sought. Consequently, she followed him as a spiritual healer and eventually forged her own path that would lead her to launch Christian Science.[7]

Mary Baker Eddy's Christian Science emerged as a prominent example of what would be known as "New Thought," a religious perspective popular in the closing decades of the nineteenth century and still followed today. Adherents to this spiritually focused "mind-over-matter" perspective emphasize a singular divine reality manifest in each individual person. They regard humans as immortal spiritual beings who are perfect in their essence and free from suffering or death.[8] For Mary Baker Eddy and others engaged with New Thought ideas, the perfection of spiritual reality allows no recognition of illness, disease, mortality, or evil in any of its many forms.

As New Thought ideas and practices spread among American metaphysical thinkers of the late nineteenth century, another offshoot of Spiritualism developed in a very different metaphysical direction. Madame Helena Blavatsky, originally from Russia, first met Henry Steel Olcott, an American Civil War veteran and lawyer, in 1874 while both were investigating Spiritualist activities in Vermont. Their friendship grew from a shared interest in the occult, and in 1875 they founded the Theosophical Society in New York City with sixteen like-minded members. Besides generating enthusiasm for esoteric knowledge and what they regarded as the universal wisdom underlying all religions, the society became a prominent outlet for popularizing Asian spiritual traditions in the United States, including the concepts of karma and reincarnation as mainstays of the American spiritual lexicon.[9]

The popularity of Theosophy also reflected to some extent nineteenth-century racial assumptions. Blavatsky, wishing to harmonize her metaphysical teachings with evolutionary theory, developed an elaborate "root race theory" that relied largely on colonial racist tropes, although to her credit, she also opposed much of the racist discourse regarding colonial India.[10] Based on her teachings, racial elements became endemic to Theosophical logic and have remained to the present, although not often in explicit terms. In the twentieth century they would become embedded in the fabric of Guy Ballard's I AM Religious Activity and its descendants.

The New Thought movement, including Mary Baker Eddy's Christian Science as well as the Theosophical teachings of Blavatsky, Olcott, and their followers, all had roots in Spiritualism.[11] By the end of the nineteenth century, many of the figures who had begun with Spiritualist interests had developed more elaborate metaphysical traditions that would become foundational for the I AM Religious Activity and consequently for the Church Universal and Triumphant. Indeed, a Spiritualist thread runs through I AM history all the way to Yellowstone.

The beginnings of the I AM Religious Activity that flourished in the United States through the 1930s trace back to Emma Curtis Hopkins, who had served a short stint in the 1880s as editor of Mary Baker Eddy's *Christian Science Journal*. Hopkins later moved to Chicago to open her own New Thought center, where she adopted much of her former mentor's Christian Science. She also incorporated other New Thought perspectives, including those of Warren Felt Evans, another student of mind healer Phineas Quimby.[12] Alluding to Exodus 3:13–14 in the Hebrew Bible, in which the Israelites' god identifies itself as "I am that I am," Evans's teachings recognize an "unchanging I AM" that each person possesses as "the Christ within us, whose divine name is Ehejah, or I Am, that is the One and the Same."[13] Hopkins would likewise declare one's identity with the I AM presence as a "universal affirmation" in her optimistic New Thought message of health, prosperity, and material success.[14]

Annie Rix Militz, a student of Hopkins, spread these teachings to the West Coast of the United States from her Home of Truth center in Los Angeles, founded in the 1890s. Militz's book *Primary Lessons in Christian Living* affirms that humans are the I AM expression of God's Being.[15] Others likewise taught the I AM presence. Charles Fillmore, another student of Hopkins who founded the Unity movement, also referenced I AM, as did Baird T. Spalding in his book *Life and Teaching of the Masters of the Far East*. By the 1920s I AM had become an established concept among American followers of metaphysical teachings.[16]

Guy W. Ballard and his wife, Edna, were well aware of these teachings.[17] He had fled their home city of Chicago under threat of criminal charges for operating a "confidence game," and he eventually settled in California; Edna remained behind in Chicago.[18] While he was living on the lam in Los Angeles, Ballard heard a "rumor," as he put it, concerning "a group of men, Divine men in Fact, called the Brotherhood of Mount Shasta, who formed a branch of the Great White Lodge, and that this Focus from very ancient times had continued unbroken down to the present day." Consequently, Ballard determined "to unravel this rumor concerning The Brotherhood."[19]

While hiking in August 1930 on the slopes of Mount Shasta in California, Ballard encountered a young man, who offered him a drink of a delicious creamy liquid that, in his recollection, had an "electrical vivifying effect in my mind and body." The young man then proceeded to share the secrets of the "Great Law" and the "Truth of Life" with the astonished Ballard. He revealed his true identity, according to Ballard's account, as "the living breathing tangible 'Presence' of the Master, Saint Germain."[20] Not a recognized "saint" in Christianity or in any other religious tradition, the historical figure of Saint Germain was Comte de Saint Germain, an eighteenth-century occultist and necromancer from the French town of Saint Germain who had gained recognition in nineteenth-century Theosophy. Helena Blavatsky described him as "the greatest Oriental Adept Europe has seen during the last centuries," and Henry Steel Olcott identified him as "a messenger and agent of the White Lodge."[21] Saint Germain's exalted position in Theosophical literature carried over into the I AM tradition, which in turn made him a central figure in CUT teachings of the latter half of the twentieth century.

Following their initial encounter on Mount Shasta, the Ascended Master Saint Germain revealed the truth of great mysteries to Ballard over the course of several months, and he eventually introduced Ballard to a host of other Ascended Masters. He also took Ballard to the Grand Teton and to Yellowstone, where they toured the hidden underground chambers. Ballard's willingness to learn and to gain spiritual insights from Saint Germain consequently proved that Ballard himself qualified as "a worthy 'Messenger' of the Great White Brotherhood and the Ascended Host."[22]

Meanwhile, at the same time that Guy Ballard's account had him learning the Great Law and Truth of Life from Saint Germain in the final months of 1930, his wife, Edna, initiated a business enterprise back in Illinois selling spiritual truths. She had been working in an occult bookstore, where she encountered a variety of Theosophical and New Age teachings. Intrigued by these traditions, Edna Ballard began publishing two periodicals based on occult topics even before her husband went to Mount Shasta. In addition, she offered secret classes on occultism.[23] As she gradually gained a significant following in Chicago, she expanded her publishing operation with the incorporation of Saint Germain Press, and by 1934 the Ballards had begun offering a series of volumes explaining the teachings of the Ascended Masters using Guy Ballard's newly designated pseudonym, Godfré Ray King. These books lay out the foundational ideas and practices of what became known as the I AM Religious Activity.[24] Book sales soared alongside the classes, lectures, and workshops that Guy and Edna Ballard offered across the United States, performing as "Accredited Messengers" who conveyed communications directly from Saint Germain, Jesus, and a host of other Ascended Masters.[25] Their popularity spread through the dismal years of the Great Depression, so that by 1939 the I AM movement boasted more than a million followers with sanctuaries in most U.S. cities.[26]

During their heyday, Guy and Edna Ballard and their son, Donald, filled large auditoriums as the sole Accredited Messengers of the Ascended Masters.[27] Initially, their movement was not known as I AM, but the New Thought notion as previously taught by Emma Curtis Hopkins and her student Annie Rix Militz coincided with the Ballards' teachings. Accordingly, the Ballards adopted I AM as the central identifying concept of their religious movement.[28] Another New Thought characteristic originating with Hopkins, "decreeing," also became a central practice of the Ballards' I AM Religious Activity. Initially, decrees involved a formal, ritualized entreaty "distinguished by its energy and focus, its concerted investment of will, in commanding—or demanding—certain outcomes for good." With the Ballards, however, decreeing evolved from its purely positive uses to a more encompassing practice that also could be used negatively in combating perceived evils.[29]

Besides its debt to New Thought, the Ballards also instituted ideas and practices drawn from twentieth-century Theosophy, specifically the emphasis on power and light. Based on their communications with the Ascended Master Saint Germain, the Ballards taught followers to unite with God through visualization and cultivation of a bodily sense of being enveloped in "Dazzling White Light." Their teachings also emphasized a cylinder of violet light representing the "consuming flame of divine love" that surrounded followers who were marked with divine presence. Additionally, other colors took on special meanings, as each of the Ascended Masters radiated their own specific color that represented some particular aspect of the divine.[30]

The remarkable success of the Ballards in building the I AM Religious Activity as a popular spiritual movement of the 1930s relied on more than their innovative blending of New Thought and Theosophical precedents. They also appealed to the white supremacist racial elements of American society in the early decades of the twentieth century. In particular, their claim of a direct relationship with the Great White Brotherhood resonated with racial overtones in the Jim Crow era of apartheid America. From the very beginning, in 1930, with Edna Ballard's "secret classes" in Chicago, a latent element of white supremacy lurked in the I AM teachings. Her ideas relied to some extent on the work of William Dudley Pelley, who himself claimed to have received messages from masters, beginning with an out-of-body experience while living alone in the Sierra Madre. Pelley had published an account of his spiritual encounter a year before Guy Ballard's claimed encounter with Saint Germain on Mount Shasta. Aside from his spiritual experiences, or perhaps thoroughly integrated with them, Pelley had gained notoriety as the founder and charismatic leader of a right-wing, pro-fascist, anti-Communist, anti–New Deal, anti-Semitic, and white supremacist group called the Silver Shirts, which had a clear and profound influence on the Ballards.[31] Indeed, the racial elements of Helena Blavatsky's "root race theory" took on new significance in the spiritual circles of twentieth-century U.S. occultism.

The Church Universal and Triumphant

The popularity of the I AM Religious Activity continued to grow through the later years of the 1930s, but the sudden death of Guy Ballard at the end of 1939 marked the beginning of its eventual decline. Following his death, the I AM organization entered a period of turmoil marked by legal problems stemming from federal mail fraud charges that the group eventually succeeded in defending.[32] After resolving the criminal cases, the I AM Religious Activity began to rebuild, but it never recovered the popularity of its heyday in the 1930s.[33] Moreover, internal discord within the I AM Religious Activity gave rise to rival groups. By the logic of communication with Ascended Masters, others were able to claim "messenger" status and form their own followings.[34] By the 1950s several groups were vying for leadership of the fractured movement.

Among the competing messengers issuing their own communications from the Ascended Masters was Mark L. Prophet, who worked from his base in Washington DC.[35] By 1958, having received communications from the Ascended Master known as El Morya, Mark Prophet had proclaimed himself a messenger of Ascended Masters patterned on the Ballard's I AM teachings. That year Prophet founded his own metaphysical organization, The Summit Lighthouse.[36]

Mark Prophet was soon gathering a following of his own through publications and speaking engagements that involved "dictations," direct communications from Ascended Masters to their designated messengers.[37] A young woman, Elizabeth Clare Ytreburg, attended one of his talks in Boston and was immediately enchanted by Prophet's claims of communications with Ascended Masters.[38] Born Elizabeth Clare Wulf as the only child of immigrant parents, she long had been a fervent spiritual seeker who was well suited to enter the metaphysical world of Mark Prophet. Her Swiss mother had studied Theosophy and the I AM teachings, inspiring the daughter's lifelong interest in the spiritual realm. Young Elizabeth suffered from petit mal epileptic seizures, a malady that plagued her throughout her life, and she found some relief as an adolescent, which she attributed to her practice of Christian Science.[39] During her college years, she undertook training to become a Christian Science practitioner and subsequently married a fellow Christian Scientist from Norway. At about the same time, she discovered for herself the teachings of the I AM movement and began attending the Boston meetings of a group that shared interests in the I AM ideas. In 1961 the group hosted Mark Prophet as its guest speaker, and upon witnessing his dictation at that first meeting, Elizabeth knew immediately that "she had found her life's calling." At once she turned her spiritual focus to the teachings of Mark Prophet.[40] Soon Mark Prophet and Elizabeth Clare Ytreburg discovered that the attraction between them went beyond their common pursuit of metaphysical truths. Acknowledging their mutual romantic interests, they both divorced their respective spouses and were married in 1963.[41]

As they settled into their Fairfax, Virginia, home, Elizabeth went to work for her new husband, whose spiritual enterprise continued to grow. She concentrated on editing and publishing Mark's work as well as over-seeing the management of The Summit Lighthouse. Mark concentrated on his role as spiritual teacher while continuing to control the major financial and logistical decisions. At the same time, Elizabeth studied spiritual teachings and practices with her husband, and within a year of their marriage, she had completed her training as a messenger for the Ascended Masters. In 1964 Elizabeth Clare Prophet took her first public dictation.[42]

Their spiritual efforts also revealed connections that went far beyond their current circumstances. Through "inner work" of private prayer and visualization, Mark and Elizabeth learned from the Ascended Masters that they had been together in past lives. Some of those past incarnations paired them as famous historical spouses, for instance, as the Egyptian pharaoh Akhenaton and his wife, Nefertiti, or the French monarchs Louis XVI and Marie Antoinette. They also determined that they had lived as the Catholic saints Bonaventure and Clare.[43] Indeed, they became convinced that finding each other in this life was no random accident of circumstance—they were destined to reunite.

Mark Prophet had established in 1961 the "Keepers of the Flame Fraternity," an elite cadre of followers regarded as especially devoted to the teachings of the Ascended Masters. He designated them as "individuals who would 'keep the flame of life,' which was seen as a source of divine power in the world" but required constant nurturing with prayers, meditation, and decrees. In 1966 he put his wife at the head of this group by designating her "Mother of the Flame" in a special ceremony at The Summit Lighthouse headquarters, which by then they had moved to Colorado Springs. Thereafter, Elizabeth Clare Prophet's followers knew her as "Mother," although she always emphasized that it was an office she held, not a title.[44]

The Summit Lighthouse continued to grow and flourish in Colorado. The organization published a weekly dispatch, *Pearls of Wisdom*, which it sent free to whomever requested it, and it brought members together with several conclaves held each year. It also instituted in 1972 an educational program, Ascended Master University (later renamed Summit University).[45] By 1973 the Prophets were among the most significant successors to Guy and Edna Ballard's I AM Religious Activity.

In an uncanny parallel to the Ballards' religious movement, the fate of The Summit Lighthouse changed suddenly and dramatically when its primary leader, Mark Prophet, died unexpectedly on February 26, 1973. His wife, Elizabeth, eased the shock for Prophet's followers by announcing a communication from him within a week of his death, explaining that she had received a dictation from her husband in his new role as Ascended Master "Lanello."[46] As Edna Ballard did following the sudden death of Guy Ballard, Elizabeth Clare Prophet elevated her husband to a prominent place in the Ascended Master pantheon.[47]

She also took control of more mundane matters as she assumed leadership of The Summit Lighthouse. Following her husband's death, Elizabeth Clare Prophet set an ambitious course for continued expansion of the movement, often coming in conflict with the organization's board of directors. In asserting her authority, she appointed staff member Randall King as president, and he became her third husband in October 1973. In the ensuing years, Elizabeth Clare Prophet adopted an increasingly more authoritarian leadership style as she gradually dismissed nearly all of Mark Prophet's appointees, including Randall King, whom she divorced in 1981, the same year she married Edward L. Francis, the sole remaining appointee from Mark's leadership.[48]

The most consequential development in the aftermath of Mark Prophet's death came in 1974 with the establishment of the Church Universal and Triumphant (incorporated May 1, 1975). The church subsequently "became the primary identity of the group."[49] A restructuring of the corporate organization created Summit International as an umbrella entity, with The Summit Lighthouse as the publishing arm of the new church. CUT also introduced ambitious plans for teaching centers to be established throughout the United States.

Elizabeth Clare Prophet consolidated her leadership of the church and its affiliated organizations. Her authority as the head of the corporate enterprise relied prominently on her spiritual leadership as the sole messenger of the Ascended Masters. A dictation in 1974, less than a year after her husband Mark's death, bestowed her with the "office of the World Mother." By the late 1970s she assumed the title of "Guru Ma" based on a dictation she received from Padma Sambhava, a well-known figure of Tibetan Buddhism.[50] Additionally, in keeping with Theosophical and New Thought history, Elizabeth Clare Prophet's eclectic religious orientation also relied on a strong Christian element. She even claimed at one point to have received a blessing of her spiritual authority and leadership in a cosmic message from the late Pope John XXIII.[51] In her teachings Elizabeth Clare Prophet was the divinely selected head of the Church Universal and Triumphant.

With the rapid growth of CUT under the leadership of Elizabeth Clare Prophet came the need for additional facilities. In 1976 the organization left Colorado for California, where so many new religious movements have germinated or relocated.[52] They settled in the Los Angeles area. After just a year of leasing space in the city of Pasadena, they purchased a 218-acre property near Malibu, where they established their headquarters, renaming the scenic location "Camelot." But with ever-increasing membership and ambitious plans for even greater growth, Camelot also soon proved insufficient, and church officials began looking for property outside of California.[53]

Other factors besides the need for additional space urged the Church Universal and Triumphant to leave California. Relations with nonmember communities had become increasingly strained, contributing to greater feelings of estrangement and a perception of religious persecution among the members. Mark Prophet's writings had warned of "spiritual wicked-ness in high places," instilling suspicions of conspiracy and feelings of besiegement in his followers. Shortly after moving to Camelot, a property dispute with the National Park Service, which held an interest in the property for future expansion of its Santa Monica Mountains Recreational Area, confirmed their apprehensions. Their dispute with the government brought attention from local news media, resulting in numerous reports of the church stockpiling weapons and encouraging members to break ties with their families.[54] These accusations coincided with the efforts of anticult activists, who increasingly targeted CUT, while former members launched a series of lawsuits against the church and its leaders. Then came the Jonestown mass suicide by followers of Jim Jones in November 1978, which heightened the sensationalist scrutiny of Elizabeth Clare Prophet and her followers.[55] As her spiritual claims incited more controversy in California, Prophet realized that the church needed to find a new home that would be less conspicuous to the prying inquiries of public inves-tigations and media attention. Leaving California for the remote wilds of Montana would offer a chance for a fresh start without the constant attention of Los Angeles media groups.

The task of locating a new property fell to Prophet's husband and coleader of the church, Edward L. Francis. He was able to find an ideal parcel of wildland bordering Yellowstone National Park in Montana. The property had become available after the failed attempt of the federal government to purchase the 12,500-acre retreat ranch from New York publishing mogul Malcolm Forbes.[56] A church-owned corporation, Royal Teton, Ltd., subsequently acquired what it regarded as "a jewel in the heart of America's wilderness preserve" on September 9, 1981.[57]

Soon after purchasing the property in Montana, Elizabeth Clare Proph-et referred to the ranch as the "Inner Retreat," a place of periodic refuge from the dark energy of the world.[58] She described it as "the Place of Great Encounters where heart-friends from around the world meet to study and apply the teachings of the Ascended Masters."[59] More important, it provided a direct connection to the Great White Brotherhood residing in their ethereal Royal Teton Retreat to the south, in the Teton Moun-tains. Church officials noted that Electric Peak in the northwest corner of Yellowstone National Park where it borders the church's Royal Teton

Ranch is, according to the church's interpretation, their "connecting point to the Grand Teton Mountain 80 miles due south."[60] "Our Inner Retreat in Montana," declared Prophet's husband, Edward Francis, "represents a bold new adventure and a vital first step in the forging of a larger community of the Great White Brotherhood."[61]

Soon a number of "dedicated Keepers of the Flame, as pioneers of the spirit," had moved to Montana "to establish the most basic elements of a self-sufficient community."[62] The church acquired additional property farther north in Montana's Paradise Valley for a residential community dubbed "Glastonbury," where members could "stake their claim in an ascended-master community, to be homesteaders" who "take personal responsibility for the forging of their own destinies."[63] But the church's initial effort focused on developing the agricultural operation, which included purchasing additional lands, specifically an additional ranch property in the northern portion of the Paradise Valley with even more acreage than its original acquisition of the Forbes ranch.[64] This later purchase included irrigated farmland "to produce an economically viable and self-sufficient agricultural base for the support and survival of our entire community as envisioned by Saint Germain," according to publicity from the church.[65]

The first major church event on their Montana property occurred in August 1982, when "Keepers of the Flame and their families communed with God and nature, angels and elemental life, and with heart-friends new and old in our very first gathering at the Inner Retreat." Retreatants camped on what they regarded as "our Western Shamballa," and for eighteen days they engaged in numerous spiritual and recreational activities as they "came to know intimately this beautiful land God has so graciously given us."[66]

Following the success of this first conference on their Montana property, church officials expected a much larger summer event the following year, which called for establishing a "wonderful wilderness conference site" in a mountain meadow that they identified as the "Heart of the Inner Retreat," located several miles up Mol Heron Creek. The new conference grounds needed major improvements, beginning with diverting a small stream and draining the soggy field. Work also involved grading and straightening the narrow winding road leading up to the secluded site as well as building accommodations for conference attendees that included a septic system that was "the largest in Park County."[67] By July 1983 church staff and community members had transformed the picturesque mountain meadow into a conference ground able to host a thousand or more devotees.

Establishing the Heart of the Inner Retreat high in the Montana mountains fulfilled church prophecies for the future of the community, but it also coincided with increasing estrangement from mainstream U.S. society and the church's ensuing paranoia about geopolitical developments of the time.[68] "Saint Germain's long-term plan for this activity and his devoted students," announced a church publication on the occasion of the 1983 summer conference, "calls for the achievement of self-sufficiency and preparedness in the face of worsening world conditions." It went on to explain, "In this time of the pouring out of the 'vials of the seven last plagues,' when mankind's accumulated karma is returning and the judgment of the Lord is at hand, Saint Germain wants his chelas [followers] to be in a position of maximum safety, protection, and independence."[69] Saint Germain had revealed in a January 1983 dictation (delivered through the messenger Elizabeth Clare Prophet) that ensuring the church's long-term survival involved a "responsibility to our children and our country to take dominion over the earth and subdue it, and to be fruitful and multiply the Christ Consciousness in body and soul." To fulfill this mandate of dominion, the church newsletter concludes, "we have undertaken our program of Lanello Reserves Emergency Food Supply, offered our series of survival seminars and wilderness survival training for Keepers of the Flame, and striven to develop the maximum agricultural utilization of the Royal Teton Ranch for the future benefit of all who may one day rely upon this retreat as the place of ultimate refuge."[70] The followers of Elizabeth Clare Prophet regarded their Inner Retreat at the upper end of the Yellowstone River Valley, north of the national park, as the refuge where they would perpetuate the teachings and realize the prophecies of the Ascended Masters.

By 1986, however, the Inner Retreat of the Royal Teton Ranch figured as more than a place of refuge and summer conferences in the future plans of the Church Universal and Triumphant. Additional pressures in California, where CUT maintained its headquarters, along with continued development of the Montana property in building "an archetypal community for the Aquarian age," urged the group to move its corporate offices to the wilds of the Rocky Mountains.[71] Legal troubles, in particular a

$1.56 million judgment in favor of a former member, had jeopardized the church's finances. Then an "unexpected offer" from a Japanese Buddhist organization, Nichiren Shoshu Soka Gakkai International, to purchase the Camelot property in Malibu provided a way out of the church's "financial pinch."[72] By December 1986 Elizabeth Clare Prophet and her staff had left the warm California winter for a new home in Montana.[73]

Apocalypse

A little more than three years after moving its headquarters to Montana, the Church Universal and Triumphant went underground—not figuratively but actually into bunkers below ground. Some 750 church members, including their leader, Elizabeth Clare Prophet, her family, and closest associates, descended into a massive underground complex of bomb shelters buried adjacent to their Heart of the Inner Retreat conference site. Fully provisioned to live up to seven years underground, heavily armed to defend themselves from marauders they suspected would seek shelter in their fortified haven, the church's most dedicated adherents awaited the nuclear holocaust that their spiritual masters had told them would occur. The air in their bunkers was heavy with anticipation as they awaited Armageddon in March 1990.[74]

A general nervousness had been circulating for months among the non-CUT residents of the Yellowstone River Valley north of the national park. The controversies that Elizabeth Clare Prophet had hoped to leave behind when she moved her church from California followed her to the northern wilds. Longtime Montana locals soon expressed their uneasiness about the arrival of the Church Universal and Triumphant, which would acquire over forty thousand acres in Park County, Montana, and bring some two thousand church members to the region. Their neighbors voiced concerns about the environmental degradations that the sudden population growth would bring. Additionally, a low-level hysteria incited by anti-cult activists who regarded CUT as a dangerous cult made for a determined antipathy toward these religious fanatics whom locals regarded as unwanted invaders of their beautiful valley.

The animosity that longtime locals felt toward the Church Universal and Triumphant was evident from the time they arrived in the early

1980s and began developing the enormous "ranch" on lands adjacent to Yellowstone National Park. Although many folks in the area reserved judgment or in common western fashion minded their own business, not giving much thought to the strangers from California, a few Montana neighbors were not ready to accept an unorthodox community like the Church Universal and Triumphant. Fear and paranoia stemming from xenophobic prejudice ran rampant among certain segments of the longer-term residents in the area. They were not about to welcome a dangerous cult to their picturesque homeland.

Local animosity grew with publicity about the Bhagwan Shree Rajneesh community in the town of Antelope, Oregon, which invited comparisons to CUT in Montana.[75] News in the early 1980s that the religious community in Oregon had taken political control of the rural town and changed its name to Rajneeshpuram alarmed Montana residents in the area, who realized that the influx of CUT members could do the same in their county. When CUT member Randolph Mack ran for commissioner of Park County, Montana, in 1990, public alarm forced him to withdraw from the race over accusations of another "Antelope incident" in the making.[76]

Besides concerns about a takeover of local politics by the newly arrived church community, environmental issues also ignited opposition to CUT and its plans for developing its Montana properties. Environmentalists were disappointed in the government's failure to acquire the Forbes acreage bordering the national park, and for the most part they opposed all development on the land. They feared that the church community's plans would threaten the Yellowstone ecosystem, specifically concerning sewage contamination of the Yellowstone River and destruction of key habitats for bison, elk, grizzly bears, and deer. Although portions of the property had seen previous developments, including two early-twentieth-century towns and a resort hotel featuring geothermal pools, most of the land in CUT's initial purchase on the Yellowstone boundary remained undeveloped wilderness, and environmentalists expressed fears about the impact that the church's plans for development would have.[77]

In addition to worries about commandeering local government or endangering the waterways and wildlife habitats in the Yellowstone River Valley, images of Jonestown heightened local animosity toward the Church Universal and Triumphant community. The followers of Jim Jones and his Peoples Temple had built a self-sufficient religious community in the South American nation of Guyana in the 1970s, not unlike what leaders of CUT envisioned for their community in Montana a decade later. Grisly scenes of murder and mass suicide at Jonestown shocked the world in November 1978 and established an enduring stereotype of religious "cults" that would haunt organizations with unorthodox religious views led by charismatic authoritarian leaders.[78] The parallels to CUT seemed obvious to many Montanans, who feared that Elizabeth Clare Prophet was bringing another Jonestown to the boundary of Yellowstone National Park.

These anxieties intensified in 1989 with the arrest of two CUT officials on weapons charges. Federal law enforcement officers apprehended Vernon Hamilton, who was attempting to purchase weaponry in Spokane, Washington, on July 7, 1989. Hamilton worked in the construction department at the Royal Teton Ranch, but he was one of the few staff members with military experience, and he served on the ranch's security detail. He and Edward Francis had discussed concerns about the ranch's vulnerability to attack by hostile outsiders, and together they had concocted a plan to acquire weapons and ammunition for defensive purposes. To avoid negative publicity about the community arming itself, they decided that Hamilton would purchase the weapons under a false identity and Francis would supply the funds.[79]

Their plan backfired as the publicity about Vernon Hamilton's arrest spread internationally. In searching Hamilton's possessions in Spokane, federal agents found nearly $100,000 in cash and gold, $100,000 worth of weapons, and 120,000 rounds of ammunition. They also discovered plans to arm two hundred CUT members in order to establish a secure perimeter around underground shelters the church was building on its Montana property.[80] This news of a heavily armed and isolated religious community naturally invited comparisons to Jim Jones and his Jonestown compound as the Church Universal and Triumphant became a headline feature in major periodicals.[81]

The federal investigation led to the arrest of Edward Francis as a coconspirator in the arms acquisition plot.[82] Eventually, Francis and Hamilton both pleaded guilty to minor offenses, but the news coverage made an indelible impression of the Church Universal and Triumphant as a dangerous cult on the border of Yellowstone National Park. Church officials worked to deflect the negative attention by insisting that Hamilton was acting alone and not representing the church.[83] For her part Elizabeth Clare Prophet claimed ignorance of the entire plot. She explained to church members a few weeks after his arrest that Hamilton "never did bring anything that he ever did to my attention or submit it to the altar or ask my counsel."[84] The church community accepted her innocence, but to the general public, Edward Francis's involvement made her claims seem disingenuous. Not only was he a top executive and board member of the church and its various enterprises; Francis was married to Elizabeth Clare Prophet. As her husband went off to serve time in a federal prison, it was hard to imagine that the church's charismatic leader had not been involved in the plot to purchase weapons.[85]

Further revelations about the Church Universal and Triumphant became public during the fiasco of the botched weapons purchase. In the fall of 1987 the Ascended Masters had revealed to the CUT community the probability of a Soviet nuclear attack on the United States. In a dictation from Saint Germain, Elizabeth Clare Prophet warned, "You have every reason to believe, to be prepared for, and to expect a first strike attack by the Soviet Union on the United States."[86] In anticipation of this inevitable catastrophe, the community began preparations. Members directed their resources and collective efforts toward constructing a massive underground shelter at the Heart of the Inner Retreat high in the mountains. Initially, the project was kept secret, but with the coverage of Vernon Hamilton's arrest, the world learned of the Church Universal and Triumphant's preparations for nuclear holocaust.

Those preparations culminated, on the night of March 14, 1990, in the core community of CUT leadership and staff going underground in "the largest private bomb shelter complex in the country, perhaps the world."[87] Crammed into the six connected H-shaped shelters buried adjacent to the Heart of the Inner Retreat on the Royal Teton Ranch were 750 anxious followers of Elizabeth Clare Prophet expecting a nuclear attack that would obliterate the world as they knew it. Other CUT members occupied dozens of smaller private shelters to the north, in the Glastonbury residential developments.[88] That night the beleaguered church community went nervously into its cramped, fortified quarters expecting to awaken to a world forever changed.[89]

Since as early as 1973, CUT had cautioned its members that great disasters were imminent and they should prepare for the worst by storing food, learning first aid, and stockpiling survival supplies.[90] But these vague warnings took on urgency in October 1987, when Elizabeth Clare Prophet conveyed a warning from El Morya predicting that a worldwide nuclear war would begin in October 1989. Another dictation from Ascended Master Saint Germain corroborated El Morya's prediction of a Soviet nuclear attack.[91]

At first little was done to heed the Ascended Masters' warnings, but the following summer, devastating fires swept through Yellowstone National Park and threatened CUT's Royal Teton Ranch, motivating the community to take more seriously these predictions of El Morya and Saint Germain. A roaring wall of flames bore down on the Heart of the Inner Retreat on the church property from the fires that burned more than a third of the acreage in the national park during the summer of 1988. Rather than following official orders to evacuate, Elizabeth Clare Prophet and a couple hundred of her followers stood their ground against the furious firestorm with "arms held out against the flames, chanting 'roll them back, roll them back,' while the flames came ever closer." Then suddenly, on the third afternoon, the winds that fed the conflagration reversed, pushing the flames away from the ranch property and allowing firefighters to gain control over the blaze.

It seemed to the CUT community that its chants and decrees had spared the property from disaster. But in a dictation from El Morya soon after, the faithful learned that the threat of the fires had been brought on by their own spiritual weakness. They were instructed to increase their confessions and spiritual disciplines. Then a subsequent blaze the following month threatened from the other side of the ranch, and they doubled down with daily decree vigils as the fire moved closer to the ranch boundary, until an early cold spell brought snow and rain to quench the flames.[92]

Members of the CUT community realized that the frightening prospect of losing their sacred ground to the holocaust of wildfire was a warning from the Ascended Masters to begin preparations for surviving the nuclear attack predicted for October 1989. They turned to El Morya for guidance on how to proceed. The Ascended Master instructed them to build six underground shelter complexes in the Heart of the Inner Retreat, to consolidate their financial resources, and to store enough food to last seven years.[93]

Work began at once in designing and building bunkers to withstand a nuclear attack and to house the community in the aftermath. But by the beginning of 1989, it was clear that construction of the shelter complex would not be completed by the October deadline. A request to El Morya to "hold back the karma for a few more months" resulted in a new deadline: March 15, 1990.[94] The pace picked up, with virtually all attention and resources focused on building and provisioning the underground complex where the community could survive the apocalypse.[95] The church spent more than twenty million dollars building the bunkers and stockpiling enough fuel, food, and all necessary goods for 750 people to remain sheltered for seven years.[96] Additionally, church followers went to great personal expense in building and stocking with supplies dozens of other underground shelters in the region, and numerous members in other areas likewise prepared for the imminent world conflagration.[97] By March 1990 the whole of the Church Universal and Triumphant braced for the onslaught.

With preparations completed, they were ready for the worst. Descending into the protection of their underground shelters on the evening of March 14, 1990, the people of the Church Universal and Triumphant fully expected the aboveground world, including the Royal Teton Ranch, their homes, their entire country, to be annihilated by a nuclear holocaust that the Ascended Masters of the Great White Brotherhood had revealed would be arriving this night. As workers finished securing the shelter, Elizabeth Clare Prophet sat on a metal folding chair facing a small group of mothers, sisters, and daughters gathered in the central "hub room" of the bunker to do the spiritual work of chanting decrees for preservation of their holy community. She was dressed simply in blue jeans, a striped shirt, and boots and adorned "with at least twenty chains of precious and semiprecious stones," in addition to Hindu and Buddhist prayer beads, plus the fifteen rings she constantly wore, displaying "diamonds, rubies, topazes, emeralds, sapphires and a large amethyst." Prophet accentuated her spiritual gifts by wielding a two-foot sharpened sword meant to amplify the power of the decrees.[98]

Led by their messenger, the spiritual leader of their church, the women chanted affirmations that they believed would attune their collective consciousness to the proper vibrational frequency that would preserve them, their families, and the entire church community from the impending nuclear attack. Afterward they returned to their designated quarters, climbing into the narrow bunks and fastening safety belts that had been installed to hold them in their beds during the attack. Eventually, the Church Universal and Triumphant community members settled down in their underground refuge that restless night to await the end of the corrupt world they had fled.[99]

When sunlight appeared over the mountain horizon to push the tense night from the Yellowstone River Valley, the familiar world of a Montana late-winter morning remained unscathed, calm, and quiet. No nuclear attack had been launched on the United States. A mood of "disappointment and relief, but not yet disillusionment" accompanied the church staff as they awoke to return to their lives above ground.[100]

Up the highway, though, at the Glastonbury residential community, fear and confusion reigned. A temporary power outage in roughly half of the homes during the night had caused panic in some of the privately owned shelters. Many had stayed up most of the night decreeing, and most of the faithful there refused to leave their shelters until they had a personal "all clear" message from Elizabeth Clare Prophet herself.[101] With rumors of war circulating among them, they waited to hear from the messenger of the Ascended Masters, the only one they could trust.

To many church members, the realization that no nuclear attack had come was a relief similar to what they had felt eighteen months earlier when faced with the wall of flames from the Yellowstone fires. Much as they had understood their efforts to turn back those conflagrations, Elizabeth Clare Prophet and her followers credited their decrees for preventing a nuclear catastrophe in March 1990. But to others it was a devastating blow to their spiritual convictions. Many had made substantial personal and financial sacrifices in preparing to go underground, and the failure of the Ascended Masters' predictions was more than a disappointment; for some it meant financial ruin.[102] A good number of CUT followers began to question their confidence in Prophet. Many would eventually leave the church altogether.[103]

Church without a Prophet

Elizabeth Clare Prophet and her followers emerged from their underground bunkers to face international scrutiny and local derision in the wake of the "disconfirmation" of her prophecies.[104] Unperturbed, the church leadership characterized the failure of the predicted nuclear attack to materialize as an expected outcome of followers' faithful devotion and obedience.[105] As one former member explained: "[Elizabeth] Clare Prophet said that the reason there was not a nuclear war was because we had all followed the orders of the Ascended Masters and gone through the entire Shelter Cycle. Because everyone was obedient, because we all prayed through the entire situation, our prayers had prevented the End. More importantly however, the collective actions of the group . . . was enough to prove there are faithful and obedient people in the world, and the apocalypse was averted."[106] Similar to their experience of the Yellowstone fires of 1988, their faith had saved the day.

They were not yet, however, in the clear. Just as the church was occupied with propping up its sagging public image, another disaster loomed. Three of their underground fuel tanks near the shelter began leaking, and over a five-day period in early April 1990, some 21,000 gallons of diesel fuel plus 11,500 gallons of gasoline escaped into the ground near Mol Heron Creek, threatening an important spawning waterway for cutthroat trout. Church officials responded quickly and decisively, digging up the faulty tanks and emptying the others of an additional 520,000 gallons of fuel. They hired a professional disaster recovery firm and worked heroically to contain the leaked fuel, to remove all contaminated soil, and to protect the creek. Remarkably, only about 10 gallons of fuel actually entered the waterway.[107] Yet the church could not contain the public relations damage. Environmental groups were outraged at the endangerment of Mol Heron Creek, and federal agencies initiated investigations into possible water quality violations. Montana congressman Pat Williams declared that the Church Universal and Triumphant was endangering "both land and lives in Montana." The state of Montana sued the church for damages and sought an injunction prohibiting additional development on CUT land.[108] It seemed that opposition to CUT in Montana and elsewhere had reached an all-time high, especially among those most concerned with environmental issues.

In response to damage done to their reputation, Elizabeth Clare Prophet undertook a national publicity campaign to repair the church's public image. It included dozens of interviews by news organizations and appearances on several prominent television talk shows.[109] Local nonmember residents were invited for informal talks over pizza, and Prophet and other church officials made presentations at local organizations.[110] The church made a concerted effort to gain acceptance as good neighbors among skeptical Montanans.

As CUT struggled to regain its footing and reestablish its credibility, a new challenge emerged regarding leadership of the church. Elizabeth Clare Prophet had served as the undisputed head of CUT's worldwide community in her role as messenger of the Ascended Masters. She had guided the church through its many controversies and conflicts, and despite much criticism and accusations by former church members and others, she was affectionately embraced by her loyal followers as Ma Guru, the wise, caring, and protective Mother of her community. But as she navigated the difficult years following the shelter cycle, Prophet also dealt with growing concerns about her health. On New Year's Day 1999 she announced to her shocked community that she had been diagnosed with Alzheimer's disease and would no longer serve as spiritual leader of the church.[111]

Even before dementia claimed its spiritual leader, the Church Universal and Triumphant was changing. Internal discord and sagging morale among staff members in the years following the shelter cycle precipitated reforms that promised momentous restructuring of their administrative organization. In June 1996 Elizabeth Clare Prophet had resigned as church president, ostensibly to devote all her energies to her spiritual leadership as the church's messenger. Taking over the top administrative role was church member Gilbert Cleirbaut, a Belgian-born Canadian management consultant, who soon instituted reforms to steer the church toward the mainstream of U.S. religious culture with more democratic governance.[112] The changes included doing away with the official code of conduct that regulated members' behavior regarding everything from dress codes to sexual practices. Cleirbaut cultivated an atmosphere of trust by instituting procedures of "due process" to end the arbitrary dismissals of members not conforming to community expectations. Although many followers welcomed these changes, including Elizabeth Clare Prophet's own children, who were still involved in the leadership of the church, the most conservative leaders of the church's "charismatic aristocracy" opposed the

FIG. 13. The Hindu deity Shiva guards the front of the main church sanctuary at Church Universal and Triumphant headquarters, with large portraits of Jesus and Saint Germain looking out over an eclectic assortment of religious objects and images, June 2, 2016. Photo by T. S. Bremer.

changes and worked to consolidate their power. They soon succeeded in restoring their authority, which allowed them to reinstitute the code of conduct and eliminate dissenters from the church, including Cleirbaut, who was expelled in 1999.[113]

In the midst of this internal strife among leaders and staff came Elizabeth Clare Prophet's "tearful goodbye" in announcing her retirement with no clear plan of succession.[114] For the first time in nearly a half-century, the movement begun by Mark Prophet in the 1950s and formally organized as the Church Universal and Triumphant by his widow would be without a spiritual leader as Elizabeth's reign came to an end in the final year of the millennium.[115]

By the turn of the millennium, the Church Universal and Triumphant had entered a new phase, becoming a smaller organization more focused on its publishing enterprise and without a spiritual leader. Efforts to be more accommodating of its neighbors and gain acceptance as permanent members of Montana society following the shelter cycle era had succeeded to some extent.[116] More than a decade into the new millennium, local residents could acknowledge, as one former critic of the church said in 2016, "Clearly, they're not the factor that they were in a lot of ways, and are more integrated with the community."[117]

A welcome change for folks worried about environmental impacts of the CUT community has been its members' greater concern as stewards of the land. One observer noted in 1999 that the church was pursuing "a new land ethic, one that focuses on preservation instead of development. The church is even selling land to the government it once reviled," adding, "The church still has plenty of critics, but lately, environmentalists have been heaping praise on CUT." This was largely due to the shift from an emphasis on agriculture to concern for wildlife preservation: "The church says it wants to remove cattle from its ranch and welcome some of Yellowstone's wandering bison."[118]

This shift in attitude about caring for the land corresponds to improved relations with the National Park Service.[119] Over the course of its residence in Montana, the Church Universal and Triumphant has had an ambivalent and sometimes contentious relationship with the national park on its boundary. Before the church purchased Malcolm Forbes's ranch, the federal government was poised to add the land to the Gallatin National Forest, but when that effort could not be concluded, CUT was able to acquire the property as the centerpiece of its Royal Teton Ranch.[120] In the early years of the church's ownership, park officials joined local environmentalists in voicing concerns about threats to the Yellowstone ecosystem, specifically concerning how church developments might disrupt geothermal features and disturb key habitats for grizzly bears, elk, bison, bighorn sheep, and pronghorn antelope.[121]

Of particular concern to the National Park Service were water rights and how greater development might affect Yellowstone's geysers and other thermal features. Robert Barbee, the park superintendent in the 1980s, when CUT was establishing its headquarters on its Montana property, commented on the threat that development posed to Yellowstone's geothermal features; he told a local television station: "These are our priceless resources in this country. As we move on into the next century in the national parks, and some of the wilderness areas and national forests, that will be all that we have. We have a sacred charge, and we take it seriously." He emphasized that the Park Service was not concerned that CUT was a religious community but only that the sudden influx of a large number of people could threaten Yellowstone's resources. In reply, Edward Francis, vice president of the church and manager of the Royal Teton Ranch, retorted, "My problem with Yellowstone Park is that I think in some cases they like to view areas outside the park not just as a neighbor but as a land that they should have some proprietary interest in."[122]

Their disagreement became urgent when the church proceeded to drill a well that tapped into the heated waters of the same aquifer that feeds the Yellowstone geysers. This prompted a Montana representative to introduce legislation in the U.S. Congress to prohibit water usage from the aquifer. In reply, CUT officials claimed that concerns about water usage amounted to usurpation of their legal water rights, but it also evidenced religious persecution aimed at thwarting their community's viability.[123]

Besides concern for protecting the park's thermal features, another urgent issue for National Park Service officials involved habitat for seasonal migrations of elk, bison, bighorn sheep, and other Yellowstone fauna. By 1999 a solution had been negotiated in a complicated, two-phase land deal between the Church Universal and Triumphant, the U.S. Department of the Interior, the U.S. Forest Service, and the Rocky Mountain Elk Foundation. In addition to acquiring property from the church through purchase and land exchanges, the agreement provides conservation easements on much of the Royal Teton Ranch land; plus, it includes a "right of first refusal" for the Elk Foundation to buy additional undeveloped lands that the church may wish to sell. The agreement also settled the controversy over CUT's use of water from the Yellowstone aquifer by turning over to the government all subsurface geothermal water rights on church property.[124]

Park officials and conservationists were pleased with the agreement. The head of the Rocky Mountain Elk Foundation remarked: "We greatly appreciated the Church's efforts to ensure a conservation outcome for these lands. These are valuable and desirable lands, and there are other buyers out there whose goals are not conservation, but exploitation and development." In reply, Kate Gordon, the church president at the time, stated: "Like many other Americans, I consider Yellowstone National Park and the surrounding lands as sacred ground. And to know that the property we're exchanging will remain forever in that tradition is a great comfort. For that reason, I'm glad we dealt with those committed to protecting the integrity of the place."[125] The years of distrust, animosity, sometimes hostility, between the Church Universal and Triumphant and the federal government seemed to have passed as they found common cause in protecting the sacred ground of Yellowstone National Park and its ecosystem.

The Sacred Ground of Yellowstone

Despite their differences with the National Park Service, the Church Universal and Triumphant had always regarded Yellowstone as sacred ground. From the time that Saint Germain revealed Yellowstone's secret mines to Ray Ballard in 1930, it had been a revered locale in the sacred geography of the I AM tradition and its descendants. When Elizabeth Clare Prophet announced in 1981 that Gautama Buddha had designated the Heart of the Inner Retreat as the Western Shamballa, Yellowstone became the auspicious link between two of the most holy sites for the Church Universal and Triumphant, its Royal Teton Ranch and the Grand Teton Mountain.

Consequently, Yellowstone has special energies for followers of CUT. One member spoke of "profound powerful forces of nature that have really been part of the park, whether it's the animals, the wildlife, the forest, the mountains, the thermal features, and all the things that we know about the park. But it just feels different, and I can't quite tell you why. . . . It's just something I feel." She went on to emphasize, however, that the Tetons are even more special to her: "Because there's a retreat of the Great White Brotherhood. And that to me, even though it's on the other side of the park, it's a very sacred place, more so for me than Yellowstone."[126]

Many CUT members connect Yellowstone to the spiritual powers of the Tetons. A former member who grew up in the church in Montana recalls that his family would visit Yellowstone National Park "constantly": "We went there a lot." He explained, "The church considered the Tetons to be holy, and so Yellowstone is just sort of that I think also for them," an extension of the holiness of the Tetons. "You go to Yellowstone, you're closer to God. You know what I kept from my time with the church?—that. You go to the Tetons, man, you can touch God right there at the Grand."[127]

The auspicious energies that connect the Tetons to Yellowstone, according to a prominent CUT member, flow through the Royal Teton Ranch in the waters of the Yellowstone River, which crosses the church's property:

> The actual Yellowstone River, there's been quite a lot spoken about that, where the actual water in the river and the streams is symbolical, and it has to do with the flowing of the energy from the Yellowstone park. The heart of the Yellowstone park is also charged from the energies in the heart of the earth, and that has to do with the Royal Teton, the etheric retreat. And so the light then gets carried out into the earth, and it goes through all of the arteries and veins of the waters and the rivers, and it actually feeds light and energy to the rest of the world. So the interesting thing is that prayers and the spiritual work we do actually goes into the Yellowstone River because it flows right past.[128]

For members of the church, the sacred river brings Yellowstone's spiritual energies to their holy ground and carries their prayers and spiritual efforts into the universe.

As heirs to the eclectic spirituality of the I AM tradition, members of the Church Universal and Triumphant experience Yellowstone far differently than most people who visit, work in, or live nearby the park. Their eyes and hearts are trained beyond the terrestrial attractions of Yellowstone to the ethereal realities revealed by their Ascended Masters. More than a beautiful place, more than the sublime experience of nature's awesome power, more than a landscape of moral lessons or nationalist pride, Yellowstone in the CUT imaginary holds secrets to the universe and the destiny of humankind. For them the world's first national park is nothing less than the sacred source of light and energy for all of the world.

POSTLUDE

An Ambivalence of Affections

Writing this book has changed how I feel about Yellowstone. Diving deeply into the history of the national park has left me with ambivalence about a place I have loved for most of my life and thought I knew well. The claims that Yellowstone has made on me once seemed absolute and unwavering, holding me in a devotion more real, more profound, more inspired, than any religion I had ever known. Now I'm less sure.

Attention to religion in Yellowstone's history has likewise deepened my ambivalence about the traditions, practices, and beliefs of faith communities in the United States. I have long maintained a strict agnosticism on all matters of religious faith, convinced that dogmatic claims of gods and spirits, miracles and afterlives, the various insinuations of alternate metaphysical realities, are all beyond the possibility of human knowing. Yet as a scholar of religions in the Americas, I know fully well the value of religious devotion, spirituality, and participation in communities of shared beliefs. Without question, religion has had a profound and defining influence on billions of lives throughout history, providing purpose, meaning, belonging, inspiration, and consolation to peoples across all human cultures. In my own life, I have been witness to the profound influences of spiritual devotions in the lives of people dear to me, and I cannot deny impactful moments in my own experience when metaphysical realities became apparent to me. I do not doubt the existence of spiritual dimensions that we have not yet begun to grasp or even to imagine.

Yet I also know that religions of all sorts have been rightly identified and criticized as perpetrators and justifications for unimaginable atrocities throughout history, from human sacrifices of ancient societies to the Holocaust of the Third Reich and continuing even today with brutal executions by groups like ISIS and the deadly persecutions of Rohingya

Muslims in the Buddhist-majority nation of Myanmar. Only the most naive and uninformed among us can deny that religion has always had blood on its hands.

At the same time, my academic studies and teaching about religions in the Americas has reminded me of the undeniable positive value of the world's religions. Virtually all religious traditions establish moral principles for their adherents' ethical guidance. Religious practices anchor the foundational cohesion of many, if not all, human communities. The mythical narratives and historical heroes of religions have inspired resilience to endure the challenges, pain, and despair of living in this world. And perhaps most valuable for humanity as a whole, religions have been perennial sources of hope for better futures. Without ignoring the violent, tragic, and traumatic histories involving the world's religions, it is clear that many peoples' lives have been made better by religious beliefs and practices. Religion has been both a negative force and a positive presence in the history of humanity.

My ambivalence about religion—the good, the bad, the ugly, the hopeful—has been brought into stark relief as I delved into the religious history of Yellowstone National Park. A religiously grounded aesthetic appreciation of the natural world has made protecting Yellowstone and other national parks a sacred commitment for substantial portions of the U.S. citizenry. At the same time, that sort of holy dedication has deepened historical racial divisions by affirming white supremacy in popular interpretations of the nation's parks. Though Native Americans have been a more visible presence in the park in recent years, the scars of past traumas from removal and exclusion run deep. Similarly, one cannot easily dismiss the unconventional doctrines and cultural paranoia evident in the history of the Church Universal and Triumphant without also acknowledging how the church has consistently delivered on the promise of community and belonging to religious seekers who too often found themselves painfully estranged from family and friends. Throughout history, religion and Yellowstone National Park have been constant but complicated companions.

This realization has confounded my own relationship with Yellowstone. My affections have deep roots. From childhood adventures with my father in the park's backcountry to first encountering the person whom I would spend my life with to the many lessons of both nature's wonders and the precariousness of all life, Yellowstone has given me so much. The park has been a profound presence in my life, one that has brought abiding joy in ways that no other place ever could. It has been a touchstone in my most valued relationships. At the same time, writing this book has also made me aware that my whiteness, my masculine identity, my socioeconomic advantages, and even my culturally acquired aesthetic values all undergird the privileges that have made possible my relationship with Yellowstone. My affections are not innocent.

The affection I continue to have for Yellowstone is now tempered with ambivalence. I cannot stop loving the park, but I do so with a more complex understanding of why and how I have found it valuable in my life. It reminds me that the relationships we have with places are just as complicated as any relationships—those we have with others, with our histories and heritages, with the future. We ignore these complications at our own peril. Indeed, accepting and embracing our ambivalence allows a richer, more sensitive and compassionate manner of being in the wonderlands of our lives.

NOTES

Prelude

1. Muir, *Our National Parks*, 1.

Introduction

1. This "mountain" was known for decades prior to the arrival of Church Universal and Triumphant (CUT) as Deaf Jim Knob. An endnote to a "dictation" from Gautama Buddha delivered at the Inner Retreat in the upper part of CUT's Royal Teton Ranch on Sunday, November 8, 1981, spoken through the spiritual messenger Elizabeth Clare Prophet, known to her followers as "Mother," explains, "Deaf Jim Knob was renamed 'Maitreya Mountain' by Mother when she took her students to the heart of the Inner Retreat." Prophet, "Call of Hierarchy," 508 n. 1.

2. According to Erin Prophet, daughter of CUT founders Mark and Elizabeth Clare Prophet, her father on the eve of his death by stroke in 1973 had instructed his followers to relocate to Montana. Prophet, *Prophet's Daughter*, 17.

3. I first introduced the notion of "a simultaneity of places" in Bremer, *Blessed with Tourists*, 4.

4. A number of influential theories of religion emphasize the formative role of religion in creating purpose and meaning in people's lives. Cultural anthropologist Clifford Geertz, for instance, describes religion as synthesizing a people's worldview with their ethos, and thus creating a meaningful world where their ways of living correspond exactly to "the way things in sheer actuality are, their most comprehensive ideas of order." See Geertz, "Religion as a Cultural System," 89. Ann Taves discusses work by Wayne Proudfoot, Phillip Shaver, Bernard Spilka, and Lee A. Kirkpatrick regarding the role of "meaning-belief systems" in attributing religious meanings to particular events and experiences. Taves, *Religious Experience Reconsidered*, 101–2.

5. "The making of place," I have previously argued, "always involves the making of identities, and, conversely, the construction of identity always involves the construction of place." Bremer, *Blessed with Tourists*, 4–5.

6. Kerry Mitchell documents how the federal government facilitates spiritual experiences of national parks in *Spirituality and the State*.

7. Although Yellowstone has been widely recognized as the world's first national park, at least two other sites set the precedent for the creation of Yellowstone National Park. The Hot Springs Reservation in Arkansas was the first national protected area, created by the U.S. Congress in 1832, forty years prior to the Yellowstone Park Act. See Heacox, *American Idea*, 229 (photo caption). Withdrawing Arkansas's natural springs from private development created a precedent for later parks, but as Alfred Runte notes, reserving Hot Springs was "in recognition of its medicinal value, not with the intent of protecting scenery." Runte, *National Park*, 26. The second federal precedent for Yellowstone was the Yosemite Valley and the Mariposa Grove of giant redwood trees in California. In 1864, despite "the distractions of the Civil War, Congress quietly passed, and President Lincoln signed, The Yosemite Park Act." Heacox, *American Idea*, 123. This legislation ceded the park to the State of California, but it imposed management restrictions that maintained Yosemite "for public use, resort and recreation," stipulating that it must remain "inalienable for all time." Historian Alfred Runte argues, "In fact, if not in name, Yosemite was the first national park." Runte, *National Parks*, 29–30.

8. Quoted in Albanese, *Nature Religion in America*, 34.

9. Stoll, *Inherit the Holy Mountain*, 21.

10. A digital copy of the Westminster Confession of Faith is available at http://www.pcaac.org/wp-content/uploads/2012/11/wcfscriptureProofs.pdf (accessed December 19, 2018).

11. Stoll, *Inherit the Holy Mountain*, 24.

12. Albanese, *Nature Religion in America*, 37.

13. Quoted in Albanese, *Nature Religion in America*, 41.

14. Stoll, *Inherit the Holy Mountain*, 56.

15. Mark Stoll observes that "Olmsted saw parks' purpose as primarily moral and social." Stoll, *Inherit the Holy Mountain*, 97. Similarly, Evan Berry recognizes Olmsted's "soteriological view of recreation." Berry, *Devoted to Nature*, 66.

16. At age seven Frederick Law Olmsted boarded in the home of Zolva Whitmore, a Congregationalist minister in the rural hamlet of North Guilford, Connecticut. There Olmsted gained religious instruction from Reverend Whitmore as part of the education he and the other twelve students received in the local one-room school. Rybczynski, *Clearing in the Distance*, 25.

17. This is from a letter Olmsted wrote in 1858 to the Board of Commissioners of Central Park, quoted in Stoll, *Inherit the Holy Mountain*, 97.

18. Stoll writes, "Central Park represented an Eden in the midst of an urban Hell." Stoll, *Inherit the Holy Mountain*, 97.

19. Quoted in Stoll, *Inherit the Holy Mountain*, 97.

20. Rybczynski, *Clearing in the Distance*, 257–58.

21. Catherine Albanese discusses the concept of "sublime" as it pertains to American cultural understandings and attitudes toward nature in the revolutionary and early republic periods and how during the nineteenth century it "lost some of its eighteenth-century trappings of fear and gloomy majesty, in a luminist perception of divine glory." Albanese, *Nature Religion in America*, 58–62 and 94.

22. Albanese documents the convergence of social and cultural developments involved in an American turn toward nature in the nineteenth century. Among them are "a lingering Calvinism, with its deep sense of evil and sin; an idealist tradition that molded Platonism and Neoplatonism to modern times and purposes; a romanticism that turned to nature no longer contained (in the Enlightenment and early revolutionary mode) but more expansive to accompany the liberation of self and society; and an emerging 'scientific' view in which mesmerism and Swedenborgianism became guiding lights." Albanese, *Nature Religion in America*, 80. Environmental historian William Cronon notes that by the end of the nineteenth century attitudes toward nature and wildlands had shifted dramatically for many Americans, "The wastelands that had once seemed worthless had for some people come to seem almost beyond price." For these partisans of conservation in the early twentieth century, Cronon concludes, "Satan's home had become God's own temple." Cronon, "Trouble with Wilderness," 70–72.

23. Journalist John O'Sullivan coined the term *Manifest Destiny* in 1845, when he proclaimed "the right of our manifest destiny to overspread and possess the whole continent which providence has given us for the development of the great experiment of liberty and federated self government." Quoted in Stephanson, *Manifest Destiny*, 42. Later nineteenth-century gender concerns tied this ideology of national destiny to measures of maleness.

24. The imagery of uncovering "the nakedness of our sleeping Yellowstone Beauty" comes from a letter from Sam Wilkeson to Jay Cooke, October 10, 1870, Jay Cooke Papers, Historical Society of Pennsylvania (HSP).

25. Nabokov and Loendorf, *Restoring a Presence*, 8.

26. Quoted in Nabokov and Loendorf, *Restoring a Presence*, 194.

27. Besides the Nabokov and Loendorf volume, see Janetski, *Indians in Yellowstone National Park*; and Loendorf and Stone, *Mountain Spirit*.

28. Frome, *Strangers in High Places*, 180.

29. Historian Robin Winks noted at a 1987 National Park Service conference on "The National Park Idea, within the Parks and Beyond" that "Yellowstone is a creation of human beings. . . . Yellowstone is a cultural artifact." A video recording of Winks's keynote address is in Yellowstone Archives (YA), Videotape Collection,

tape 036. Many others before and since have emphasized the cultural nature of national parks. Examples include John Sears' chapter on "Yellowstone and the 'Wild West,'" in Sears, *Sacred Places*, 156–81; Schullery, *Searching for Yellowstone*; and Barringer, *Selling Yellowstone*.

30. Justin Farrell argues that intractable conflicts in the Greater Yellowstone Ecosystem involve "a struggle over moral truths." Farrell, *Battle for Yellowstone*, 10.

1. Where Hell Bubbled Up

1. Kuppens, "On the Origin of the Yellowstone National Park," 400. The Pikuni people (sometimes spelled *Piikani*) are most commonly referred to as "Piegan" in nineteenth-century and later references. The Pikuni are one of three divisions of the Blackfeet tribe. Like many of the names that Euro-Americans applied to indigenous peoples, the term *Blackfeet* is a misleading term that the people to whom it applies never used. Euro-Americans used it to refer to a sizable native group that inhabited the Northern Rocky Mountain region of northern Idaho and Montana and stretching well into Canada. Many of the contemporary members of this group prefer their traditional name, Natsitapii. Nabokov and Loendorf, *Restoring a Presence*, 91.

2. Kuppens, "On the Origin of the Yellowstone National Park," 400. Besides Kuppens's recollections, my speculations of his first learning about Yellowstone from his Indian hosts relies on descriptions of Pikuni people in the writings of artist George Catlin, in *Letters and Notes*, 61. I also consulted references about the Pikuni leader Chief Big Lake in the writings of James Willard Schultz, a nineteenth-century fur trapper who married into the Pikuni tribe and was given the name Apikuni. Schultz, *Blackfeet and Buffalo*.

3. The account that Francis X. Kuppens wrote of his trip to Yellowstone leaves the details of what he saw and experienced there to others: it explains, "I shall not attempt to describe it, that has been done by many abler pens than mine." Kuppens, "On the Origin of the Yellowstone National Park," 401. As with all early sources on Yellowstone, readers need to regard Kuppens's account with some skepticism, as does George Black, who doubts that Kuppens's testimony can be trusted. Black, *Empire of shadows*, 458 n. 27.

4. Details of Kuppens's life here and in subsequent paragraphs come from Garraghan, *Jesuits of the Middle United States*, 2:587–89.

5. Axtell, *Invasion Within*, 68.

6. Kuppens, "On the Origin of the Yellowstone National Park," 400.

7. Kuppens, "On the Origin of the Yellowstone National Park," 400.

8. Kuppens, "On the Origin of the Yellowstone National Park," 401.

9. Regarding the persistent myth that American Indians feared Yellowstone, see Weixelman, "Fear or Reverence"; and Whittlesey, "Native Americans, the Earliest Interpreters."

10. How Indians felt about Yellowstone has long been a topic of conjecture on the part of non-native chroniclers of the region. Regarding the specific beliefs of Pikuni people, or Piegans, there is some evidence that they never claimed Yellowstone as their own sacred place, but because they recognized it as sacred to other people, they treated it with respect, usually with prayers and tobacco offerings. Nabokov and Loendorf, *Restoring a Presence*, 93.

11. Swagerty, *Indianization of Lewis and Clark*, 56.

12. Ambrose, *Undaunted Courage*, 399.

13. Colter left no written record of his explorations; this quotation comes from Washington Irving's reworking of a manuscript given to him by an army captain regarding his adventures in the West. Irving, *Adventures of Captain Bonneville*, 120.

14. Victor, *River of the West*, 79–80. According to the Wyoming State Historic Preservation Office, Colter's Hell is located on the western outskirts of Cody, Wyoming. See https://wyoshpo.wyo.gov/index.php/programs/national-register/wyoming -listings/view-full-list/729-colter-s-hell (accessed August 14, 2023).

15. Haines, *Yellowstone Story*, 1:41–42.

16. Potts's letter appeared in the *Philadelphia Gazette & Daily Advertiser*, November 14, 1826; a transcript is available online at https://user.xmission.com/~drudy /mtman/html/potts2.html.

17. Potts's second published letter appeared in the *Philadelphia Gazette & Daily Advertiser*, September 27, 1827; the transcript is available online at https://user .xmission.com/~drudy/mtman/html/potts3.html. His other letters can be found at https://user.xmission.com/~drudy/mtman/html/pottsltr.html (accessed July 6, 2019).

18. Haines, *Yellowstone Story*, 1:39.

19. Gunnison, *Mormons*, 161.

20. Aubrey Haines identifies Ferris as "the first tourist to visit the Yellowstone wonders." He also notes that Ferris was the first to give an adequate description of a geyser in Yellowstone, and he was the first to apply the term *geyser* to the Yellowstone thermal features. Haines, *Yellowstone Story*, 1:47.

21. Ferris, *Life in the Rocky Mountains*, 296.

22. Ferris, *Life in the Rocky Mountains*, 297.

23. Ferris, *Life in the Rocky Mountains*, 298.

24. For a summary of "Attitudes about Yellowstone Imputed to Indians," see Nabokov and Loendorf, *Restoring a Presence*, 274–77. Yellowstone author Paul Schullery

states, "There is overwhelming evidence that most of the tribes that used the Yellowstone area (especially the hot springs and geyser basins) saw it as a place of spiritual power, of communion with natural forces, a place that inspired reverence." Schullery, *Searching for Yellowstone*, 29.

25. Russell, *Journal of a Trapper*, 46.

26. Russell, *Journal of a Trapper*, 63.

27. "The Yellowstone," *Montana Post*, July 28, 1866, 4, in Rare Books Collection. Huntington Library (HL).

28. Baumler, "Cross in the Wilderness," 19; and Salish-Pend d'Oreille Culture Committee, *Salish People*, 111.

29. The discussion of American Indians from the intermountain West requesting Christian missionaries and the respective versions of the tale told by Protestants and Catholics is adapted from Bremer, "Black Robes and the Book of Heaven," which includes a more detailed analysis of the events and the beginnings of U.S. Christian missionary activity in the Upper Rocky Mountains.

30. Barrows, *Oregon*, 104.

31. Barrows, *Oregon*, 105.

32. Barrows, *Oregon*, 109.

33. Barrows, *Oregon*, 109.

34. Barrows, *Oregon*, 110–11.

35. Barrows, *Oregon*, 111–12. The artist George Catlin, in his Letter Number 48, describes meeting these two Indian delegates on the trip up the Missouri River: "I travelled two thousand miles, companion with these two young fellows, towards their own country, and became much pleased with their manners and dispositions." Catlin goes on to report, "The last mentioned of the two, died near the mouth of the Yellow Stone River on his way home, with disease which he had contracted in the civilized district; and the other one I have since learned, arrived safely amongst his friends, conveying to them the melancholy intelligence of the deaths of all the rest of his party." See Catlin, *Letters and Notes*, 561–62.

36. In regard to how Barrows was concerned with current interests, an early review by Bret Harte in *Overland Monthly and Out West Magazine* in February 1884 notes that his book "was evidently designed to be picturesque, filled with striking scenes, and for this purpose the earliest missions had less to offer" (212–14).

37. Garraghan, *Jesuits of the Middle United States*, 2:236–37.

38. Garraghan, *Jesuits of the Middle United States*, 2:238.

39. Garraghan, *The Jesuits of the Middle United States*, 2:240–41.

40. The letter of Bishop Rosati, dated December 31, 1831, is quoted in Garraghan, *Jesuits of the Middle United States*, 2:237–38.

41. Garraghan, *Jesuits of the Middle United States*, 2:242. Garraghan also reports that there is no evidence in the historical record that the two survivors ever made it back to their homes in the Columbia Valley.

42. Quoted in Garraghan, *Jesuits of the Middle United States*, 2:237–38.

43. It may have also been a case of other priorities, since much of their energy and resources at the time went to building up their new school, St. Louis University. De Smet, *Life, Letters and Travels*, 1:28.

44. Garraghan, *Jesuits of the Middle United States*, 2:247.

45. Issuing passports for the Jesuits to travel in Indian Territory in 1838 would be one of the last official acts of the aging explorer and former territorial governor William Clark, as he died later that year. Garraghan, *Jesuits of the Middle United States*, 2:432.

46. Garraghan, *Jesuits of the Middle United States*, 2:432 n. 23.

47. De Smet's letter of August 20, 1838, quoted in Garraghan, *Jesuits of the Middle United States*, 2:436.

48. De Smet, *Life, Letters and Travel*, 1:29–30.

49. Garraghan, *Jesuits of the Middle United States*, 2:248–49.

50. This translation appears in Davis, "Peter John De Smet," 41–42.

51. Regarding De Smet's sojourn west in 1840, see Garraghan, *Jesuits of the Middle United States*, 2:252–54. See also Davis, "Peter John De Smet."

52. Peterson and Peers, *Sacred Encounters*, 23.

53. Quoted in Peterson and Peers, *Sacred Encounters*, 97.

54. The Historic St. Mary's Mission and Museum at the site of the original mission features this claim of "where Montana began" on its website at http://www .saintmarysmission.org/index.html (accessed July 6, 2019).

55. Although not the first time Yellowstone appeared in cartographic representations of the American West, Bridger's hand-drawn map contains "many firsts for Yellowstone National Park cartography," including more of the thermal features than any previous map; many of the tributaries of the Yellowstone, Madison, and Gallatin Rivers; and the first illustration of the Grand Canyon of the Yellowstone River. Blevins, *Mapping Yellowstone*, 21–22. The original map is now part of the De Smetiana Map Series collection in the Jesuit Archives, Central United States, St. Louis MO. Bridger may not have drawn the map himself, and certainly he did not label it, as he remained illiterate his entire life. Aubrey Haines states that Father De Smet drew it based on information from Bridger when they met at an Indian Council near Fort Laramie in 1851. Haines, *Yellowstone Story*, 1:85.

56. De Smet, *Western Missions and Missionaries*, 87.

57. According to a contemporaneous report in the *Montana Post*, July 27, 1867, 8, available in HL.

58. Tuttle, "Early History of the Episcopal Church in Montana," 204.

59. The funeral notice was published in the *Montana Post*, December 28, 1867, 8, available in HL.

60. "Christianity added to, but did not replace, Indian ways of thinking about the sacred." Peterson and Peers, *Sacred Encounters*, 97.

2. For the Benefit of the People

1. Cooke, *Jay Cooke's Memoir*, 10.

2. Cooke, *Jay Cooke's Memoir*, 10 and 166.

3. Clinton Lloyd, the former chief clerk of the House of Representatives, quoted in an undated news clipping from the *Washington Post*, on file in Jay Cooke Collection, Rutherford B. Hayes Presidential Library and Museum (HPL).

4. Journalist John O'Sullivan coined the term *Manifest Destiny* in 1845 in his proclamation of the American people as a chosen nation with "the right of our manifest destiny to overspread and to possess the whole continent which providence has given us for the development of the great experiment of liberty and federated self government." Stephanson, *Manifest Destiny*, 42.

5. Anders Stephanson notes that the conclusion of the Civil War "soon allowed the victorious North to regain its destinarian footing. . . . The United States would be born again, 'a mountain of holiness for the dissemination of light and purity to all nations,' as one Reverend in Philadelphia decreed. With the end in sight, the Unionist cause could be interpreted as divine vindication. Thus the Civil War revitalized confidence in the American mission, now properly national and northern." Stephanson, *Manifest Destiny*, 65. This revitalization of U.S. Manifest Destiny also had a strongly racial element. As Edward Blum points out, postbellum national reunification relied to a large extent on the shared racial identity of white Christians. Blum, *Reforging the White Republic*, 6–7.

6. Cooke, *Jay Cooke's Memoir*, 2.

7. The partnership agreements are in the H. D. Cooke Collection, folder HM 47681, HL.

8. Oberholtzer, *Jay Cooke, Financier of the Civil War*, 1:487–90 and 96. Jay Cooke served as vice president of the American Sunday School Union for thirty-five years. At the time of his death, in 1905, the recording secretary of the union wrote that Mr. Cooke "was deeply interested in the benevolent and missionary work of the Society, and, from personal observation, esteemed it the most important of the evangelizing agencies at work in the new and rural sections of our country." His support included the purchase of large orders of American Sunday School Union literature to distribute in areas that he thought were "in need of healthful literature." Letter from J. M. Andrews, recording secretary of the American

Sunday School Union, to Mrs. Charles Barney, daughter of Jay Cooke, May 11, 1905, HPL.

9. Oberholtzer, *Jay Cooke, Financier of the Civil War*, 1:485.

10. Historian George Black notes that when Nathaniel Langford visited Jay Cooke in the summer of 1870, he offered the banker an "enticement" of Yellowstone's potential to attract "thousands of curious Easterners" who would ride the Northern Pacific Railroad to experience this natural wonderland. George Black, *Empire of Shadows*, 278.

11. Langford worked in the bank owned by his brother-in-law William R. Marshall, who would later serve as governor of Minnesota. When the bank failed in 1860, Langford began to turn his vision westward. Black, *Empire of Shadows*, 101.

12. Another of Langford's brothers-in-law, James Wick Taylor, was an acquaintance of Salmon P. Chase, who served as secretary of the treasury in the Lincoln administration and was responsible for enlisting Jay Cooke to finance the war effort. Taylor's influence with Chase led to Langford's appointment as the government's revenue agent in Montana and later made him the leading candidate for appointment as territorial governor. Haines, "Foreword," in Langford, *Discovery of Yellowstone Park*, viii–ix.

13. An 1866 newspaper article in the *Montana Post* asserts that "long before any other benevolent institutions, or even churches, were established here, the benign influences of Masonry were felt and acknowledged." "Masonry in Montana" in the *Montana Post*, August 11, 1866, 4, available in the bound collection of the *Montana Post, 1866–1868*, HL.

14. Michael A. Leeson's 1885 book on Montana history states, "The history of Masonry in Montana is coeval with the discovery of her gold mines." He quotes the claim of Nathaniel Langford that he and two other new arrivals "opened and closed the first Lodge ever assembled in Montana" in September 1862. Leeson, *History of Montana*, 375.

15. Ridley, *Masons*, 42.

16. Albanese, *Republic of Mind and Spirit*, 124; and Vaughn, *Antimasonic Party*, 10–11.

17. Catherine L. Albanese notes that by the end of the eighteenth century Freemasonry in America had become "thoroughly biblicized," with "lodge prayers that skillfully combined the Bible of the past with the deism of the eighteenth-century Masonic present." Albanese, *Republic of Mind and Spirit*, 128.

18. Albanese, *Republic of Mind and Spirit*, 131–32.

19. Regarding the "Morgan affair" scandal and its consequences for Freemasonry in America, see Vaughn, *Antimasonic Party*.

20. Gardiner, "Death and Masonic Funerals," 383.

21. Leeson, *History of Montana*, 375. A contemporary article titled "Masonry in Montana" in the *Montana Post*, August 11, 1866, 4, corroborates Langford's view of Freemasonry's role in early Montana settlement: "Coeval with the spread of civilization over the fair and beautiful Territory of the mountains came Masonry as the *avant courier* of all that is pure in morality and beneficial to the eternal happiness of mankind." The article states that the first petition for a lodge in Virginia City was sent in October 1853 (an apparent typographical error, which should read 1863, when Virginia City was first established); a Grand Lodge was established in January 1866, and by August 1866 there were seven lodges in Montana Territory. The article is in the bound collection of the *Montana Post, 1866–1868*, HL.

22. Langford, *Vigilante Days and Ways*, 324. Daniel Gardiner concludes: "To men such as Langford the fraternity was a stabilizing influence. It brought respectable proceedings to fledgling communities." Gardiner, "Death and Masonic Funerals," 393.

23. This view of the Masonic purpose, written by Cornelius Hedges in 1874, is quoted in White, "Cornelius Hedges," 149.

24. The announcement appeared March 16, 1867, in the *Montana Post*, 8, and can be found in the bound collection of the *Montana Post, 1866–1868*, HL.

25. *Montana Post*, December 28, 1867, 1, in the bound collection of the *Montana Post, 1866–1868*, HL. Also see Leeson, *History of Montana*, 780.

26. In fact, Langford needed to engage in some unpleasant Masonic business before departing on the Yellowstone expedition, closing down the Bozeman lodge due to an irreconcilable internal dispute among its local members. See Black, *Empire of Shadows*, 2–3.

27. Black, *Empire of Shadows*, 338. Cornelius Hedges, like Langford, "played an integral part" in the founding of the Grand Lodge of Montana in 1866. Following his term as Most Worshipful Grand Master of the Grand Lodge of Montana, Hedges held the position of grand secretary of the Grand Lodge of Montana from 1872 until his death in 1907. See White, "Cornelius Hedges," 131–34.

28. Lubetkin, *Jay Cooke's Gamble*, 23–24. Governor Marshall welcomed the participation of Langford on the Canadian expedition with "relief and satisfaction, for I felt that I needed a companion to whom I had . . . confidence." Entry in "Journal of an expedition to Pembina and Fort Garry. Made in April and May 1870. By Wm. R. Marshall and Nathaniel P. Langford. At the request of, and made on instructions from Jay Cooke Esq. Phila.," April 4, 1870, HPL.

29. Letter from William R. Marshall (written on State of Minnesota Executive Department stationery) to Jay Cooke, May 29, 1870, HSP.

30. Aubrey Haines cites Langford's diary at the Minnesota Historical Society in St. Paul in Haines, *Yellowstone Story*, 1:105.

31. Haines, "Foreword," in Langford, *Discovery of Yellowstone Park*, ix.

32. Haines, *Yellowstone Story*, 1:108. Sometimes called the Washburn-Doane expedition or the Washburn-Langford-Doane expedition, I will refer to this 1870 exploratory excursion simply as the "Washburn expedition."

33. Haines, *Yellowstone Story*, 1:108–9.

34. Langford, *Vigilante Days and Ways*, 1 and 324; and Leeson, *History of Montana*, 375.

35. Langford, *Discovery of Yellowstone Park*, 117–18.

36. Langford's account, as will be explained shortly, is not to be trusted. As Yellowstone historian Paul Schullery concludes, "Langford was a tireless and unethical self-promoter who left a legacy of shifty dealings and indignant business associates." Schullery, *Searching for Yellowstone*, 57. For a thorough analysis of the campfire story and its legacy, see Schullery and Whittlesey, *Myth and History*.

37. The story of a campfire discussion concerning the future of Yellowstone served for decades as the official origin story of the national park idea. It was even promoted in the early years of the National Park Service by the agency's leaders; no less an iconic figure than Horace Albright, the second director of the National Park Service who set many of the enduring precedents and traditions for the Park Service and remained "still a vital presence in the conservation community in the 1960s," was a vocal advocate of the campfire story; according to Paul Schullery, he "fought bitterly and effectively against the demythologizing of the campfire creation story. He, more than anyone else, had employed the moral purity of the story to promote the goodness of the parks and had turned the story into a secular genesis for the conservation movement. It was unthinkable to him that Yellowstone did not start at Madison Junction." Schullery, *Searching for Yellowstone*, 61.

    Over the years the story had been repeated in countless Park Service campfire programs and even celebrated with historic reenactments at the site of the expedition's final campsite near Madison Junction in Yellowstone. Clayton, *Wonderlandscape*, 78–95. However, most historians who have studied this version of how the idea for making Yellowstone a national park originated are in agreement that the historical evidence for such a conversation is inconclusive at best. Marlene Merrill expresses a widely held view when she characterizes Langford's account of the campfire conversation as "akin to a raconteur's tale and suggests that Langford greatly revised, if not rewrote, whatever might have been in his now-missing journal." Merrill, *Yellowstone and the Great West*, 237–38 n. 24. On the other hand, Lynn Ross-Bryant discusses the tale as an "origin story" of "mythic qualities" in Ross-Bryant, *Pilgrimage to the National Parks*, 50–51.

But this origin story was not actually too original. Five years before the purported campfire conversation, landscape architect Frederick Law Olmsted had warned in his management proposal for Yosemite Park that the scenic wonders "might become private property" and thereby "their value to posterity be injured." He recommended that Congress provide "that the premises should be segregated from the general domain of the public lands, and devoted forever to popular resort and recreation." Quoted in Grusin, *Culture, Technology, and the Creation of America's National Parks*, 25.

38. Katherine Early, as one example, concludes that the original proponents of the national park "were operating under the impetus of development, and to them, the preservation of Yellowstone promised, not a threat to their ethic, but an opportunity to implement it." See Early, *Benefit and Enjoyment of the People*, 71–72. Gareth John concludes that "the establishment of the park in 1872 was fully intended by its political supporters and activists to preserve the commodity value of the Yellowstone-as-landscape for incipient corporate interests—in particular, financiers of the NPRR." John, "Yellowstone as 'Landscape Idea,'" 20.

39. Letter from Sam Wilkeson to Jay Cooke, October 10, 1870, HSP. Wilkeson, formerly a journalist and close confidant of Cooke, served as secretary of the Northern Pacific Railroad and directed publicity for the railroad. Lubetkin, *Jay Cooke's Gamble*, 19.

40. Langford wrote to Jay Cooke on March 4, 1871, from Utica, New York, explaining that he had been suffering there for five weeks under a physician's care for "a severe sore throat." HSP.

41. Langford, "Wonders of the Yellowstone," May and June 1871.

42. Mark Stoll discusses the Calvinist underpinnings of nineteenth-century American attitudes that regarded nature in both aesthetic and scientific terms. He explains how early Reformed Protestants regarded nature as a holy book to be read; nature, according to Stoll, became "Calvinists' second scripture." Stoll, *Inherit the Holy Mountain*, 10–53 and 41–42.

43. Langford, "Wonders of the Yellowstone," May 1871, 1.

44. Langford, "Wonders of the Yellowstone," May 1871, 5.

45. The location of this geological oddity is on property owned by the Church Universal and Triumphant (discussed in chapter 6 of this book), whose members refer to it as "Angel's Ascent" rather than Devil's Slide.

46. Langford, "Wonders of the Yellowstone," May 1871, 6–7. Park historian Lee Whittlesey has found "no less than 56 devil, 6 hell, and 3 Satan place names in Yellowstone history" (these do not include places like Devil's Slide that lie

outside of the national park boundaries). He goes on to explain that most of these names disappeared in the efforts of United States Geological Survey official Arnold Hague, who was responsible for establishing many of Yellowstone's place names in the 1880s and 1890s. Hague, according to Whittlesey, harbored a "personal philosophy of getting rid of all names that contained 'Hell' or 'Devil.'" Whittlesey, *Wonderland Nomenclature*, xxxix. Joel Daehnke explains the prevalence of Christian underworld references in the early place names of Yellowstone according to how the region defied American Christian ideas about nature. "The region seemed best expressed in the terminology of the profane," he observes, "rather than the sacred, and it is characteristic that, while it was often contained within the prevalent Christian values informing the interpretation of American landscape, Yellowstone nomenclature and imagery so often found its way to the unregenerate world of the Fall." Daehnke, *In the Work of Their Hands*, 69.

47. Langford, "Wonders of the Yellowstone," May 1871, 12–13.
48. Langford, "Wonders of the Yellowstone," June 1871, 116.
49. Langford, "Wonders of the Yellowstone," May 1871, 5.
50. Langford, "Wonders of the Yellowstone," June 1871, 119.
51. Langford, "Wonders of the Yellowstone," June 1871, 123.
52. Langford, "Wonders of the Yellowstone," June 1871, 125.
53. Joel Daehnke emphasizes the redemptive nature of American expansionism. He observes, "The 'peculiar fusion' of providential and republican ideologies at the core of Manifest Destiny makes it difficult to separate the notion of Christian virtue from a concept of civic virtue, or a concept of the life of toil from the cursed nature of a fallen human condition." Daehnke, *In the Work of Their Hands*, 15.
54. As noted earlier, this is the phrase that journalist John O'Sullivan used to coin the term *Manifest Destiny* in 1845. Stephanson, *Manifest Destiny*, 42.
55. Langford, "Wonders of the Yellowstone," June 1871, 128.
56. This "grand plan" is tied to American imperial conquests justified by Manifest Destiny. As Richard White emphasizes: "The railroads reconstructed space into empire. Railroads were tools of dispossession and possession alike." White also notes the racial intentions of the Northern Pacific Railroad in particular; he quotes W. Milnor Roberts, chief engineer of the Northern Pacific, who wrote that the completion of the railroad "will forever settle the question of white supremacy over an area of country covering 450,000 square miles." White, *Railroaded*, 46.
57. Katherine Early notes that Nathaniel Langford's 1871 speaking tour about the wonders of Yellowstone coincided with a major bond drive for the Northern Pacific Railroad. Early, *Benefit and Enjoyment of the People*, 28.
58. Haines, *Yellowstone Story*, 1:138. Gareth John characterizes Ferdinand V. Hayden as the personification of "the universalizing and synthetic approach to western

exploration" whose scientific expeditions "bolstered the nationalist cause of Manifest Destiny." John, "Yellowstone as 'Landscape Idea,'" 8–9.

59. Foster, *Strange Genius*, 203.

60. Quoted in Foster, *Strange Genius*, 207.

61. John observes that "pictorial practices" of nineteenth-century exploration of North American territories "were constitutive of a visual discourse on the West, including more specifically Yellowstone, and were integral to scientific explorative practice and the constitution of geographical knowledge." John, "Yellowstone as 'Landscape Idea,'" 9.

62. Hales, *William Henry Jackson*, 85.

63. Hales, *William Henry Jackson*, 100; Foster, *Strange Genius*, 169; and Hassrick, *Drawn to Yellowstone*, 45.

64. Jay Cooke had chosen Moran based on the artist's reputation as a "rare genius" who Cooke realized would be useful in promoting the railroad with paintings of western landscapes. Wilkins and Hinkley, *Thomas Moran*, 80. Gen. Alvred B. Nettleton, Cooke's close associate and office manager, arranged for Moran to accompany the expedition "on less than two weeks' notice." His subsequent letter introducing Moran to Hayden explained that the artist "goes out under the patronage of Messrs. Scribner and Co., Publishers, NY and our Mr. Cooke on whom . . . you will confer a great favor by receiving Mr. Moran into your party." Quoted in Early, *Benefit and Enjoyment of the People*, 66.

65. Moran borrowed five hundred dollars from Jay Cooke for his expenses to accompany Hayden on the expedition to Yellowstone. Moran later produced a watercolor series of sixteen Yellowstone landscapes for Cooke, "commissioned no doubt to settle his debt to the financier." Wilkins and Hinkley, *Thomas Moran*, 96–97.

66. Quoted in Wilkins and Hinkley, *Thomas Moran*, 95.

67. Katherine Early relates that when Thomas Moran joined the Hayden expedition in the summer of 1871, the artist was "an inexperienced woodsman who had never before ridden a horse." Early, *Benefit and Enjoyment of the People*, 66.

68. On several occasions Moran and Jackson departed from the others to photograph and sketch the scenery and features of Yellowstone. At the Grand Canyon of the Yellowstone River, for instance, they remained for an additional four days after the rest of the survey company had moved on. See Wilkins and Hinkley, *Thomas Moran*, 91.

69. Katherine Early says of the 1871 Hayden survey of Yellowstone, "The specimens, reports and photographs provided the 'objective' proof which was necessary in the campaign to set Yellowstone aside. Jackson and Moran's images proved the area's beauty, and with this mixture of aesthetic, scientific and political support,

the drive to preserve Yellowstone began." Early, *Benefit and Enjoyment of the People*, 17. John Clayton points out that Hayden's ostensible pursuit of scientific knowledge realized important cultural objectives as he articulated "how an unfamiliar landscape could be folded into the era's dominant culture." Clayton, *Wonderlandscape*, 5.

70. Haines, *Yellowstone Story*, 1:155. Nettleton's letter credits the idea for a national park to Judge William D. Kelley, and it mentions the precedent of Yosemite.

71. Haines, *Yellowstone Story*, 1:166–69. Patin notes how the artistic visual representations of Yellowstone were instrumental in passing the Yellowstone Act "since painting conflated the natural wonders of the west and nineteenth-century American culture." By domesticating the wildlands of Yellowstone as a "park," the legislators initiated "the open secret" of wilderness, "that the garden has been designed and placed where the Other (Wilderness) is supposed to be." Patin, "Exhibitions and Empire," 57 and 58. Patin cites the work of William Chaloupka and R. McGreggor Cawley, "The Great Wild Hope: Nature, Environmentalism, and the Open Secret."

72. Haines, *Yellowstone Story*, 1:169.

73. For a discussion of the legislative process that passed the Yellowstone Act, see Haines, *Yellowstone Story*, 1:166–72. George Black also discusses the lobbying effort and legislative debate over the Yellowstone Act in Black, *Empire of Shadows*, 353–54.

74. Art historian Joni Kinsey notes how Moran's paintings in particular transformed popular perceptions of Yellowstone; she concludes that "what had been perceived as distant, sinister, and hellish places before 1870 became, through his portrayals, places of magnificence and wonder that could stand as important symbols of America's uniqueness." Kinsey, "Thomas Moran's Surveys," 34.

75. For the unveiling of Moran's twelve-by-seven-foot painting on May 2, 1872, see Wilkins and Hinkley, *Thomas Moran*, 3–5; and Kinsey, *Thomas Moran and the Surveying of the American West*, 64.

76. Moran reported in a letter to Hayden that just before the official unveiling of his *Grand Cañon of the Yellowstone* painting in 1872, officials of the Northern Pacific Railroad, including the president, vice president, and several directors, had visited him to view the painting and expressed their enthusiasm. Merrill, *Yellowstone and the Great West*, 209.

77. Wilkins and Hinkley, *Thomas Moran*, 4. Wilkins and Hinkley describe Moran's painting as his "Great Picture," referencing the nineteenth-century convention of "a very large painting exhibited publicly and conceived in subject to appeal to a wide spectrum of public taste" (315 n. 2). As he created the painting, according to Gareth John, "Moran's greatest challenge . . . was in recreating the novel and

seemingly unnatural coloration of various geological forms." John, "Yellowstone as 'Landscape Idea,'" 16.

78. Referencing W. J. T. Mitchell's idea of "imperial landscape," Thomas Patin highlights how "landscape becomes an instrument of social and cultural constructs and relations and through which social and subjective identities are formed." Consequently, through the representational rhetoric of nature and national parks, "natural wonders can be converted into national heritage." Patin, "Exhibitions and Empire," 41–42 and 43. With reference to Denis E. Cosgrove's notion of the "landscape idea as 'a way of seeing,'" Gareth John emphasizes how "landscape discourse comprised a range of historical-geographical practices—from the commissioning, production, publication, and circulation of landscape paintings, sketches, and descriptions to the conducting of scientific exploration and the resultant production of maps and publication of scientific data—all drawing or pressing upon to varying degrees prevailing constructs of nationhood, race, and gender . . . as well as conventions of authorship and authority." John, "Yellowstone as 'Landscape Idea,'" 21 n. 3.

79. Hassrick, *Drawn to Yellowstone*, 42. Moran's painting exemplifies what Albert Boime describes as the "magisterial gaze" of nineteenth-century American landscape painting that utilizes an elevated perspective representing from above "not only a visual line of sight but an ideological one as well." This gaze, as depicted in literature and art of the nineteenth century in terms of a "commanding view," involves "the perspective of the American on the heights searching for new worlds to conquer," becoming, in Boime's estimation, a "metonymic image . . . of the desire for dominance." As a literary and artistic representation of Manifest Destiny, "the magisterial gaze embodied the exaltation of a cultured American elite before the illimitable horizon that they identified with the destiny of the American nation." Boime, *Magisterial Gaze*, 2, 20–21, and 38.

80. Neither the far-off hot springs nor the Teton Mountains are actually visible from the Grand Canyon of the Yellowstone, but according to his biographers, Moran "did not hesitate to take liberty with the facts of topography." Wilkins and Hinkley, *Thomas Moran*, 100. Grusin discusses the "composite nature" of the *Grand Cañon of the Yellowstone* painting as a faithful rendition that "allows Moran to represent elements that reflected not only the temper of his mind on that day but also the temper of the survey more generally." Grusin, *Culture, Technology, and the Creation of America's National Parks*, 90. Moran himself explained: "Every form introduced into the picture is within view from a given point, but the relations of the separate parts to one another are not always preserved. . . . My aim was to bring before the public the character of that region." Quoted in John, "Yellowstone as 'Landscape Idea,'" 18.

81. Hassrick, *Drawn to Yellowstone*, 42.
82. Bedell, *The Anatomy of Nature*, 134.
83. John, "Yellowstone as 'Landscape Idea,'" 18–19.
84. John Clayton concludes that "Moran's work tied together the unique, the natural, and the vast in a way that people could interpret as implying God's grace even in the West. Yellowstone, in his vision, was super-sublime." In particular, Clayton continues, Moran's artistry portrayed a land that "could speak for God. And God, Americans of the time believed, had a plan for this nation. It was a Manifest Destiny for the special people of this special country to occupy these landscapes from sea to sea." Clayton, *Wonderlandscape*, 15. For Moran's propensity "to suggest the late nineteenth-century concept of the Far West as Eden" in his Yellowstone paintings, see Morand, "Thomas Moran," 18.
85. Americans in the 1870s, according to Clayton, viewed Yellowstone as an expression of Manifest Destiny. "Yellowstone," he declares, "stood for what America thought was best about itself." Clayton, *Wonderlandscape*, 15. What nineteenth-century Americans "thought was best about itself" informed a "spiritual aesthetic" that "led painters to create landscape art that was charged with the task of reproducing nature as 'a holy text which revealed truth and also offered it for interpretation.'" Daehnke, *In the Work of Their Hands*, 68, quoting Barbara Novak.
86. Wilkins and Hinkley, *Thomas Moran*, 5; and Hassrick, *Drawn to Yellowstone*, 42.
87. McCarron-Cates, "Best Possible View," 107. Garreth John compares the cultural impact of Moran's nineteenth-century painting to the impact in the twentieth century of the first photographs of Earth from the moon. John, "Yellowstone as 'Landscape Idea,'" 17.
88. John, "Yellowstone as 'Landscape Idea,'" 4.
89. Richard Grusin characterizes U.S. national parks as "technologies that work in concert with other cultural forces to enmesh the unclaimed and undeveloped wilderness lands of the American West into the social, political, and economic networks of Eastern capitalism." Grusin, *Culture, Technology, and the Creation of America's National Parks*, 10–11. Similarly, in her analysis of the photographs of Tseng Kwong Chi, Iyko Day observes, "An uninhabited space where a pure white wilderness exists as a refuge from corrupting human influences," as national parks have been characterized from their earliest years, actually involves instead "the capitalist conversion of Indigenous territory into tourist sites." Day, "Tseng Kwong Chi," 106.
90. As explained earlier, this is how John O'Sullivan defined *Manifest Destiny* when he coined the term in 1845. Also mentioned earlier is Joel Daehnke's observation of "the 'peculiar fusion' of providential and republican ideologies at the core of Manifest Destiny." Daehnke, *In the Work of Their Hands*, 15.

91. Regarding the role of scenic wonders in U.S. national identity, Iyko Day cites Patrick Wolfe to conclude, "In Canada and the United States, British settler nations whose colonial objective was primarily land appropriation rather than the exploitation of Indigenous labor, national identity has often been defined as a product of the landscape." Day, "Tseng Kwong Chi," 95.

92. Gene Edward Veith demonstrates the religious and spiritual associations of early American art. For nineteenth-century artists and critics, he argues, "aesthetic issues themselves were understood to have spiritual meaning." Veith, *Painters of Faith*, 13. Thomas Moran in particular exemplifies the landscape artists' attention to geological science in their attempt to convey moral and spiritual lessons in their paintings. As Rebecca Bedell emphasizes, these artists took earnest interest in the geological sciences, best demonstrated in the close relationship between Moran and Hayden (and later Moran's association with John Wesley Powell). They maintained, however, a decidedly conservative view of geology "that found evidence of God's shaping hand in the fabric of the earth, a geology that could draw moral and spiritual lessons from stones." Ultimately, in Bedell's opinion, it was a "valiant yet ultimately futile effort to preserve the unity of God and nature." Bedell, *Anatomy of Nature*, xi. "Moran, far more successfully than his predecessors," concludes John Clayton, "could see Western landscapes—with their unsurpassed vastness and grandeur largely unspoiled by Anglo development—as profound and divine." Clayton, *Wonderlandscape*, 14.

93. In partnership with scientists, especially geologists, nineteenth-century landscape artists played a crucial role in revealing the aesthetic and spiritual value of the land to the U.S. public; as Rebecca Bedell observes, "Their work was directed toward the same ambitious ends: the observation, collection, and analysis of information that would elucidate the American land, chart its ancient history and topography, map its natural resources, detail its scenic attractions, in short, make it known." Bedell, *Anatomy of Nature*, 124. Floramae McCarron-Cates concludes, "Taken together, the paintings, drawings, and oil sketches of iconic scenery and views by Church, Homer, and Moran, along with the photographs and wood engravings of these same locations, reinforced the intellectual concept of a heritage shared by all Americans." McCarron-Cates, "Best Possible View," 107. Specifically in regard to Yellowstone and subsequent national parks, Gareth John regards Moran's *Grand Cañon of the Yellowstone* as "symptomatic and representative of a broader landscape movement or tradition that . . . contributed in a critical way to the establishment of America's first national park and consequently to the national park system." John, "Yellowstone as 'Landscape Idea,'" 6.

94. Stephanson, *Manifest Destiny*, 66.

95. Raab, "Panoramic Vision, Telegraphic Language," 496.

96. A description and interpretation of Gast's painting appears in Raab, "Panoramic Vision, Telegraphic Language," 505–10.

97. The racial implications of western settlement became explicit in Croffutt's 1876 guide, in which he exclaims that the American West "has been occupied by over half a million of the most adventurous, active, honest, and progressive white people that the world can produce." Quoted in Raab, "Panoramic Vision, Telegraphic Language," 499.

98. Albert Boime points out that Gast's painting illustrates the sort of promotional hype that railroads and tour operators indulged in to boost profits. Boime, *Magisterial Gaze*, 133. The woman at the center of Gast's painting, in the view of Jennifer Raab, represents an "allegorical figure of nation and empire" that appears as "the physical manifestation of an immaterial belief, the embodiment of manifest destiny." She occupies a "panoramic position" that, according to Raab, "aestheticizes the racial and environmental destruction occurring beneath her" and where "the messiness of history and politics is purified." Raab, "Panoramic Vision, Telegraphic Language," 506–8.

99. Though we can identify the signing of the Yellowstone Act as the exact moment of transformation, Gareth John regards the transformation of Yellowstone "from Wilderness to Wonderland" as a two-year process involving four expeditions to the headwaters of the Yellowstone River and culminating with the unveiling of Moran's "Big Picture." He contends that "after 1869, numerous accounts and images transformed [Yellowstone] from a mythical wilderness, a fearful place where hell bubbled to the surface, to a scientifically validated, nationally revered 'spectacle of nature.'" John, "Yellowstone as 'Landscape Idea,'" 4. More generally, William Cronon's influential essay about the American conceptualization of wilderness notes how spectacular scenery (e.g., Niagara Falls, the Catskills, the Adirondacks, Yosemite, and Yellowstone) became appealing tourist destinations for "a growing number of citizens [who] had to visit and see them for themselves." Cronon, "Trouble with Wilderness," 72.

100. Frederick Law Olmsted, for instance, envisioned New York's Central Park as an Edenic refuge for the urban working class. Stoll, *Inherit the Holy Mountain*, 97. Regarding the transformation of Yellowstone from wild land to civilized park, Lynn Ross-Bryant notes that white Americans desired to experience the wonders of nature "from the protection of civilization." She quotes Truman Everts, the member of the Washburn expedition who became lost and nearly died in Yellowstone, who predicted in 1871 that "the wonders of the Yellowstone will be made accessible to all lovers of sublimity, grandeur and novelty in natural scenery, and its majestic waters become the abode of civilization and refinement." Ross-Bryant, *Pilgrimage to the National Parks*, 61–62.

3. Pilgrimage to Wonderland

1. Wheeler, *6,000 Miles through Wonderland*, 82.

2. Cornelius Hedges, the Montana Freemason who participated in the Washburn expedition of 1870, predicted the sort of reverence that pilgrim-tourists like Wheeler would experience at the Grand Canyon of the Yellowstone. Hedges wrote, in an article published in the *Helena Daily Herald* shortly after returning from the 1870 expedition, that the Lower Falls of the Yellowstone River were "surely destined at no distant day to become a shrine for a world-wide pilgrimage." Quoted in Schullery, *Searching for Yellowstone*, 283–84 n. 17.

3. Lynn Ross-Bryant argues that its popularity as a pilgrimage destination for nineteenth-century American travelers hinges on Yellowstone's embodiment of "the value issues at the heart of late nineteenth-century American culture—and at least created the possibility of tourists reflecting on these dilemmas through the power—both demonic and wonderful—of the National Park." Ross-Bryant, *Pilgrimage to the National Parks*, 70.

4. Historian Paul Schullery notes that in the early years of the park, "the only way to move large numbers of people through Yellowstone and allow them the opportunity to view the recognized 'wonders' (primarily the geological and geothermal features) was through industrial tourism." Schullery, *Searching for Yellowstone*, 101.

5. This chapter focuses mainly on park visitors from the United States, but Yellowstone was also an appealing destination for nineteenth-century European travelers. Among the most celebrated were Windham Thomas Wyndam-Quin, the fourth Earl of Dunraven, who toured the park in 1874. See Dunraven, *Great Divide*. Another British writer, Rudyard Kipling, visited in 1889; his account is reprinted in Schullery, *Old Yellowstone Days*, 85–114. Regarding nineteenth-century German tourists to Yellowstone, see Pfund, "Western Nature."

6. Haines, *Yellowstone Story*, 1:171–72.

7. Norton, *Wonder-Land Illustrated*, 11.

8. Norton, *Wonder-Land Illustrated*, 16.

9. Norton, *Wonder-Land Illustrated*, 23.

10. Norton, *Wonder-Land Illustrated*, 28.

11. Norton, *Wonder-Land Illustrated*, 38–39.

12. Norton, *Wonder-Land Illustrated*, 78.

13. Norton, *Wonder-Land Illustrated*, 44.

14. Stanley, *Rambles in Wonderland*, 61. Reverend Stanley's book enjoyed a favorable reception among nineteenth-century readers, perhaps in part, as Yellowstone historian Lee Whittlesey notes, "because men of the cloth were often educated

and credible during a time when many other persons were not." Whittlesey credits Stanley's travelogue for inspiring "other clerics who seized upon Yellowstone almost immediately as a vehicle from which to 'celebrate the glories of the Creator.'" Whittlesey, *Storytelling in Yellowstone*, 75–76.

15. Stanley, *Rambles in Wonderland*, 60.

16. Stanley, *Rambles in Wonderland*, 65.

17. Stanley, *Rambles in Wonderland*, 71.

18. Stanley, *Rambles in Wonderland*, 95.

19. Stanley, *Rambles in Wonderland*, 71–72.

20. Stanley, *Rambles in Wonderland*, 77–78.

21. Stanley, *Rambles in Wonderland*, 135.

22. Stanley, *Rambles in Wonderland*, 140.

23. Stanley, *Rambles in Wonderland*, 96.

24. Sears, *Sacred Places*, 10.

25. Davidson et al., *Frederic Church, Winslow Homer, and Thomas Moran*, 4–6. William Cronon notes how spectacular scenery (e.g., Niagara Falls, the Catskills, the Adirondacks, Yosemite, and Yellowstone) became appealing tourist destinations in nineteenth-century America for "a growing number of citizens [who] had to visit and see them for themselves." Cronon, "Trouble with Wilderness," 72.

26. Quoted in Schullery, *Searching for Yellowstone*, 100.

27. As early as 1867, the indescribable wonder of Yellowstone was recognized in the *Virginia City (MT) Post* in an article exclaiming that "language is not adequate to convey an idea of the marvelous beauty of scenery, which is beyond the power of descriptions, and begets a wonderful fascination of the mind of the beholder who reverently gazes at the snow crowned summits." Quoted in John, "Yellowstone as 'Landscape Idea,'" 10.

28. A similar frustration also dogged some artists. While touring Yellowstone in 1893, artist Frederic Remington remarked about the view of the Golden Gate Pass, in the northern part of the park: "It is one of those marvellous [*sic*] vistas of mountain scenery utterly beyond the pen or brush of any man. Paint cannot touch it, and words are wasted." Quoted in Hassrick, *Drawn to Yellowstone*, 117.

29. Hassrick, *Drawn to Yellowstone*, 94.

30. Daehnke, *In the Work of Their Hands*, 87–88. The Kipling quotation is in Schullery, *Old Yellowstone Days*, 98.

31. Emerson, *Nature, Addresses and Lectures*, 62.

32. Thoreau, *Walden*, 350. Thoreau would eventually be recognized as a foundational figure in the American environmental movement. As historian Mark Stoll states, "During the countercultural 1960s and 1970s Thoreau was canonized as the greatest saint in the environmental pantheon." Stoll, *Inherit the Holy Mountain*, 215.

33. Whitman, *Leaves of Grass*, iii and 52.

34. William Cronon writes, "Sublime landscapes were those rare places on earth where one had more chance than elsewhere to glimpse the face of God." Cronon, "Trouble with Wilderness," 73.

35. Norton, *Wonder-Land Illustrated*, 39.

36. This is according to environmental historian Roderick Nash, who also concludes, "Sublimity suggested the association of God and wild nature." Nash, *Wilderness and the American Mind*, 45–46.

37. Katherine Early identifies how a "romantic understanding of nature issued in dichotomies" among the genteel class of nineteenth-century Americans. For them nature was, on the one hand, pastoral and benevolent, while at the same time it was wild, uncultivated, and malevolent. Both views of nature were valued, but the sublime was prized more than the beautiful, "since it inspired such deep emotions within the beholder." Early notes that the sublime also was dichotomous, as it evoked feelings of awe and terror, even though appreciating nature had become a cultural duty of educated Americans. She concludes: "This ambivalence toward nature, even in romanticism, helps to explain why conservation and development were still so closely linked in the 1870s. People were beginning to appreciate both aspects of nature, the wild and the tame, but overall, the need to dominate the wild side was still stronger than the urge to appreciate it." Early, *"For the Benefit and Enjoyment of the People,"* 23–24.

38. Stonerook, *Off the Beaten Track*, 34–35.

39. Yellowstone was known as "Wonderland" from its earliest days as a national park and even before. An 1871 *New York Times* editorial on Yellowstone bore the headline "The New Wonderland." John, "Yellowstone as 'Landscape Idea,'" 12. The Northern Pacific Railroad adopted *Wonderland* as its promotional moniker to encourage visitation to the Pacific Northwest as a whole but especially for Yellowstone. Schullery, *Searching for Yellowstone*, 89.

40. Stanley, *Rambles in Wonderland*, 154.

41. Culpin, *"For the Benefit and Enjoyment of the People,"* 9–38.

42. Stanley, *Rambles in Wonderland*, 7.

43. In their book on Christian pilgrimage traditions, anthropologists Victor and Edith Turner observe, "Some form of deliberate travel to a far place intimately associated with the deepest, most cherished, axiomatic values of the traveler seems to be a 'cultural universal.' If it is not religiously sanctioned, counseled, or encouraged, it will take other forms." Turner and Turner, *Image and Pilgrimage*, 241. Lynn Ross-Bryant includes American national parks in this universal practice of travel to places that embody "the values that orient the culture." Ross-Bryant, *Pilgrimage to the National Parks*, 7.

44. This and the following paragraphs are adapted from Bremer, "Tourism and Pilgrimage."

45. Turner and Turner, *Image and Pilgrimage*, 20.

46. Regarding the historical relationships between pilgrimage traditions and modern tourism, see Badone and Roseman, *Intersecting Journeys*; Bremer, "Touristic Spirit in Places of Religion"; Bremer, "Worshiping at Nature's Shrine"; Feifer, *Going Places*; and Kaelber, "Paradigms of Travel." Historian John Sears considers nineteenth-century American tourist attractions as pilgrimage destinations, concluding that "tourist attractions suggested transcendent meanings and functioned as the sacred places of nineteenth-century American society." Sears, *Sacred Places*, 7. Joel Daehnke notes how the practice of tourism for an elite class of nineteenth-century Americans "was an activity particularly suited to a moral ideology of leisure, given its advocacy of a sustained withdrawal from the affairs of business and its reverence toward the natural," as it invested these Victorian travelers "with what amounted to a near religious experience of an abstention from labor and the pursuit of wealth." Daehnke, *In the Work of Their Hands*, 72.

47. Brown, *Inventing New England*, 1–14.

48. For a history of train travel to Yellowstone, see Waite, *Yellowstone by Train*. On the history of transcontinental railroads and their role in developing the American West, see White, *Railroaded*.

49. Paul Schullery notes that once railroad service reached Yellowstone's boundary, a visit to the park, "whether it took five days, seven days, or several weeks, contained the same elements." Schullery, *Searching for Yellowstone*, 101. William J. Hunt Jr. describes the transformation of the visitor experience in the first two decades of the park from "rough and ready" tourism in a roadless expanse of wilderness to a conventional itinerary that introduced "thousands of tourists each year to an area so fantastic it became generally known as 'Wonderland.'" Hunt, "Heart of the Park," 80–81.

50. The town of Cinnabar, Montana, sprung up in 1883 as the terminus of the Northern Pacific Railroad's Yellowstone branch line when the railroad could not acquire the right-of-way to Gardiner at the park's north entrance. Just as quickly as it materialized, though, Cinnabar disappeared soon after the rail lines were at last able to extend the last three miles to Gardiner, in 1903. See Dick, "Cinnabar," 15–24.

51. The National Hotel opened in 1883 but struggled through bankruptcy and a workers' strike in its first two years of operation. See Culpin, *History of Concession Development*, 25–27.

52. Quoted in Meyer, *Spirit of Yellowstone*, 92.

53. Miller, *Adventures in Yellowstone*, 195.

54. Miller, *Adventures in Yellowstone*, 190–91.

55. Harrison, *Summer's Outing*, 62.

56. Harrison, *Summer's Outing*, 80.

57. Harrison, *Summer's Outing*, 61.

58. Gillis, *Another Summer*, 29.

59. Bremer, "Worshiping at Nature's Shrine," 5.

60. Cynthia Hahn notes that Christian pilgrimage objects from late antiquity were regarded by pilgrims of the time "as repositories of the *eulogiae* or 'blessings' that the pilgrims sought to obtain from their visits to the *loca sancta* of the Holy Land." Hahn, "Loca Sancta Souvenirs," 86. Similarly, Gary Vikan, a scholar of Byzantine culture, remarks in a book relating Elvis Presley's Memphis, Tennessee, home of Graceland to medieval Christian pilgrimage destinations that "all *loca sancta* from the earliest centuries of Christianity to the present day" are places "not only to see and touch relics, [but also] to acquire sacred souvenirs." Vikan, *From the Holy Land to Graceland*, 158. Beverly Gordon explains, "People feel the need to bring things home with them from the sacred, extraordinary time or space, for home is equated with ordinary, mundane time and space. They can't hold on to the non-ordinary experience, for it is by nature ephemeral, but they can hold on to a tangible piece of it, an object that came from it." Gordon, "Souvenir," 136. In her philosophical contemplation of souvenirs, Susan Stewart emphasizes how the material object "authenticates the experience." "We might say," she notes, "that this capacity of objects to serve as traces of authentic experience is, in fact, exemplified by the souvenir. The souvenir distinguishes experiences." Stewart, *On Longing*, 134–35.

61. Norris, "Meanderings of a Mountaineer," 57.

62. Haines, *Yellowstone Story*, 1:204–5.

63. Stanley, *Rambles in Wonderland*, 109.

64. The 1873 "Bozeman Memorial," quoted in Haines, *Yellowstone Story*, 1:214.

65. Quoted in Haines, *Yellowstone Story*, 1:200. Haines recognizes Captain Ludlow's scientific elitism in criticizing common tourists while ignoring the scientific removal of specimens. "These people were vandals all," Haines writes, "whether their trophies served a parlor knick-knack cabinet or a museum exhibit case."

66. Gregory, "Report," 28.

67. Anderson, "Protection of the Yellowstone National Park," 381.

68. Walter Scribner Schuyler manuscript journal of a surveying trip to Yellowstone for the U.S. Army in the summer of 1880, 19, HL.

69. Stonerook, *Off the Beaten Track*, 24–25.

70. Montana Historical Society, *F. Jay Haynes*, 12 and 77; Culpin, *History of Concession Development*, 25; and Tilden, *Following the Frontier*, 139. Besides his photography

enterprise, Haynes also operated transportation services in the park. Culpin, *History of Concession Development*, 44; and Tilden, *Following the Frontier*, 389–90.

71. Montana Historical Society, *F. Jay Haynes*, 14.

72. Montana Historical Society, *F. Jay Haynes*, 16.

73. Besides their own reliance on artists and writers to promote Yellowstone, Peter Hassrick notes that the railroad's "vast advertising literature" instigated an exponential growth in book and magazine publications seeking "to feed their readers an appealing diet of richer and richer Yellowstone fare." Hassrick, *Drawn to Yellowstone*, 94.

74. Haines, *Yellowstone Story*, 1:144. Matthew McGuirk built the health spa camp, called "Chestnutville," on the Boiling River near its effluence into the Gardiner River beginning in 1871. He attempted to claim the land in 1872, just one week after enactment of the Yellowstone Act, for the "improvements" to "McGuirk's Medicinal Springs," consisting of a house, ditch, fence, and barn. McGuirk operated his camp until 1874. Culpin, *History of Concession Development*, 2. These were not the first uses of the hot springs for bathing and healing. Evidence indicates that local American Indian tribes had used Yellowstone's thermal attractions for "spiritual bathing" long before Euro-Americans arrived in the region. According to Nez Perce historian Adeline Fredin, "geysers / hot springs were a ceremonial and religious part in our history/prehistory. . . . It was one place where the Great Spirit existed and we could bath [*sic*] the body and spirit directly." This is from a correspondence with Joseph Weixelman that he included in his master's thesis, "The Power to Evoke Wonder: Native Americans and the Geysers of Yellowstone National Park" (Montana State University, 1992), quoted in Black, *Empire of Shadows*, 496 n. 1.

75. Stanley, *Rambles in Wonderland*, 57–58.

76. Harrison, *Summer's Outing*, 70. Yellowstone's thermal waters were used for therapeutic purposes well into the early twentieth century. For instance, when the Fountain Hotel opened in 1891, it had a separate plumbing system that delivered the medicinal properties of the nearby hot springs to guests. But as Paul Schullery notes, "Yellowstone never suffered the kind of wholesale destruction and alteration visited upon other geothermal areas, probably because park managers [by the end of the nineteenth century] had already developed a sense of the worth of the unhindered expression of nature in at least this one respect." Schullery, *Searching for Yellowstone*, 142.

77. Stonerook, *Off the Beaten Track*, 5.

78. Stanley, *Rambles in Wonderland*, 20.

79. Stanley, *Rambles in Wonderland*, 37.

80. Stanley, *Rambles in Wonderland*, 37–38.

81. Robert Berkhofer discusses the ambivalence of attitudes toward Native Americans in terms of white American constructions of their own identity. Berkhofer, *White Man's Indian*, 27–31.

82. Norris's editorial appeared in September 1876, little more than a year following George Armstrong Custer's final defeat, which enraged American citizens against all native peoples. It can be found in Norris, "Meanderings of a Mountaineer."

83. Regarding the Nez Perce in Yellowstone, see Haines, *Yellowstone Story*, 1:219–37.

84. "Report upon the Yellowstone National Park to the Secretary of the Interior" by P. W. Norris, superintendent for the Year 1877, 842, copy in YA.

85. Norris, "Report upon the Yellowstone National Park," 981.

86. Norris, "Meanderings of a Mountaineer," 90.

87. Grant's third State of the Union address delivered December 4, 1871, is available online at https://millercenter.org/the-presidency/presidential-speeches/december-4-1871-third-annual-message (accessed October 17, 2024).

88. Mark Stoll draws attention to how a "Reformed Edenic landscape manifested itself in state and national parks, beginning with the first park, Yosemite in 1864." Stoll, *Inherit the Holy Mountain*, 98.

89. Art historian Albert Boime identifies the "magisterial gaze" of nineteenth-century American landscape painting with "the desire for dominance" inherent in the logic of Manifest Destiny. Boime, *Magisterial Gaze*, 21.

90. Harrison, *Summer's Outing*, 28.

91. Harrison, *Summer's Outing*, 37.

92. Regarding the persistent myth that American Indians feared Yellowstone, see Weixelman, "Fear or Reverence"; and Whittlesey, "Native Americans, the Earliest Interpreters."

93. Wheeler, *6,000 Miles through Wonderland*, 82.

4. Sacred Nature and the White Race

1. Whittlesey and Schullery, "Roosevelt Arch," 9.

2. Whittlesey and Schullery, "Roosevelt Arch," 6.

3. Whittlesey and Schullery, "Roosevelt Arch," 12.

4. Whittlesey and Schullery, "Roosevelt Arch," 13.

5. Whittlesey and Schullery, "Roosevelt Arch," 12–13.

6. Whittlesey and Schullery, "Roosevelt Arch," 13, quoting news reports.

7. Whittlesey and Schullery, "Roosevelt Arch," 13.

8. A transcript of Roosevelt's speech at the dedication of the arch is in Whittlesey and Schullery, "Roosevelt Arch," 14–15.

9. Whittlesey and Schullery, "Roosevelt Arch," 14.

10. From the diary of visitor Dorothy Brown Pardo (1911), quoted as the epigraph to Anderson, "Monumental Idea."

11. As Katherine Early observes, at its creation as a national park, Yellowstone "was not intended to advance the concept of conservation." It appears to be a "conservation watershed only in retrospect." In creating the park were "elements of conservation, but most were linked to development." Early, *Benefit and Enjoyment of the People*, 5–6. Roderick Nash likewise notes that the Yellowstone Act of 1872 was intended to protect "curiosities"—such as the geysers and other thermal features as well as the impressive landscapes that tourist visitors desired—and that preservation of wilderness was only incidental to these other purposes. Nash, *Wilderness and the American Mind*, 108. In fact, Nathaniel P. Langford wrote to Columbus Delano, secretary of the Interior, shortly after his appointment as the park's first superintendent asking for clarification of his authority in that role in providing "for the protection of the rights of visitors [for instance, against exorbitant tolls on private roads], and the establishment of such rules as will conduce to their comfort and pleasure," indicating that the first priority of the new national park was for the well-being of visitors rather than for the protection of nature. Letter to the Hon. C. Delano, secretary of the Interior, from N. P. Langford, May 20, 1872, typescript copy in Horace Marden Albright Papers (HMAP), box 27.

12. Whittlesey and Schullery, "Roosevelt Arch," 3.

13. Burroughs, *Camping & Tramping with Roosevelt*, 66–67.

14. Burroughs, *Camping & Tramping with Roosevelt*.

15. Renehan, *John Burroughs*, 77.

16. Quoted in Renehan, *John Burroughs*, 5.

17. Renehan, *John Burroughs*, 6.

18. Warren, *John Burroughs and the Place of Nature*, 150.

19. Quoted in Renehan, *John Burroughs*, 243.

20. Renehan, *John Burroughs*, 242.

21. Quoted in Nash, *Wilderness and the American Mind*, 122.

22. Renehan, *John Burroughs*, 253.

23. Renehan, *John Burroughs*, 213.

24. Renehan, *John Burroughs*, 243.

25. Nash, *Wilderness and the American Mind*, 122.

26. Donald Worster has described Muir as "a prophet, a creative spiritual leader responding to his times with a vision of ultimate meaning and purpose. . . . In Muir's eye, the entire world of nature was suffused with divinity." Worster, "John Muir and the Religion of Nature," 27.

27. Nash, *Wilderness and the American Mind*, 123.

28. Worster, *Passion for Nature*, 37–39.

29. Quoted in Worster, *Passion for Nature*, 48.

30. Stoll, *Inherit the Holy Mountain*, 147.

31. Worster, *Passion for Nature*, 76.

32. Stoll, *Inherit the Holy Mountain*, 148. Stoll documents how "a very large majority of the [early] figures of the standard histories of environmentalism grew up in just two denominations, Congregationalism and Presbyterianism, both in the Calvinist tradition." He characterizes Muir's religious journey as following "a well-worn Scottish Presbyterian path from religion to natural history." Stoll, *Inherit the Holy Mountain*, 2 and 145.

33. As historian of religions Catherine L. Albanese states, "Emerson's *Nature* was to have a profound effect on many, even outside Transcendentalist circles." Albanese, *Nature Religion in America*, 80.

34. Worster, *Passion for Nature*, 209–10.

35. Worster, *Passion for Nature*, 211. In 1893 Muir would make a pilgrimage to Concord, Massachusetts, where he toured Emerson's house and study before paying his respects at the gravesites of both Emerson and Thoreau. Worster, *Passion for Nature*, 335.

36. Worster, *Passion for Nature*, 211–12.

37. Muir, *My First Summer in the Sierra*, 82.

38. Muir, *Our National Parks*, 334.

39. Muir, *Our National Parks*, 303–4.

40. Worster identifies the Yosemite Valley as "the spiritual center" of Muir's home in *Passion for Nature*, 149.

41. Regarding Muir's national reputation as an author, see Worster, *Passion for Nature*, 241.

42. Worster, *Passion for Nature*, 299.

43. Muir, *Our National Parks*, 74.

44. Muir biographer Donald Worster notes that the spiritual aspect in Muir's writings changed as he aged. The somewhat pantheistic views of his younger years, when he declared that "all is beauty, all is God," became more muted in his later writings as he sought to reassure his more conventionally religious Christian readers that beauty is made *by* God rather than being God itself. Worster, *Passion for Nature*, 374–75.

45. Bremer, "Icons of Whiteness." Much of the discussion of John Muir, Theodore Roosevelt, and others in this chapter is adapted from this essay.

46. Muir recounts his sojourn to the American South in *Thousand-Mile Walk*.

47. Worster, *Passion for Nature*, 91.

48. Worster, *Passion for Nature*, 127.

49. Quoted in Worster, *Passion for Nature*, 128. Worster concludes, with a somewhat apologetic tone, that on balance "Muir accepted blacks as part of the family of man and did not come down on the side of southern or northern racists or white supremacists." Worster, *Passion for Nature*, 137.

50. Muir, *My First Summer in the Sierra*, 78.

51. Rebecca Solnit argues in an essay published in the magazine of the Sierra Club, a group that celebrates Muir as its founding president, the absence of native peoples in his depiction of wildlands has had "three terrible impacts": the denial of rights for Native Americans; an impoverished and distorted white understanding of nature and environmental history; and implications for land management policies. Solnit, "John Muir in Native America," 7.

52. Brinkley, *Wilderness Warrior*, 545.

53. Brinkley, *Wilderness Warrior*, 546.

54. Quoted in Brinkley, *Wilderness Warrior*, 184.

55. Quoted in Worster, *Passion for Nature*, 369. Muir's opposition to hunting did not extend to hunting animals for sustenance. Worster, *Passion for Nature*, 355–56. Although he did not share Roosevelt's hypermasculinity, Muir had inconsistent gender assumptions about "Nature," which he often referred to as feminine but also stated that Nature labors "like a man." Daehnke, *In the Work of Their Hands*, 72.

56. Miller, *Gifford Pinchot*, 155.

57. Mintz, "Taking Stock," 45; and Brinkley, *Wilderness Warrior*, 642.

58. Mintz, "Taking Stock," 45.

59. Stoll, *Inherit the Holy Mountain*, 52.

60. Quoted in Wohlforth, *Fate of Nature*, 171–72. W. Paul Reeve's discussion of Theodore Roosevelt and "race suicide" includes a reprint of a 1904 cartoon showing Roosevelt applauding "No Race Suicide" among the Mormons in Utah. Reeve, *Religion of a Different Color*, 250.

61. Charles Wohlforth acknowledges that although Roosevelt clearly supported eugenics as a way to create a white national identity, he also spoke eloquently about the ability of nationalism to transcend race. Wohlforth, *Fate of Nature*, 174. As governor of New York, he sought to ban racial segregation and discrimination in public schools, and as president of the United States, he hosted Booker T. Washington, a leading African American intellectual, at the White House, a gesture that outraged Jim Crow southerners and cost Roosevelt virtually all political support in southern states. Roosevelt also championed anti-lynching laws and supported efforts to end sharecropping practices that continued the economic enslavement of southern African Americans. Brinkley, *Wilderness Warrior*, 373, 404–6, and 433.

62. Quoted in Wohlforth, *Fate of Nature*, 170.

63. "National Conservation Commission," 996.

64. Wohlforth, *Fate of Nature*, 170–71.

65. Brinkley, *Wilderness Warrior*, 276–80; and Wohlforth, *Fate of Nature*, 174.

66. Allen, "Culling the Herd," 62.

67. Allen, "Culling the Herd," 61.

68. Allen, "Culling the Herd," 33.

69. White, *Looking Back from Beulah*, 343.

70. White, *With God in the Yellowstone*, 135.

71. Though Alma White named her denomination "the Pentecostal Union," she came out of the Wesleyan Holiness tradition and had bitter disagreements with rival Pentecostals. These disputes led Vinson Synan to describe White as "the most critical anti-Pentecostal writer of the century." Synan, *Holiness-Pentecostal Tradition*, 202.

72. White, *Titanic Tragedy*, 6.

73. Joel Daehnke describes White's Yellowstone book as "a sustained polemic against the secular complaisance she witnessed among Yellowstone tourists trying hard to enjoy themselves on holiday." It "betrays the urgency of her own millennial outlook, and she claimed the park's true value lay in its proselytizing landscape." Daehnke, *In the Work of Their Hands*, 88.

74. White, *With God in the Yellowstone*, 30–31.

75. White, *With God in the Yellowstone*, 91.

76. White, *With God in the Yellowstone*, 3.

77. White, *With God in the Yellowstone*, 42–43.

78. White, *With God in the Yellowstone*, 43.

79. White, *With God in the Yellowstone*, 54.

80. White, *Voice of Nature*, 30.

81. Stanley, *Feminist Pillar of Fire*, 1.

82. Neal, "Christianizing the Klan," 357.

83. Neal, "Christianizing the Klan," 354.

84. White, *Ku Klux Klan in Prophecy*, 135–36.

85. White, *With God in the Yellowstone*, 67.

86. Muir, *Our National Parks*, 15.

87. Muir, *Our National Parks*, 1–2.

88. Renehan, *John Burroughs*, 5–6.

89. Miller, *Gifford Pinchot*, 154–55.

90. Quoted in Miller, *Gifford Pinchot*, 141.

91. Wohlforth, *Fate of Nature*, 170–71.

92. Muir, *My First Summer in the Sierra*, 82.

5. Evangelizing Wonderland

1. Haines, *Yellowstone National Park Chapel*, 9. Haines notes that the location of this first church is a landmark along the road from Yellowstone to Livingston, Montana.

2. Haines, *Yellowstone Story*, 2:178.

3. Part 3 of Aubrey Haines's two-volume history of Yellowstone National Park discusses the presence of the U.S. Army in the park. For the history of Fort Yellowstone, see Haines, *Yellowstone Story*, 2:162–69.

4. Haines, *Yellowstone National Park Chapel*, 9–10.

5. Haines, *Yellowstone National Park Chapel*, 10.

6. Lauer, "Gardiner Church."

7. Stanley, *Rambles in Wonderland*, 61.

8. Haines, *Yellowstone National Park Chapel*, 11.

9. The building's exterior is native sandstone that was quarried from within the park; Douglas fir was used for the framing of the roof and floors as well as for the finishing of the chapel's interior, and the building had a slate roof. Haines, *Yellowstone National Park Chapel*, 13.

10. Haines, *Yellowstone National Park Chapel*, 14.

11. Haines, *Yellowstone National Park Chapel*, 17. Reverend Pritchard held a service in the chapel while vacationing in Yellowstone in the summer of 1930, and he returned again to preach there a final time in August 1931. Haines, *Yellowstone National Park Chapel*, 20.

12. Haines, *Yellowstone National Park Chapel*, 17. The term *Mormon* is the common colloquial reference to members of the Church of Jesus Christ of Latter-day Saints.

13. Aubrey Haines writes that in 1946 "Superintendent Edmund B. Rogers organized a Church Committee on November 5." Haines, *Yellowstone National Park Chapel*, 22. However, Rogers merely reconstituted an existing committee. A memo from chief park naturalist C. Max Bauer dated October 16, 1946, states that for the previous thirteen years, he had "served on the committee for the management of the chapel." His memo recounts some of the issues relating to the chapel that the committee addressed during that time, and it ends by noting that the other two members of the committee had already left and that he was expecting to be transferred soon. The memo is in YA, box A320, "Church Committee" folder.

14. Haines, *Yellowstone National Park Chapel*, 22.

15. Bremer, *Formed from This Soil*, 352–54.

16. Ost, "Living over the Store," 8.

17. As the name of Ost's organization indicates, A Christian Ministry in the National Parks concentrated on placing its volunteers in U.S. national parks, but over the years it also had operations in national forests, ski resorts, and other sites of outdoor recreation.

18. Typescript copy of "Interview" between Warren Ost and Robert C. Haraden, January 19, 1976, at Yellowstone National Park, in YA, box A-320, "Church Committee, 1972–1978" folder, 4–5.

19. Condon may have first heard of getting seminarians to lead worship in Yellowstone from L. Helmstetter, chairman of the Mission Board for the Montana District of the Evangelical Lutheran Synod, who had sent a letter of April 16, 1948, to Edmund B. Rogers, Yellowstone National Park superintendent, suggesting "a proposition where by an undergraduate of a theological Seminary might be employed in some of the work in the park. He could have church services at various places in the park and at times most suitable to tourists." Superintendent Rogers cordially declined Mr. Helmstetter's proposition, although he likely would have consulted Condon about the idea. The correspondence is in YA, folder 856, "Religious Services," box A-168.

20. For details of a tense meeting of the Park County Ministerial Association, Livingston, Montana, that David de L. Condon, chair of the Superintendent's Church Committee, attended on August 7, 1947, that involved discussion of compensation for ministers conducting services in the park, plus a follow-up request from the Ministerial Association on April 29, 1948, see YA, box A-168, folder 856, "Religious Services."

21. The details of this early history of ACMNP is in "The Administrative Manual: A Christian Ministry in the National Parks," from Central Department of Evangelism, National Council of Churches, n.d. (approx. 1960), 2–3; a copy is in YA, box C-18, "History–GM Winter Ministry" folder.

22. "A Training Manual for A Christian Ministry in the National Parks" (1957), 2; a copy is in YA, box A-322, "Church Committee 1957–59" folder.

23. Hansen, *As It Was in the Beginning*, 9. Albright's role in facilitating the Rockefeller gift is indicated in a letter from H. Conrad Hoyer of the National Lutheran Council to Horace M. Albright, August 12, 1959, in HMAP, box 32, folder 2. In a notice to friends of A Christian Ministry in the National Parks, Warren Ost announced Rockefeller's gift and stated that the funds were "designated especially to provide additional staff expansion." A copy of the announcement is in YA, box C-18, "Church Committee 1957–1959" folder.

24. According to their 1959 recruitment brochure, A Christian Ministry in the National Parks sought to place 142 students in thirty National Park Service units that year. A copy of the brochure is in YA, box C-18, "Church Committee 1957–1959" folder.

25. Hansen, *As It Was in the Beginning*, 7.

26. Ost's 1960 sabbatical report is titled "Worker-Witness in the National Parks." A copy of the printed but unpaginated report is in Warren W. Ost Papers (wwo), box 3.

27. Ost, "Worker-Witness in the National Parks," wwo, box 3.

28. Ost, "Worker-Witness in the National Parks," wwo, box 3.

29. These numbers are from A Christian Ministry in the National Parks recruiting brochure for the 1961 season, available in hmap, box 32, folder 1.

30. A Christian Ministry in the National Parks recruiting brochure for the 1974–76 seasons, available in hmap, box 32, folder 1.

31. Hansen, *As It Was in the Beginning*, 19.

32. Mrs. Blecher's complaint and Stanley Canter's reply are in ya, box a-160, folder a8223, "Special Events 1968: Religious Services, Church Affairs."

33. The Girshmans' account of their encounter with A Christian Ministry in the National Parks is in their essay "Do the National Parks Need a Christian Ministry?"

34. Girshman, "Do the National Parks Need a Christian Ministry."

35. Girshman, "Do the National Parks Need a Christian Ministry."

36. Keith Epstein, "Does Religion Belong in National Parks?" *High Country News* (Paonia co), October 2, 1995.

37. Epstein, "Does Religion Belong in National Parks."

38. A copy of the settlement agreement in the case of Karl M. Girshman, et al. v. Roger G. Kennedy, Director of the National Park Service, and Bruce Babbitt, Secretary, United States Department of the Interior, is available on the Freedom from Religion Foundation website, http://ffrf.org/publications/freethought -today/item/16789-religion-in-national-park-service-regulated (accessed August 2, 2023).

39. Hansen, *As It Was in the Beginning*, 20.

40. "About A Christian Ministry in the National Parks," http://www.acmnp.com /about (accessed October 24, 2024).

41. Author interview with Rev. Dr. William R. Young, Mammoth Hot Springs, Yellowstone National Park wy, August 3, 2006.

42. Interview with Rev. Dr. William R. Young, 2006.

43. Interview with Rev. Dr. William R. Young, 2006.

6. New Age Yellowstone

1. Author interview with Peter Duffy, May 31, 2016.

2. King, *Unveiled Mysteries*, 62.

3. King, *Unveiled Mysteries*, 62.

4. Prophet, Prophet, and Booth, *Masters and Their Retreats*, 490–91.

5. Regarding the Fox sisters and the beginnings of the Spiritualism craze in America, see Braude, *Radical Spirits*, 10–25. It even reached the White House, where First Lady Mary Todd Lincoln hosted séances following her young son Willie's death. Temple, *Abraham Lincoln*, 196–203.

6. Conkin, *American Originals*, 231–32. Mesmerism, based on Anton Mesmer's eighteenth-century metaphysical philosophy of animal magnetism, became established in the United States following the 1836 New England lecture tour of French mesmerist Charles Poyen. Albanese, *Republic of Mind and Spirit*, 190–94.

7. Conkin, *American Originals*, 231.

8. "Spirit is immortal Truth," Mary Baker Eddy writes in *Science and Health*; "matter is mortal error." Eddy, *Science and Health*, 468.

9. Schmidt, *Restless Souls*, 158–60.

10. Prophet, "Theosophical Root Race Theory."

11. In practice New Thought and Theosophy were not entirely separate traditions. They sometimes blended, as in the work of Theosophist Annie Besant, who imported New Thought ideas into Theosophical practices of meditation and yoga. Schmidt, *Restless Souls*, 161–62.

12. Albanese concludes, "Evidence of the reliance of Emma Curtis Hopkins on Evans is compelling." Albanese, *Republic of Mind and Spirit*, 313–16.

13. Quoted in Albanese, *Republic of Mind and Spirit*, 311–12.

14. Albanese, *Republic of Mind and Spirit*, 321.

15. Melton, "Church Universal and Triumphant," 6.

16. Braden, *These Also Believe*, 291.

17. The Ballards were close associates of Spalding, who even lived with them for a while. Braden, *These Also Believe*, 265.

18. Ballard left Chicago about 1928; a grand jury in Chicago indicted him in March 1929, but he was never apprehended on warrants stemming from the indictment. He had settled in Los Angeles prior to the indictment, possibly using an assumed name. Braden, *These Also Believe*, 266.

19. King, *Unveiled Mysteries*, 8.

20. King, *Unveiled Mysteries*, 15.

21. Braden, *These Also Believe*, 293–94.

22. King, *Unveiled Mysteries*, 128.

23. Braden, *These Also Believe*, 267–68.

24. Melton, "Church Universal and Triumphant," 8.

25. Braden, *These Also Believe*, 292.

26. Braden, *These Also Believe*, 263.

27. Albanese, *Republic of Mind and Spirit*, 469. Although the I AM movement recognized all three Ballards as "Accredited Messengers," the son, Donald, never communicated any messages from Ascended Masters. Braden, *These Also Believe*, 270.

28. Braden notes that the term *I AM* does not appear anywhere in Guy Ballard's first book, *Unveiled Mysteries*, detailing his encounters with Saint Germain and introducing the teachings of the Ascended Masters. It was only later that the Ballards adopted the New Thought notion of *I AM* for their movement, which included a complicated and not entirely coherent pantheon drawn from eclectic sources, including Theosophy, classical mythology, astrology, and the Christian Bible. Braden, *These Also Believe*, 291–92. Albanese points out that although it is unclear whether Guy Ballard knew or studied with Annie Rix Militz or her students while he was in Los Angeles, his views accord well with Militz's late teachings about ascension as the ultimate goal of human life in overcoming the cycles of reincarnation. Albanese, *Republic of Mind and Spirit*, 468. Paul Starrs and John Wright connect the Ballards' movement to the 1920s publications by Baird T. Spalding that discuss Ascended Masters as part of an I AM movement. Starrs and Wright, "Utopia, Dystopia, and Sublime Apocalypse," 106. Erin Prophet credits the Ballards with transforming the Theosophical "masters," especially the Mahatmas identified by Helena Blavatsky, "from living adepts into 'Ascended Masters.'" Prophet, "Elizabeth Clare Prophet," 55–56.

29. Albanese, *Republic of Mind and Spirit*, 469.

30. Albanese, *Republic of Mind and Spirit*, 470.

31. Albanese, *Republic of Mind and Spirit*, 468. Pelley's organization even accused Edna Ballard of plagiarizing Pelley's work; they claimed that she had been a student of Pelley's teachings and that her own writings and teachings "are full of material which she appropriated from Mr. Pelley's writings." Quoted in Braden, *These Also Believe*, 268.

32. Edna Ballard and her son, Donald, along with numerous other prominent leaders in the movement were indicted on federal mail fraud charges in 1940. Braden, *These Also Believe*, 284. Their conviction was eventually overturned in a monumental 1944 U.S. Supreme Court decision that ruled emphatically, "Heresy trials are foreign to our Constitution." Regarding the I AM movement's legal troubles of the 1940s, see Schultz, "Bad Faith," 163–67.

33. The rebuilding of the I AM Religious Activity included the purchase of an office building in Chicago's Loop District in 1948, and the organization also established a resort-retreat center near Mount Shasta in California. Melton, "Church Universal and Triumphant," 13.

34. As Albanese notes, "Continuing revelation meant that Ascended Masters could talk freely to whom they chose, and new groups and lineages could be created." Albanese, *Republic of Mind and Spirit*, 471.

35. Melton, "Church Universal and Triumphant," 14. Mark Prophet's given surname was of Scottish origin, "but he also believed it reflected his life's calling." Prophet, "Elizabeth Clare Prophet," 55.

36. Prophet, "Elizabeth Clare Prophet," 55. As Gordon Melton points out, El Morya had long been known in Theosophical circles for his communications with Helena Blavatsky. Melton, "Church Universal and Triumphant," 13–14. According to his son Sean Prophet, Mark initially may not have welcomed El Morya when the apparition first came to him, but then "El Morya 'appeared' to him a second time and convinced him of his reality. My dad then went on to found The Summit Lighthouse on August 7, 1958." BlackSun (pseudonym of Sean Prophet), "El Morya, You Have No Power!" *Black Sun Journal*, posted July 2, 2007, www .blacksunjournal.com/religion/820_el-morya-you-have-no-power_2007.html.

37. Dictations for Mark Prophet and later his wife, Elizabeth Clare Prophet, were often public, "with the messenger standing before a group and speaking as a master in the first person," but they sometimes were conducted in private, "with the messenger writing by hand, typing, or speaking into a tape recorder." Prophet, "Elizabeth Clare Prophet," 55.

38. Although nearly every account of her early life refers to her by her given name of Elizabeth Clare Wulf, she had been recently married when she first met Mark Prophet in 1961. According to a brief biography that appeared in a news periodical at the time of her retirement in 1999, "Her first marriage, at the age of 20, was to Dag Ytreburg, a Norwegian-born lawyer." Scott McMillion, "Selling Off the Promised Land," *High Country News*, March 15, 1999, sidebar: "A Biography of Prophet's Most recent Life," https://www.hcn.org/issues/150/4851.

39. Prophet, "Elizabeth Clare Prophet," 54.

40. Prophet, "Elizabeth Clare Prophet," 53–55.

41. Melton, "Church Universal and Triumphant," 14–15.

42. Prophet, "Elizabeth Clare Prophet," 56.

43. Prophet, "Elizabeth Clare Prophet," 56.

44. Prophet, "Elizabeth Clare Prophet," 56–57.

45. Melton, "Church Universal and Triumphant," 15.

46. Prophet, "Elizabeth Clare Prophet," 57. "According to Church [CUT] teachings, Mark Prophet ascended immediately [following his death in 1973] and is now known as Ascended Master Lanello, the Ever-Present Guru." Melton, "Church Universal and Triumphant," 15. His teachings as dictated through Elizabeth Clare Prophet were compiled in Prophet, *Cosmic Consciousness*.

47. Within days of her husband's death, Edna Ballard declared on January 1, 1940, "Our Blessed Daddy Ballard made his Ascension last night at twelve o'clock from the Royal Teton Retreat, and is now an Ascended Master." Braden, *These Also Believe*, 283.

48. Prophet, "Elizabeth Clare Prophet," 58. After divorcing Randall King and briefly dating others, Elizabeth Clare Prophet "fixed her sights on Edward [Francis], telling him that the masters wanted him to become the messenger's husband and help lead the organization into the future." Although initially hesitant, Francis subsequently agreed, and they were married in 1981. Prophet, *Prophet's Daughter*, 98–99.

49. Prophet, "Elizabeth Clare Prophet," 59.

50. This coincided with an orientalist inclination that Elizabeth Clare Prophet displayed in her preference for saffron or purple robes and Indian saris. Prophet, "Elizabeth Clare Prophet," 53, 56–57.

51. Elizabeth Clare Prophet made this claim in court testimony while defending a lawsuit against the Church Universal and Triumphant by a former member. According to news reports on the trial, Prophet testified, "I received a dictation from the ascended Pope John XXIII conveying the authority for the Church Universal and Triumphant and my leadership in it." Patricia Ward Biederman, "Pope John XXIII Gave Authority to Her, Guru Ma Testifies at Trial," *Los Angeles Times*, February 19, 1986, https://www.latimes.com/archives/la-xpm-1986-02-19 -me-9581-story.html.

52. Bennett, "California Cultbusters."

53. Melton, "Church Universal and Triumphant," 16.

54. Whitsel, *Church Universal and Triumphant*, 51–52. Whitsel notes that although some of the speculation "may have been sensationalized," some of it proved accurate. For instance, church leaders acknowledged in an interview with the *Los Angeles Times* that some members had undergone survival training, and although the church repeatedly denied claims of stockpiling arms, former members reported that "the organization had been secretly hoarding weapons and ammunition since its days in Colorado Springs." Whitsel, *Church Universal and Triumphant*, 52.

55. Whitsel, *Church Universal and Triumphant*, 54.

56. DeHaas, "Mediation of Ideology and Public Image," 29. A news report in December 1980 explains that the U.S. Forest Service had successfully negotiated a deal with the Nature Conservancy to acquire the Forbes land, initially purchasing it and the Forest Service later acquiring it from the Nature Conservancy. However, "the election of Ronald Reagan as president and the Republican capture of the U.S. Senate [in the November 1980 election] 'caused considerable deterioration' in

the likelihood that the Forest Service would get the money to acquire the ranch from the Conservancy," effectively ending the government effort to purchase the land. A clipping of the December 24, 1980, article in the *Missoulian* newspaper along with correspondence regarding the land negotiations are in YA, box L-68, "CUT–Royal Teton Ranch" folder.

57. Church Universal and Triumphant, *Royal Teton Ranch News* 1, no. 1, 5 (photo caption), copy in YA, box A-407, "CUT—correspondence" folder.

58. Prophet, *Prophet's Daughter*, 18.

59. Church Universal and Triumphant, *Royal Teton Ranch News* 1, no. 1, 16 (photo caption).

60. Church Universal and Triumphant, *Royal Teton Ranch News* 1, no. 1, 5 (photo caption). The Grand Teton Mountain is actually closer to one hundred miles south of the Royal Teton Ranch.

61. Church Universal and Triumphant, *Royal Teton Ranch News* 1, no. 1, 1.

62. Church Universal and Triumphant, *Royal Teton Ranch News* 1, no. 1, 1.

63. Church Universal and Triumphant, *Royal Teton Ranch News* 1, no. 1, 1.

64. According to a church publication, they were initially prevented from acquiring the additional ranch by their real estate agent based on what CUT regarded as "religious discrimination"—the agent apparently feared that his reputation would be damaged if he were seen as complicit in the establishment of the Church Universal and Triumphant in Montana. Ultimately, a subsequent investor sold the ranch to the church. Church Universal and Triumphant, *Royal Teton Ranch News* 1, no. 1, 13–14.

65. Church Universal and Triumphant, *Royal Teton Ranch News* 1, no. 1, 14—a complete description of the new ranchland is on p. 15.

66. Church Universal and Triumphant, *Royal Teton Ranch News* 1, no. 1, 6.

67. Church Universal and Triumphant, *Royal Teton Ranch News* 1, no. 1, 7–9.

68. Erin Prophet reveals that the night before he died, her father, Mark Prophet, had told her mother "that if anything happened to him, she should take all of us and go to Montana." Elizabeth Clare Prophet subsequently regarded his statement as "the final instructions of the prophet, given with foreknowledge of his death." Prophet, *Prophet's Daughter*, 17.

69. *Chela* is a Sanskrit term referring to a devoted follower, disciple, or student.

70. Church Universal and Triumphant, *Royal Teton Ranch News* 1, no. 1, 1, 10–11. It's worth recalling that immediately following her husband's death, Elizabeth Clare Prophet had declared Mark Prophet's new status as Ascended Master Lanello. Thus, the emergency food supply presumably carried the blessings, if not the mandate, of the former leader of the movement.

71. Church Universal and Triumphant, *Royal Teton Ranch News* 2, no. 1, 1, copy in YA, box A-407, "CUT—correspondence" folder.

72. Prophet, *Prophet's Daughter*, 99–100.

73. According to news reports, the Church Universal and Triumphant sold its Malibu property in 1986 to Soka University of Tokyo for $15.5 million, with plans for the church to complete its move to Montana by December 1986. "The Controversial Church Universal and Triumphant Has Sold Its Headquarters," July 5, 1986, UPI Archives, https://www.upi.com/Archives/1986/07/05/The-controversial-Church -Universal-and-Triumphant-has-sold-its/2215520920000.

74. For an insider's account of the experience of going underground from someone who was a central figure in CUT's "shelter cycle," see Prophet, *Prophet's Daughter*, 1–15.

75. For a detailed study of Bhagwan Shree Rajneesh, see Gordon, *Golden Guru*.

76. DeHaas, "Mediation of Ideology and Public Image," 26–27.

77. DeHaas, "Mediation of Ideology and Public Image," 29–30. Richard Parks of Gardiner, Montana, spoke to me about concerns in the 1980s and 1990s regarding CUT's lack of planning for adequate sewage treatment and its sometimes contradictory statements about its development plans. Author interview with Richard Parks, June 3, 2016, Gardiner.

78. For a detailed account of Jim Jones and the mass suicide at his Jonestown community, see Chidester, *Salvation and Suicide*.

79. Prophet, *Prophet's Daughter*, 183.

80. Whitsel, *Church Universal and Triumphant*, 106. Whitsel reports that Hamilton had only twenty-six thousand dollars in cash and gold; the larger figure comes from Prophet, *Prophet's Daughter*, 191.

81. "*Newsweek, Time, U.S. News and World Report, Macleans*, and a number of other national and international media sources offered profiles on 'the Church with an arsenal.'" Whitsel, *Church Universal and Triumphant*, 108. Regarding the comparison to Jim Jones, Oprah Winfrey's show on CUT in September 1989 opened with footage of the church's Montana property "intercut with bloating bodies at Jonestown, rotting in the South American sun." Prophet, *Prophet's Daughter*, 196.

82. The purchase of arms itself was not illegal, but Hamilton's use of a false identity to make the purchases, a plan concocted with Edward Francis to hide the church's involvement, violated federal law. Prophet, *Prophet's Daughter*, 183–84.

83. CUT's initial statement to the press insisted that "the church does not own weapons but individual members do. Mr. Hamilton was not on official church business, nor did he use any church funds in his purchases." Prophet, *Prophet's Daughter*, 192.

84. Prophet, *Prophet's Daughter*, 204.

85. In fact, Elizabeth Clare Prophet's claims of innocence were misleading at best. In her memoir Erin Prophet, daughter of Elizabeth Clare Prophet and at the time an aspiring messenger of the Ascended Masters, reveals that her mother knew in advance of the plan to purchase guns and asked Erin to consult with Ascended Master El Morya. "I received an impression of a 'green light' from El Morya," Erin Prophet states, "and a verbal 'go ahead.'" Prophet, *Prophet's Daughter*, 184.

86. Prophet, *Prophet's Daughter*, 132–33.

87. Prophet, *Prophet's Daughter*, 1. Prophet describes the experience of the CUT community taking refuge in their underground shelter on the night of March 14, 1990, in the opening chapter of her book.

88. CUT members built forty-four independent private shelters in the Glastonbury developments, with capacities ranging from 4 to 126 occupants. Prophet, *Prophet's Daughter*, 224. Leighton Quarles, who grew up in the church community, reports that his family stayed that night in a shelter beneath "King Arthur's Court," the main church site above the Yellowstone River in Corwin Springs, Montana. Personal correspondence with the author.

89. A staff member later admitted that "everyone who went into the shelter that night was scared to death." They engaged in all-night prayer sessions and emerged the next morning "emotionally exhausted." Whitsel, *Church Universal and Triumphant*, 110.

90. DeHaas, "Mediation of Ideology and Public Image," 27; and Whitsel, *Church Universal and Triumphant*, 108.

91. Prophet, *Prophet's Daughter*, 132–33.

92. Prophet, *Prophet's Daughter*, 146–48.

93. Prophet, *Prophet's Daughter*, 154–55.

94. According to Erin Prophet, the extension of the deadline was not publicly announced, although CUT members were informed that "they would not die if they did not have their shelters completed by October 2, 1989." Prophet, *Prophet's Daughter*, 176.

95. Whitsel, *Church Universal and Triumphant*, 109. Church staff and members "worked long, hard sixteen-hour days to get it ready in time. It was mind-numbing work, but we knew it had to be completed," one senior staff member recalled several years later. Whitsel, *Church Universal and Triumphant*, 118.

96. Prophet, *Prophet's Daughter*, 238. Provisions included arming the bunker with assault weapons and other guns, although Whitsel concludes that CUT never assembled an armed contingent—the weapons were for self-defense as a matter of group survival following the anticipated nuclear disaster. Whitsel, *Church Universal and Triumphant*, 122–23. Erin Prophet reveals, "Underneath the floor

of the Deep Cor [*sic*] shelter [the underground storage unit for supplies] was a secret twenty-five-foot-long tank filled with fifty AR-15 rifles . . . along with tens of thousands of rounds of ammunition. Stored in the same tank as the weapons was a hoard of coins—more than $5 million in gold and silver, and $25,000 in pennies specially ordered from the Federal Reserve Bank." Prophet, *Prophet's Daughter*, 7.

97. DeHaas, "Mediation of Ideology and Public Image," 28–29.

98. Prophet, *Prophet's Daughter*, 10–11.

99. A detailed account of the experience in the CUT bunkers on the night of March 14, 1990, appears in Prophet, *Prophet's Daughter*, 1–15.

100. Prophet, *Prophet's Daughter*, 224.

101. Prophet, *Prophet's Daughter*, 224–25.

102. The financial losses stung the local economy as well. "Both the Church and its members had run up mountains of unpaid bills," including $100,000 of bad checks, of which a local grocery held $35,000. Building contractors filed $56,000 worth of property liens for unpaid construction bills. Prophet, *Prophet's Daughter*, 235.

103. Bradley Whitsel reports, "By some accounts, half of the three to four thousand CUT adherents who had come to Montana . . . suddenly left the area once expectations for a massive Soviet strike dissipated." Whitsel, *Church Universal and Triumphant*, 115. Erin Prophet estimates that in the aftermath of the shelter episode, the church lost "up to a third of its members." Prophet, "Charisma and Authority," 45.

104. In the aftermath of the failure of the prophecies, local residents openly ridiculed church followers, whom they called "the doomsdayers," and held "'end of the world' parties . . . to mock Prophet and her followers." Whitsel, *Church Universal and Triumphant*, 117.

105. Erin Prophet observes that CUT "survived the disconfirmation of prophecy through rationalization and spiritualization of the prophecies." Prophet, "Charisma and Authority," 45.

106. Quoted in Wojcik, "Avertive Millennialism," 82.

107. Prophet, *Prophet's Daughter*, 235–36; DeHaas, "Mediation of Ideology and Public Image," 30.

108. Prophet, *Prophet's Daughter*, 236–37. The state convinced the judge initially to prohibit church members from occupying the shelter or continuing construction at the site until the state could complete a thorough environmental review. Timothy Egan, "Guru's Bomb Shelter Hits Legal Snag," *New York Times*, April 24, 1990, A16. Church officials blamed the fuel leaks on manufacturing defects in the tanks, and they eventually recovered an undisclosed amount from the

manufacturer. Prophet, *Prophet's Daughter*, 237. The church subsequently settled the lawsuit with the state in an agreement that acknowledged it had not broken any laws in building its shelters or installing the tanks, but the church agreed to pay penalties plus the cost of the cleanup. DeHaas, "Mediation of Ideology and Public Image," 30–31. The lawsuit and cleanup costs amounted to nearly a million dollars, an amount that, according to Erin Prophet, "nearly pushed us over the edge financially." Prophet, *Prophet's Daughter*, 237.

109. DeHaas, "Mediation of Ideology and Public Image," 31–32.

110. DeHaas, "Mediation of Ideology and Public Image," 32. Prophet's outreach included her participation in a Montana State University forum on media coverage of the church.

111. This announcement came at the church's New Year's conference in Miami. Whitsel, *Church Universal and Triumphant*, 150.

112. Whitsel, *Church Universal and Triumphant*, 137; Prophet, *Prophet's Daughter*, 257. A news report described Cleirbaut as an "efficiency expert and corporate downsizer." McMillion, "Selling Off the Promised Land."

113. Prophet, "Charisma and Authority," 45. In her memoir Erin Prophet reports that internal discord during this period led to schism: "At one time, as many as seventeen schismatic groups sought authority within the CUT tradition, several with their own 'messengers.'" Prophet, "Charisma and Authority," 45. Among these charismatic leaders claiming Messenger status was Gilbert Cleirbaut, "who took heavily accented dictations from the Virgin Mary." Prophet, *Prophet's Daughter*, 269.

114. Prophet, *Prophet's Daughter*, 264. Following her retirement, daughter Erin and church leader Murray Steinman were appointed co-guardians of Elizabeth Clare Prophet. She eventually took up residence in a basement apartment at the Steinman's home in Bozeman, Montana, where "she seemed happier than she had been for some time," but she also "quickly stopped using her altar or making invocations, and forgot even the names of the masters." Prophet, *Prophet's Daughter*, 268. Elizabeth Clare Prophet died in Bozeman on October 18, 2009. Her obituary in the *Los Angeles Times*, October 19, 2009, can be viewed at https://www.latimes.com/local/obituaries/la-me-elizabeth-clare-prophet19-2009oct19-story.html.

115. Elizabeth Clare Prophet made her final public appearance at CUT's 2000 July conference at the Royal Teton Ranch. Prophet, *Prophet's Daughter*, 273.

116. Anthropologist Jocelyn DeHaas notes that when faced with repression, social movements can choose either greater accommodation or greater radicalism. She concludes that CUT chose accommodation, working to make peace with its neighbors. DeHaas, "Mediation of Ideology and Public Image," 22. In a conciliatory gesture, Elizabeth Clare Prophet made clear in 1991 the church's

determination to remain in the area when she remarked: "We like it here and we intend to stay. We're going to continue to be good neighbors and hope that our neighbors are good to us. We just want to be treated like ordinary people." Quoted in DeHaas, "Mediation of Ideology and Public Image," 37.

117. Author interview with Richard Parks, June 3, 2016.

118. McMillion, "Selling Off the Promised Land." In later years the "wandering bison" issue would become more controversial and less acceptable among many of CUT's Montana members.

119. Former member Leighton Quarles, who was raised in the Church Universal and Triumphant in Montana, recalled that church members were very much "at odds" with the Park Service, and in their decrees they often prayed that conflicts with the Park Service would be resolved in the church's favor. "It seemed like a difficult if not hostile relationship," he said. Author interview with Leighton Quarles, February 1, 2016.

120. The government's aborted attempt to purchase Forbes's ranch is detailed in a December 24, 1980, article in the *Missoulian* newspaper that is included with correspondence regarding the land negotiations involving the U.S. Forest Service and the Nature Conservancy in YA, box L-68, "CUT–Royal Teton Ranch" folder. Although Forbes's use of the property as a vacation retreat included a luxury cabin and other improvements, most of the land remained wild and undeveloped when CUT gained ownership. DeHaas, "Mediation of Ideology and Public Image," 29–30.

121. A Briefing Statement of July 12, 1990, from Yellowstone National Park to the U.S. secretary of the Interior regarding Church Universal and Triumphant, notes that as CUT began developments on its Montana property, "local citizens, governments, conservation organizations, and the park became concerned over the types of impacts they were and would be creating." The statement includes details regarding two major issues, geothermal development and wildlife management. A copy of the Briefing Statement is available in YA, box L-68, "CUT–Briefing Statement, July 1990" folder.

122. The remarks of both Barbee and Francis were featured in a news report on KTVQ Television in Billings, Montana, in June 1987. A video recording of the broadcast is in YA, Videotape Collection, tape 007. Also in YA, box N-136, folder N3039 "Geological Features and Studies 1987," a letter of May 12, 1987, from Superintendent Barbee to Edward L. Francis, concludes that the church's plan to develop a geothermal well "would pose an unacceptable risk to geothermal features in Yellowstone National Park," regardless of the church's pledge to halt pumping from the well in the case of "detrimental impacts on Park geothermal features."

123. The "Old Faithful Protection Act" was introduced in the House and Senate several times but did not pass and therefore was never enacted. In response to the proposed legislation, Elizabeth Clare Prophet sent written testimony to Congress characterizing the bill as the result of religious prejudice and discrimination. A subsequent federal study concluded that the church's well would likely not have "any discernible effect on Yellowstone's geothermal features," although park officials worried more about the precedent it would set. John D. Varley, chief of research at Yellowstone National Park, remarked at the time, "If everybody did what the church wants to do, then we could have a real problem on our hands." John Woestendiek, "Sect Taps Waters of Controversy: Plans for a Thermal Spring Opposed as a Threat to Yellowstone Geysers," *Philadelphia Inquirer*, November 17, 1992, A1. Edward Francis testified on behalf of the church at a joint congressional hearing on October 31, 1991. His statement details the church's position regarding its legal water rights, and he concludes with a conciliatory assessment that "the concerns over additional geothermal developments are matters that can be resolved through communication, cooperation and binding agreements with Yellowstone Park and the other appropriate federal and state agencies." A copy of Francis's statement to Congress can be found in YA, box W-240, "HR 3359–Old Faithful Protection Act" folder.

124. Author's copy of the news release issued on August 29, 1999, from the Rocky Mountain Elk Foundation includes details of the exchange.

125. Author's copy of the Rocky Mountain Elk Foundation news release August 29, 1999.

126. Author interview with Marcia Beese, June 1, 2016.

127. Author interview with Leighton Quarles, February 1, 2016.

128. Author interview with Neroli Duffy, May 31, 2016.

BIBLIOGRAPHY

Archives

Horace Marden Albright Papers (HMAP). Collection 2056: 1918–72. Charles E. Young Research Library, Department of Special Collections, University of California, Los Angeles.

Jay Cooke Collection. Rutherford B. Hayes Presidential Library and Museum (HPL), Fremont OH.

Jay Cooke Papers. Collection 0148. Historical Society of Pennsylvania (HSP), Philadelphia.

Rare Books Collection. Huntington Library (HL), San Marino CA.

Warren W. Ost Papers (WWO). Theodore Sedgwick Wright Library Special Collections and Archives. Princeton Theological Seminary, Princeton NJ.

Yellowstone Archives (YA). Yellowstone Heritage and Research Center, Gardiner MT.

Published Works

Albanese, Catherine L. *Nature Religion in America: From the Algonkian Indians to the New Age*. Chicago History of American Religion. Chicago: University of Chicago Press, 1990.

———. *A Republic of Mind and Spirit: A Cultural History of American Metaphysical Religion*. New Haven CT: Yale University Press, 2007.

Allen, Garland E. "'Culling the Herd': Eugenics and the Conservation Movement in the United States, 1900–1940." *Journal of the History of Biology* 46, no. 1 (2013): 31–72.

Ambrose, Stephen E. *Undaunted Courage: Meriwether Lewis, Thomas Jefferson, and the Opening of the American West*. New York: Simon & Schuster, 1996.

Anderson, George S. "Protection of the Yellowstone National Park." In *Hunting in Many Lands: The Book of the Boone and Crockett Club*, edited by Theodore Roosevelt and George Bird Grinnell, 377–402. New York: Forest and Stream, 1895.

Anderson, Roger J. "A Monumental Idea." *Yellowstone Science* 11, no. 3 (Summer 2003): front matter.

Axtell, James. *The Invasion Within: The Contest of Cultures in Colonial North America*. New York: Oxford University Press, 1985.

Badone, Ellen, and Sharon R. Roseman, eds. *Intersecting Journeys: The Anthropology of Pilgrimage and Tourism*. Urbana: University of Illinois Press, 2004.

Barringer, Mark Daniel. *Selling Yellowstone: Capitalism and the Construction of Nature*. Lawrence: University Press of Kansas, 2002.

Barrows, William. *Oregon: The Struggle for Possession*. Boston: Houghton Mifflin, 1883.

Baumler, Ellen. "A Cross in the Wilderness: St. Mary's Mission Celebrates 175 Years." *Montana: The Magazine of Western History* (Montana Historical Society) 66, no. 1 (Spring 2016): 18–38.

Bedell, Rebecca. *The Anatomy of Nature: Geology & American Landscape Painting, 1825–1875*. Princeton NJ: Princeton University Press, 2001.

Bennett, James. "California Cultbusters: The West Coast Origins of the Modern Anti-Cult Movement." In *Religion in the U.S. West: Empire and Caretaking*, edited by Brandi Denison and Brett Hendrickson. Chapel Hill: University of North Carolina Press, 2026.

Berkhofer, Robert F., Jr. *The White Man's Indian: Images of the American Indian from Columbus to the Present*. New York: Knopf, 1978.

Berry, Evan. *Devoted to Nature: The Religious Roots of American Environmentalism*. Oakland: University of California Press, 2015.

Black, George. *Empire of Shadows: The Epic Story of Yellowstone*. New York: St. Martin's Press, 2012.

Blevins, Bruce H. *Mapping Yellowstone: A History of the Mapping of Yellowstone National Park*. Mansfield Center CT: Martino, 2014.

Blum, Edward J. *Reforging the White Republic: Race, Religion, and American Nationalism, 1865–1898*. Baton Rouge: Louisiana State University Press, 2005.

Boime, Albert. *The Magisterial Gaze: Manifest Destiny and American Landscape Painting, c. 1830–1865*. Washington DC: Smithsonian Institution Press, 1991.

Braden, Charles Samuel. *These Also Believe: A Study of Modern American Cults & Minority Religious Movements*. New York: Macmillan, 1949.

Braude, Ann. *Radical Spirits: Spiritualism and Women's Rights in Nineteenth-Century America*. Boston: Beacon Press, 1989.

Bremer, Thomas S. "Black Robes and the Book of Heaven: When Christianity Went West." *Church History and Religious Culture* 101, no. 1 (February 2021): 80–100.

———. *Blessed with Tourists: The Borderlands of Religion and Tourism in San Antonio*. Chapel Hill: University of North Carolina Press, 2004.

———. *Formed from This Soil: An Introduction to the Diverse History of Religion in America*. Oxford UK: Wiley Blackwell, 2015.

———. "Icons of Whiteness: Race and Religion in U.S. National Parks." In *Religion in the U.S. West: Empire and Caretaking*, edited by Brandi Denison and Brett Hendrickson. Chapel Hill: University of North Carolina Press, 2026.

———. "Sacred Spaces and Tourist Places." In *Tourism, Religion and Spiritual Journeys*, edited by Dallen J. Timothy and Daniel H. Olsen, 25–35. New York: Routledge, 2006.

———. "Tourism and Pilgrimage." In *Encyclopedia of Religion in America*, edited by Charles H. Lippy and Peter W. Williams, 2197–2205. Washington DC: CQ Press, 2010.

———. "Worshiping at Nature's Shrine." *Practical Matters Journal*, no. 9 (2016): 1–12. https://practicalmattersjournal.ecdsdev.org/wp-content/uploads/2016/03/Bremer -Worshiping-at-Natures-Shrine.pdf.

Brinkley, Douglas. *The Wilderness Warrior: Theodore Roosevelt and the Crusade for America*. New York: Harper, 2009.

Brown, Dona. *Inventing New England: Regional Tourism in the Nineteenth Century*. Washington DC: Smithsonian Institution Press, 1995.

Burroughs, John. *Camping & Tramping with Roosevelt*. Boston: Houghton Mifflin, 1907.

Catlin, George. *Letters and Notes on the Manners, Customs, and Conditions of the North American Indians. Written during Eight Years' Travel (1832–1839) amongst the Wildest Tribes of Indians in North America*. Philadelphia: J. W. Bradley, 1859.

Chidester, David. *Salvation and Suicide: An Interpretation of Jim Jones, the Peoples Temple, and Jonestown*. Bloomington: Indiana University Press, 1991.

Clayton, John. *Wonderlandscape: Yellowstone National Park and the Evolution of an American Cultural Icon*. New York: Pegasus Books, 2017.

Conkin, Paul Keith. *American Originals: Homemade Varieties of Christianity*. Chapel Hill: University of North Carolina Press, 1997.

Cooke, Jay. "Jay Cooke's Memoir." 1895. Jay Cooke Collection. HPL.

Cronon, William. "The Trouble with Wilderness; or, Getting Back to the Wrong Nature." In *Uncommon Ground: Rethinking the Human Place in Nature*, edited by William Cronon, 69–90. New York: Norton, 1996.

Culpin, Mary Shivers. *"For the Benefit and Enjoyment of the People": A History of Concession Development in Yellowstone National Park, 1872–1966*. Yellowstone National Park WY: National Park Service, Yellowstone Center for Resources, 2003.

Daehnke, Joel. *In the Work of Their Hands Is Their Prayer: Cultural Narrative and Redemption on the American Frontiers, 1830–1930*. Athens: Ohio University Press, 2003.

Davidson, Gail S., Floramae McCarron-Cates, Barbara Bloemink, Sarah Burns, and Karal Ann Marling. *Frederic Church, Winslow Homer, and Thomas Moran: Tourism and the American Landscape*. New York: Bulfinch Press, 2006.

Davis, W. L. "Peter John De Smet: The Journey of 1840." *Pacific Northwest Quarterly* 35, no. 1 (1944): 29–43.

Day, Iyko. "Tseng Kwong Chi and the Eugenic Landscape." *American Quarterly* 65, no. 1 (2013): 91–118.

De Smet, Pierre-Jean. *Life, Letters and Travels of Father Pierre-Jean de Smet, SJ, 1801–1873; Missionary Labors and Adventures among the Wild Tribes of the North American Indians.* Vol. 1. Edited by Hiram Martin Chittenden. New York: F. P. Harper, 1905.

———. *Western Missions and Missionaries: A Series of Letters.* New York: J. B. Kirker, late E. Dunigan and Brother, 1863.

DeHaas, Jocelyn H. "The Mediation of Ideology and Public Image in the Church Universal and Triumphant." In *Church Universal and Triumphant: In Scholarly Perspective,* edited by James R. Lewis and J. Gordon Melton, 21–37. Stanford CA: Center for Academic Publication, 1994.

Dick, David Scott. "Cinnabar: Archaeology and History of Yellowstone's Lost Train Town." Master's thesis, University of Montana, 2010.

Dunraven, Windham Thomas Wyndham-Quin, Earl of. *The Great Divide: Travels in the Upper Yellowstone in the Summer of 1874.* London: Chatto and Windus, 1876.

Early, Katherine E. *"For the Benefit and Enjoyment of the People": Cultural Attitudes and the Establishment of Yellowstone National Park.* Washington DC: Georgetown University Press, 1984.

Eddy, Mary Baker. *Science and Health: With Key to the Scriptures.* Boston: First Church of Christ, Scientist, 1994.

Emerson, Ralph Waldo. *Nature, Addresses and Lectures.* Boston: Phillips, Sampson, 1850.

Farrell, Justin. *The Battle for Yellowstone: Morality and the Sacred Roots of Environmental Conflict.* Princeton NJ: Princeton University Press, 2015.

Feifer, Maxine. *Going Places: The Ways of the Tourist from Imperial Rome to the Present Day.* London: Macmillan, 1985.

Ferris, Warren Angus. *Life in the Rocky Mountains; a Diary of Wanderings on the Sources of the Rivers Missouri, Columbia, and Colorado from February, 1830, to November, 1835.* Edited and introduced by Leroy R. Hafen. Denver: F. A. Rosenstock Old West Publishing, 1940.

Foster, Mike. *Strange Genius: The Life of Ferdinand Vandeveer Hayden.* Niwot CO: Roberts Rinehart Publishers, 1994.

Frome, Michael. *Strangers in High Places: The Story of the Great Smoky Mountains.* 1966. Revised, Knoxville: University of Tennessee Press, 1980.

Gardiner, Daniel. "Death and Masonic Funerals in Territorial Idaho and Montana." In *Freemasonry on the Frontier,* edited by John S. Wade, 371–97. St. Neots, Cambridgeshire UK: Lewis Masonic, 2021.

Garraghan, Gilbert J. *The Jesuits of the Middle United States*. Vol. 2. 3 vols. New York: America Press, 1938.

Geertz, Clifford. "Religion as a Cultural System." *The Interpretation of Cultures: Selected Essays*, 87–125. New York: Basic Books, 1973.

Gillis, Charles J. *Another Summer: The Yellowstone Park and Alaska*. New York: printed for private distribution, 1893. Huntington Library.

Girshman, Karl, and Rita Girshman. "Do the National Parks Need a Christian Ministry?" *Freethought Today* 11, no. 8 (1994): n.p.

Gordon, Beverly. "The Souvenir: Messenger of the Extraordinary." *Journal of Popular Culture* 20, no. 3 (1986): 135–46.

Gordon, James S. *The Golden Guru: The Strange Journey of Bhagwan Shree Rajneesh*. Lexington MA: S. Greene Press, 1987.

Gregory, James F. "Report of Lieut. Col. James F. Gregory." In *Report of an Exploration of Parts of Wyoming, Idaho, and Montana in August and September, 1882*, edited by Philip Henry Sheridan, 19–35. Washington DC: Government Printing Office, 1882.

Grusin, Richard. *Culture, Technology, and the Creation of America's National Parks*. New York: Cambridge University Press, 2004.

Gunnison, J. W. *The Mormons, or, Latter-Day Saints, in the Valley of the Great Salt Lake: A History of Their Rise and Progress, Peculiar Doctrines, Present Condition, and Prospects, Derived from Personal Observation, during a Residence among Them*. Philadelphia: Lippincott, Grambo, 1852.

Hahn, Cynthia. "Loca Sancta Souvenirs: Sealing the Pilgrim's Experience." In *The Blessings of Pilgrimage*, edited by Robert G. Ousterhout, 85–96. Urbana: University of Illinois Press, 1990.

Haines, Aubrey L. *A History of the Yellowstone National Park Chapel, 1913–1916*. Rev. ed. Yellowstone Park WY: Yellowstone National Park, 1963.

———. "Foreword." In *The Discovery of Yellowstone Park: Journal of the Washburn Expedition to the Yellowstone and Firehole Rivers in the Year 1870*, by Nathaniel P. Langford, vii–xxi. Lincoln: University of Nebraska Press, 1972.

———. *The Yellowstone Story: A History of Our First National Park*. Vol. 1. 2 vols. Rev. ed. Niwot: University Press of Colorado, 1996.

———. *The Yellowstone Story: A History of Our First National Park*. Vol. 2. 2 vols. Rev. ed. Niwot: University Press of Colorado, 1996.

Hales, Peter B. *William Henry Jackson and the Transformation of the American Landscape*. Philadelphia: Temple University Press, 1988.

Hansen, G. Holger. *As It Was in the Beginning: A History of A Christian Ministry in the National Parks*. Freeport ME: A Christian Ministry in the National Parks, 2001.

Harrison, Carter H. *A Summer's Outing and The Old Man's Story*. Chicago: Dibble Publishing, 1891.

Hassrick, Peter H. *Drawn to Yellowstone: Artists in America's First National Park*. Los Angeles: Autry Museum of Western Heritage, in association with University of Washington Press, 2002.

Heacox, Kim. *An American Idea: The Making of the National Parks*. Washington DC: National Geographic Society, 2001.

Hunt, William J., Jr. "The Heart of the Park: The Historical Archaeology of Tourism in the Lower Geyser Basin, 1872–1917." In *People and Place: The Human Experience in Greater Yellowstone: Proceedings*, edited by Paul Schullery and Sarah Stevenson, 80–99. Yellowstone National Park WY: National Park Service, Yellowstone Center for Resources, 2004.

Irving, Washington. *Adventures of Captain Bonneville, or Scenes beyond the Rocky Mountains of the Far West*. Paris: A. and W. Galignani, 1837.

Janetski, Joel C. *Indians in Yellowstone National Park*. Salt Lake City: University of Utah Press, 2002.

John, Gareth E. "Yellowstone as 'Landscape Idea': Thomas Moran and the Pictorial Practices of Gilded-Age Western Expansion." *Journal of Cultural Geography* 24, no. 2 (2007): 1–29.

Kaelber, Lutz. "Paradigms of Travel: From Medieval Pilgrimage to the Postmodern Virtual Tour." In *Tourism, Religion and Spiritual Journeys*, edited by Dallen J. Timothy and Daniel H. Olsen, 49–63. New York: Routledge, 2006.

King, Godfré Ray [Guy Warren Ballard, pseud.]. *Unveiled Mysteries*. Blacksburg VA: Wilder Publications, 2011.

Kinsey, Joni. *Thomas Moran and the Surveying of the American West*. Washington DC: Smithsonian Institution Press, 1992.

———. "Thomas Moran's Surveys of Yellowstone and the Grand Canyon: The Coalition of Art, Business, and Government." In *Splendors of the American West: Thomas Moran's Art of the Grand Canyon and Yellowstone: Paintings, Watercolors, Drawings, and Photographs from the Thomas Gilcrease Institute of American History and Art*, edited by Anne Morand, Joni Kinsey, and Mary Panzer, 29–41. Birmingham AL: Birmingham Museum of Art, 1990.

Kuppens, Francis X. "On the Origin of the Yellowstone National Park." *Woodstock Letters* 26, no. 3 (1897): 400–402.

Langford, Nathaniel P. *The Discovery of Yellowstone Park: Journal of the Washburn Expedition to the Yellowstone and Firehole Rivers in the Year 1870*. Lincoln: University of Nebraska Press, 1972.

———. *Vigilante Days and Ways: The Pioneers of the Rockies; the Makers and Making of Montana, Idaho, Oregon, Washington, and Wyoming*. Vol. 1. 2 vols. Boston: J. G. Cupples, 1890.

———. "The Wonders of the Yellowstone [Part 1]." *Scribner's Monthly, an Illustrated Magazine for the People* 2 (May 1871): 1–17.

———. "The Wonders of the Yellowstone [Part 2]." *Scribner's Monthly, an Illustrated Magazine for the People* 2 (June 1871): 113–28.

Lauer, Edna. "The History of the Gardiner Church." Typescript, n.d. In the bound scrapbook "Gardiner Community Church Yesterday and Today." Yellowstone Archives, Gardiner MT, box A-354.

Leeson, Michael A. *History of Montana, 1739–1885: A History of Its Discovery and Settlement, Social and Commercial Progress, Mines and Miners, Agriculture and Stock-Growing, Churches, Schools and Societies, Indians and Indian Wars, Vigilantes, Courts of Justice, Newspaper Press, Navigation, Railroads and Statistics: With Histories of Counties, Cities, Villages and Mining Camps: Also, Personal Reminiscences of Great Historic Value, Views Characteristic of the Territory in Our Own Times, and Portraits of Pioneers and Representative Men in the Professions and Trades.* Chicago: Warner, 1885.

Loendorf, Lawrence L., and Nancy Medaris Stone. *Mountain Spirit: The Sheep Eater Indians of Yellowstone.* Salt Lake City: University of Utah Press, 2006.

Lubetkin, M. John. *Jay Cooke's Gamble: The Northern Pacific Railroad, the Sioux, and the Panic of 1873.* Norman: University of Oklahoma Press, 2006.

McCarron-Cates, Floramae. "The Best Possible View: Pictorial Representation in the American West." In *Frederic Church, Winslow Homer, and Thomas Moran: Tourism and the American Landscape,* by Davidson, McCarron-Cates, Bloemink, Burns, and Marling, 75–117. New York: Bulfinch Press, 2006.

Melton, J. Gordon. "The Church Universal and Triumphant: Its Heritage and Thought-world." In *Church Universal and Triumphant: In Scholarly Perspective,* edited by James R. Lewis and J. Gordon Melton, 1–20. Stanford CA: Center for Academic Publication, 1994.

Merrill, Marlene. *Yellowstone and the Great West: Journals, Letters, and Images from the 1871 Hayden Expedition.* Lincoln: University of Nebraska Press, 1999.

Meyer, Judith L. *The Spirit of Yellowstone: The Cultural Evolution of a National Park.* Lanham MD: Roberts Rinehart, 2003.

Miller, Char. *Gifford Pinchot and the Making of Modern Environmentalism.* Washington DC: Island Press / Shearwater Books, 2001.

Miller, M. Mark, ed. *Adventures in Yellowstone: Early Travelers Tell Their Tales.* Guilford CT: TwoDot, 2009.

Mintz, Steven. "'Taking Stock of Our Resources': A Request from Theodore Roosevelt, 1908." *OAH Magazine of History* 21, no. 2 (2007): 45–48.

Montana Historical Society. *F. Jay Haynes, Photographer.* Helena: Montana Historical Society Press, 1981.

Morand, Anne. "Thomas Moran: Yellowstone and the Grand Canyon—in the Field and from the Studio." In *Splendors of the American West: Thomas Moran's Art of the Grand Canyon and Yellowstone: Paintings, Watercolors, Drawings, and Photographs from the Thomas Gilcrease Institute of American History and Art*, edited by Anne Morand, Joni Kinsey, and Mary Panzer, 11–27. Birmingham AL: Birmingham Museum of Art, 1990.

Muir, John. *My First Summer in the Sierra*. Boston: Houghton Mifflin, 1911.

———. *Our National Parks*. Boston: Houghton Mifflin, 1901.

———. *A Thousand-Mile Walk to the Gulf*. Edited by William Frederic Badè. Boston: Houghton Mifflin, 1916.

Nabokov, Peter, and Lawrence Loendorf. *American Indians and Yellowstone National Park: A Documentary Overview*. Yellowstone National Park WY: National Park Service Yellowstone Center for Resources, 2002.

———. *Restoring a Presence: American Indians and Yellowstone National Park*. Norman: University of Oklahoma Press, 2004.

Nash, Roderick. *Wilderness and the American Mind*. 4th ed. New Haven CT: Yale University Press, 2001.

"The National Conservation Commission." *Science*, n.s., 27, no. 704, June 26, 1908, 994–96.

Neal, Lynn S. "Christianizing the Klan: Alma White, Branford Clarke, and the Art of Religious Intolerance." *Church History* 78, no. 2 (June 2009): 350–78.

Norris, Philetus W. "Meanderings of a Mountaineer, or, the Journals and Musings (or Storys) of a Rambler over Prairie (or Mountain) and Plain." Collection of newspaper clippings, 1870–75, annotated by Norris, 1885. Huntington Library.

Norton, Harry J. *Wonder-Land Illustrated; or, Horseback Rides through the Yellowstone National Park*. Virginia City MT: Harry J. Norton, 1873.

"Notes from [Yellowstone Women's] Guild Records." N.d. Box C-18, Yellowstone Park Chapel folder, Yellowstone Archives.

Oberholtzer, Ellis Paxson. *Jay Cooke, Financier of the Civil War*. Vol. 1. 2 vols. Philadelphia: G. W. Jacobs, 1907.

Ost, Warren W. "Living over the Store." In *To Live over the Store: Essays on the Experience of A Christian Ministry in the National Parks, a Tribute to Forty Years, 1952–1992*, edited by William L. Baumgaertner, 8–14. New York: A Christian Ministry in the National Parks, 1993.

Patin, Thomas. "Exhibitions and Empire: National Parks and the Performance of Manifest Destiny." *Journal of American Culture* 22, no. 1 (1999): 41–60.

Peterson, Jacqueline, and Laura L. Peers. *Sacred Encounters: Father De Smet and the Indians of the Rocky Mountain West*. Norman: University of Oklahoma Press, 1993.

Pfund, Johanna Maria. "Western Nature—German Culture: German Representations of Yellowstone, 1872–1910." Master's thesis, Montana State University, 1994.

Prophet, Elizabeth Clare. "The Call of Hierarchy: We Hallow Space and Dedicate It to the Invincible Light-Bearer." In *Where the Eagles Gather: Book Two*, edited by Elizabeth Clare Prophet, 499–508. Corwin Springs MT: Summit University Press, 1989.

Prophet, Erin L. "Charisma and Authority in New Religious Movements." In *The Oxford Handbook of New Religious Movements*, edited by James R. Lewis and Inga Bårdsen Tøllefsen, 2:36–49. 2nd ed. New York: Oxford University Press, 2016.

———. "Elizabeth Clare Prophet: Gender, Sexuality, and the Divine Feminine." In *Female Leaders in New Religious Movements*, edited by Inga Bårdsen Tøllefsen and Christian Giudice, 51–77. Cham, Switzerland: Palgrave Macmillan, 2017.

———. *Prophet's Daughter: My Life with Elizabeth Clare Prophet inside the Church Universal and Triumphant*. Guilford CT: Lyons Press, 2009.

———. "Theosophical Root Race Theory as Syncretic Theology in the Context of Hermeticism and Nineteenth-Century Biology." Unpublished conference paper. Presented at Center for the Study of World Religions, Cambridge MA, 2019.

Prophet, Mark L. *Cosmic Consciousness: One Man's Search for God*. Los Angeles: Summit University Press, 1986.

Prophet, Mark, Elizabeth Clare Prophet, and Annice Booth. *The Masters and Their Retreats*. Corwin Springs MT: Summit University Press, 2003.

Raab, Jennifer. "Panoramic Vision, Telegraphic Language: Selling the American West, 1869–1884." *Journal of American Studies* 47, no. 2 (2013): 495–520.

Reeve, W. Paul. *Religion of a Different Color: Race and the Mormon Struggle for Whiteness*. New York: Oxford University Press, 2015.

Renehan, Edward J., Jr. *John Burroughs: An American Naturalist*. Post Mills VT: Chelsea Green, 1992.

Ridley, Jasper Godwin. *The Freemasons: A History of the World's Most Powerful Secret Society*. New York: Arcade, 2001.

Ross-Bryant, Lynn. *Pilgrimage to the National Parks: Religion and Nature in the United States*. New York: Routledge, 2013.

Runte, Alfred. *National Parks: The American Experience*. 2nd rev. ed. Lincoln: University of Nebraska Press, 1987.

Russell, Osborne. *Osborne Russell's Journal of a Trapper*. Edited by Aubrey L. Haines. Lincoln: University of Nebraska Press, 1965.

Rybczynski, Witold. *A Clearing in the Distance: Frederick Law Olmsted and America in the Nineteenth Century*. New York: Scribner, 1999.

Salish-Pend d'Oreille Culture Committee *and* Elders Cultural Advisory Council (Confederated Salish & Kootenai Tribes of the Flathead Reservation). *The Salish People and the Lewis and Clark Expedition*. Lincoln: University of Nebraska Press, 2005.

Schmidt, Leigh Eric. *Restless Souls: The Making of American Spirituality*. San Francisco: HarperSanFrancisco, 2005.

Schullery, Paul, ed. *Old Yellowstone Days*. Boulder: Colorado Associated University Press, 1979.

———. *Searching for Yellowstone: Ecology and Wonder in the Last Wilderness*. Boston: Houghton Mifflin, 1997.

Schullery, Paul, and Lee H. Whittlesey. *Myth and History in the Creation of Yellowstone National Park*. Lincoln: University of Nebraska Press, 2003.

Schultz, James Willard. *Blackfeet and Buffalo: Memories of Life among the Indians*. Norman: University of Oklahoma Press, 1962.

Schultz, William. "Bad Faith: Religious Fraud and Religious Freedom in the 'Mighty I AM' Case." In *The Changing Terrain of Religious Freedom*, edited by Heather J. Sharkey and Jeffrey E. Green, 153–69. Philadelphia: University of Pennsylvania Press, 2021.

Sears, John F. *Sacred Places: American Tourist Attractions in the Nineteenth Century*. New York: Oxford University Press, 1989.

Sellars, Richard West. *Preserving Nature in the National Parks: A History*. New Haven CT: Yale University Press, 1997.

Solnit, Rebecca. "John Muir in Native America." *Sierra: The Magazine of the Sierra Club* 106, no. 1 (April 2021), https://www.sierraclub.org/sierra/2021-2-march-april/feature/john-muir-native-america.

Stanley, Edwin James. *Rambles in Wonderland: Or, Up the Yellowstone, and among the Geysers and Other Curiosities of the National Park*. New York: D. Appleton, 1878.

Stanley, Susie Cunningham. *Feminist Pillar of Fire: The Life of Alma White*. Cleveland: Pilgrim Press, 1993.

Starrs, Paul, and John Wright. "Utopia, Dystopia, and Sublime Apocalypse in Montana's Church Universal and Triumphant." *Geographical Review* 95, no. 1 (2005): 97–121.

Stephanson, Anders. *Manifest Destiny: American Expansionism and the Empire of Right*. New York: Hill and Wang, 1995.

Stewart, Susan. *On Longing: Narratives of the Miniature, the Gigantic, the Souvenir, the Collection*. Baltimore: Johns Hopkins University Press, 1984.

Stoll, Mark. *Inherit the Holy Mountain: Religion and the Rise of American Environmentalism*. New York: Oxford University Press, 2015.

Stonerook, S. B. *Off the Beaten Track: Through the Big Bald, Big Horn, Shoshone, and the Rocky Mountains to Yellowstone National Park: An Accurate and Concise Description of the Entire Trip from Ottumwa, Iowa, to Yellowstone National Park and Return*. Burlington IA: Conrad Lutz, 1896.

Swagerty, William R. *The Indianization of Lewis and Clark.* 2 vols. Norman OK: Arthur H. Clark, 2012.

Synan, Vinson. *The Holiness-Pentecostal Tradition: Charismatic Movements in the Twentieth Century.* 2nd ed. Grand Rapids MI: W. B. Eerdmans, 1997.

Taves, Ann. *Religious Experience Reconsidered: A Building Block Approach to the Study of Religion and Other Special Things.* Princeton NJ: Princeton University Press, 2009.

Temple, Wayne Calhoun. *Abraham Lincoln: From Skeptic to Prophet.* 3rd ed. Mahomet IL: Mayhaven, 2013.

Thoreau, Henry David. *Walden; or, Life in the Woods.* Boston: Houghton Mifflin, 1906.

Tilden, Freeman. *Following the Frontier with F. Jay Haynes, Pioneer Photographer of the Old West.* New York: Knopf, 1964.

Turner, Victor, and Edith Turner. *Image and Pilgrimage in Christian Culture: Anthropological Perspectives.* New York: Columbia University Press, 1978.

Tuttle, Daniel S. "Early History of the Episcopal Church in Montana." *Contributions to the Historical Society of Montana; With Its Transactions, Officers and Members* 5 (1904): 289–324.

Vaughn, William Preston. *The Antimasonic Party in the United States, 1826–1843.* Lexington: University Press of Kentucky, 1983.

Veith, Gene Edward. *Painters of Faith: The Spiritual Landscape in Nineteenth-Century America.* Washington DC: Regnery, 2001.

Victor, Frances Fuller. *The River of the West: Life and Adventure in the Rocky Mountains and Oregon; Embracing Events in the Life-Time of a Mountain-Man and Pioneer: With the Early History of the North-Western Slope, Including an Account of the Fur Traders, the Indian Tribes, the Overland Immigration, the Oregon Missions, and the Tragic Fate of Rev. Dr. Whitman and Family. Also, a Description of the Country, Its Condition, Prospects, and Resources; Its Soil, Climate, and Scenery; Its Mountains, Rivers, Valleys, Deserts, and Plains; Its Inland Waters, and Natural Wonders.* Hartford CT: Columbian Book Company, 1870.

Vikan, Gary. *From the Holy Land to Graceland: Sacred People, Places and Things in Our Lives.* Washington DC: American Association of Museums, 2013.

Waite, Thornton. *Yellowstone by Train: A History of Rail Travel to America's First National Park.* Missoula MT: Pictorial Histories, 2006.

Warren, James Perrin. *John Burroughs and the Place of Nature.* Athens: University of Georgia Press, 2006.

Weixelman, Joseph. "Fear or Reverence? Native Americans and the Geysers of Yellowstone." *Yellowstone Science* 9, no. 4 (Fall 2001): 2–10.

———. "The Power to Evoke Wonder: Native Americans and the Geysers of Yellowstone National Park." Master's thesis, Montana State University, 1992.

Wheeler, Olin D. *6,000 Miles through Wonderland: Being a Description of the Marvelous Region Traversed by the Northern Pacific Railroad*. Chicago: Rand, McNally, 1893.

White, Alma. *The Ku Klux Klan in Prophecy*. Zarephath NJ: Good Citizen, 1925.

———. *Looking Back from Beulah, on the Overruling and Forming Hand of God in the Poverty and Struggles of Childhood, the Hardships of Later Years; the Battles, Victories and Joys of the Sanctified Life*. Bound Brook NJ: Pillar of Fire, 1909.

———. *The Titanic Tragedy: God Speaking to the Nations*. Bound Brook NJ: Pentecostal Union (Pillar of Fire), 1913.

———. *The Voice of Nature*. Zarephath NJ: Pillar of Fire, 1930.

———. *With God in the Yellowstone*. Zarephath NJ: Pillar of Fire, 1920.

White, Richard. *Railroaded: The Transcontinentals and the Making of Modern America*. New York: Norton, 2011.

White, Thomas Edward. "Cornelius Hedges: Uncommon Hero of the Common Life." Master's thesis, Montana State University, 1963.

Whitman, Walt. *Leaves of Grass*. Brooklyn: Printed by Andrew and James Rome, 1855.

Whitsel, Bradley C. *The Church Universal and Triumphant: Elizabeth Clare Prophet's Apocalyptic Movement*. Syracuse NY: Syracuse University Press, 2003.

Whittlesey, Lee H. "Native Americans, the Earliest Interpreters: What Is Known about Their Legends and Stories of Yellowstone National Park and the Complexities of Interpreting Them." *George Wright FORUM* 19, no. 3 (2002): 40–51.

———. *Storytelling in Yellowstone: Horse and Buggy Tour Guides*. Albuquerque: University of New Mexico Press, 2007.

———. *Wonderland Nomenclature: A History of the Place Names of Yellowstone National Park, Being a Description of and Guidebook to Its Most Important Natural Features, Together with Appendices of Related Elements*. Helena: Montana Historical Society Press, 1988.

Whittlesey, Lee H., and Paul Schullery. "The Roosevelt Arch." *Yellowstone Science* 11, no. 3 (Summer 2003): 2–24.

Wilkins, Thurman, and Caroline Lawson Hinkley. *Thomas Moran: Artist of the Mountains*. 2nd ed. Norman: University of Oklahoma Press, 1998.

Wohlforth, Charles P. *The Fate of Nature: Rediscovering Our Ability to Rescue the Earth*. New York: Thomas Dunne Books / St. Martin's Press, 2010.

Wojcik, Daniel. "Avertive Millennialism." In *The Oxford Handbook of Millennialism*, edited by Catherine Wessinger, 66–88. New York: Oxford University Press, 2011.

Worster, Donald. "John Muir and the Religion of Nature." *Historically Speaking* 10, no. 2 (2009): 27–28.

———. *A Passion for Nature: The Life of John Muir*. New York: Oxford University Press, 2008.

INDEX

Page numbers in italics indicate illustrations.

Hedges, Cornelius, 49, 50, 51, 52, 95, 178n27, 188n2

hell. *See* underworld imagery

Hell-Broth Springs, 73

Hetch Hetchy Valley, 115–16

Hinduism, 6, 81, 156

Hopkins, Emma Curtis, 140, 142–43

Hot Springs Reservation, 170n7

Hudson River School, 62, 76

Hudson River Valley, 76

Humboldt, Alexander von, 107–8

hunting, 30, 44, 98, 106–7. *See also* recreation

I AM, 140–41, 142, 203n28

I AM Religious Activity, 6, 136, 137, 140–41, 142–43, 144, 146, 164

Ignace, Young, 36. *See also* La Mouse, Ignace

Inner Retreat. *See* Heart of the Inner Retreat; Royal Teton Ranch

Iroquois, 31, 35, 37

Jackson, William Henry, 58, 59, 86

Jay Cooke and Company, 45–46, 52–53, 57–58

Jesuits, 19–22, 30, 35–40, 41

Jesus Christ, 20, 21, 119, 124, 142, *160*

John XXIII (Catholic pope), 147

Jones, Jim, 148, 152–53

Jonestown, 148, 152–53

Judaism, 127, 129, 131–32

Kant, Immanuel, 78

karma, 140, 156

Keepers of the Flame, 145–46, 149, 150

King, Randall, 146

Kiowa, 15

Kipling, Rudyard, 77

Kootenai, 15

Ku Klux Klan, 113, 116

Kuppens, Francis, 19, 40, 42

Lake of the Woods, 82

La Mouse, Ignace, 35, 36

landscape architecture, 13–14

Lanello (ascended master), 146

Langford, Nathaniel P., 52, 53–57; and Freemasonry, 47, *48*, 49, 95; and Jay Cooke, 47, 50–51; as Yellowstone park superintendent, 69, 80, 90, 95, 195n11

Lewis and Clark expedition, 24, 32

Lincoln, Abraham, 45

Lincoln, Mary Todd, 202n5

Louisiana Purchase, 23

Lower Falls of the Yellowstone River, 54, 61–62, 78

Lower Geyser Basin, 74, 82, 83

Ludlow, William, 85

Lutherans, 120, 200n19

Mack, Randolph, 152

Madison River, 27, 52, 175n55

magisterial gaze, 184n79

Maitreya Mountain, 5, 6, 138, 169n1

Malibu CA, 147, 151

Mammoth Hot Springs, 72, 72–73, 82, 84, 86, *87*, 88, 118; chapel, 120–22, *121*, *126*, 199n9

Manifest Destiny, 45, 52, 63, 66, 93, 171n23; as divine purpose for the nation, 14, 16, 43, 56, 62, 64, 92; and gender, 14, 171n23; and race, 60, 62, 64, 66

Marsh, George Perkins, 100

Marshall, William R., 50–51

Masons. *See* Freemasonry

Mather, Cotton, 11

McGuirk, Matthew, 193n74

IN THE AMERICA'S PUBLIC LANDS SERIES

Sacred Wonderland: The History of Religion in Yellowstone
THOMAS S. BREMER

The First Atomic Bomb: The Trinity Site in New Mexico
JANET FARRELL BRODIE

The Bears of Grand Teton: A Natural and Cultural History
SUE CONSOLO-MURPHY

Restoring Nature: The Evolution of Channel Islands National Park
LARY M. DILSAVER AND TIMOTHY J. BABALIS

Framing Nature: The Creation of an American Icon at the Grand Canyon
YOLONDA YOUNGS

To order or obtain more information on these or other University of Nebraska Press titles, visit nebraskapress.unl.edu.

www.ingramcontent.com/pod-product-compliance
Lightning Source LLC
Chambersburg PA
CBHW031552080825
30826CB00002B/19